MASTERING

ACCOUNTING

MACMILLAN MASTER SERIES

Accounting
Arabic
Astronomy
Australian History
Background to Business
Basic English Law
Basic Management
Biology
British Politics
Business Communication
Business Law
Business Microcomputing
Catering Science
Catering Theory
Chemistry
COBOL Programming
Commerce
Computer Programming
Computers
Data Processing
Economic and Social History
Economics
Electrical Engineering
Electronics
English as a Foreign Language
English Grammar
English Language
English Literature
Financial Accounting
French
French 2
German
German 2
Hairdressing
Italian
Italian 2
Japanese
Keyboarding
Marketing
Mathematics
Modern British History
Modern European History
Modern World History
Nutrition
Office Practice
Pascal Programming
Philosophy
Physics
Practical Writing
Principles of Accounts
Restaurant Service
Social Welfare
Sociology
Spanish
Spanish 2
Spreadsheets
Statistics
Statistics with your Microcomputer
Study Skills
Typewriting Skills
Word Processing

MASTERING ACCOUNTING

GEORGE BRIGHT
and
MICHAEL HERBERT

M
MACMILLAN

First published by Pan Books Ltd in 1983 and 1987 as *Practical Accounts 1* and *2* in the Breakthrough Series.

Fully revised and updated edition first published in 1990 by
MACMILLAN EDUCATION LTD
Houndmills, Basingstoke, Hampshire RG21 2XS
and London
Companies and representatives
throughout the world

Typeset by TecSet Ltd, Wallington, Surrey

Printed in Hong Kong

British Library Cataloguing in Publication Data
Bright, George
[Practical accounts] Mastering accounting.
1. Accounting
I. [Practical accounts] II. Title III. Herbert,
Michael
657
ISBN 0-333-51197-2
ISBN 0-333-51198-0 Pbk
ISBN 0-333-51199-9 Pbk export

CONTENTS

CONTENTS

II ACCOUNTING FOR DIFFERENT ORGANISATIONS

CONTENTS

PREFACE

This book aims to provide you with a comprehensive introduction to the principles and practice of book-keeping and accounting. Part I introduces you to the world of double entry book-keeping and the important techniques involved in the preparation of the final accounts of a business. Part II moves on to the preparation of final accounts for a range of different organisations including partnerships, limited companies, manufacturing firms and clubs. Part III introduces you to the world of cost and management accounting and covers important topics such as the analysis of business performance, cash flow, product costing and budgetary control. This range of subject-matter makes the book relevant to many people already working in business as well as to the student of accounting.

The book is genuinely capable of use as a self-contained course of study or as a classroom text. It has a number of important features.

1 We have made extensive use of case studies. These are based on real situations and are intended to illustrate the way in which accounting is relevant to the business world.
2 Each chapter concentrates on the main principles of the topic being dealt with - unnecessary detail is omitted. This makes it easier for you to identify the main points and to gain confidence in the subject.
3 A lot of practical exercises are included both in and at the end of each chapter. An answer section is given at the back of the book. It is important for your learning that you make a good effort at each question before checking your answer.
4 The book also includes a number of activities. These have either been used to ask you to think about a situation drawing upon your own experience and imagination or to ask you to carry out researches of various kinds which would help you to relate the material in the book to the business world.
5 The Appendix contains an extensive range of GCSE examination questions.

The book covers material which is found in all the major introductory level accounting syllabuses, including GCSE, RSA I and II, LCCI 1 and 2 and GCE A level. We have tried to make the content as interesting and as straightforward as possible to help you achieve real confidence in mastering this important and challenging subject.

George Bright
Michael Herbert

ACKNOWLEDGEMENTS

The authors and publishers wish to thank the following who have kindly given permission for the use of copyright material from questions from specimen and part examination papers:

London East Anglian Group; Midland Examining Group; Northern Examining Group comprised of Associated Lancashire Schools Examining Board, Joint Matriculation Board, North Regional Examinations Board, North West Regional Examinations Board and Yorkshire and Humberside Regional Examinations Board; Northern Ireland Schools Examinations Council; Southern Examining Group and Welsh Joint Education Committee.

Every effort has been made to trace all the copyright-holders, but if any have been inadvertently overlooked the publishers will be pleased to make the necessary arrangement at the first opportunity.

PART I

BOOK-KEEPING AND ACCOUNTING FOR A SOLE TRADER

CHAPTER 1

BUSINESSES AND BALANCE SHEETS

1.1 THE NEED FOR ACCOUNTS

Most people associate accounting with the world of business. To see what it involves we can divide it into three parts.

First, it concerns the recording of transactions. This aspect is known as book-keeping because, at one time, most records or accounts were kept in books. Second, it involves reporting to people wanting information about the state of the business. This is called financial accounting because such reporting provides information in monetary or financial terms. Third, it is associated with controlling what is happening within a business. This is generally known as management accounting because managers are the people responsible for making the decisions which control what goes on.

There is nothing so special about accounting that it must be done only by accountants. We all do it, or could do it. Take for example John, a sixth-form student who works in a shop each Saturday. Most of his earnings used to disappear fairly quickly on clothes, records and concerts. Recently, however, John started to save. He wanted a motorbike. His parents agreed to buy him one for his next birthday, which was six months away, provided that by that time he could show them that he would be able to pay all the usual expenses involved in running a bike.

To help John do this, his mum gave him a pocket book. He wrote down his earnings each week and kept a note of his spending. When his birthday came he was able to show his parents exactly how much he had saved and how he had done it. By then he had also looked into the costs of running a motorbike including fuel, road tax, insurance and repairs. Writing down his savings for the previous six months on one side of a sheet of paper and the estimated running costs on the other, he was able to prove to his parents that he would indeed be able to run the bike – just.

John got his bike. He didn't throw away his pocket book, though. He soon found how useful it was in helping to keep a check on what it cost him to run the bike. He was often having to decide things like whether he should use the bike every day to travel to school (his bus pass was free); when to have the bent mud-guard repaired; who would service the bike most thoroughly and yet not charge too much; and how much he could put towards the crash helmet his girlfriend needed. He was able to use the information in his pocket book to help him make these decisions.

Exercise 1.1

When did John act as (a) book-keeper; (b) financial accountant; (c) management accountant?

Even if you do not use what you learn from this book in a business situation you may find it useful in your personal life. See if you can prove this yourself by attempting the following.

Activity

Make a list of ways in which you could (or already do) benefit from using basic accounting techniques.

There are many benefits you might mention. On the book-keeping side it is always helpful to keep records of receipts and payments made through a bank account. When you receive your statement it is then much easier to check it. A record of spending on particular items might also be useful, e.g. heating, motoring or purchases of food for the freezer. It is sometimes helpful to prpare a clear statement of your financial position. Such a statement may help to persuade a bank manager to give you a loan or it might help to prove to yourself or others how much better off you are after giving up smoking. So drawing up a report rather like a financial accountant is useful. Everybody has to make decisions and very often these involve money. A housewife who is finding it difficult to make ends meet might be faced with the task of deciding whether her children should have school lunches or take their own. Another might have to decide whether they can afford a holiday this year and, if so, what sort. Simple records and brief statements will be very useful in making such decisions. No matter that they are written on the back of an envelope! Perhaps management accounting seems too grand a title for it. What's in a name? The word 'economics' derives from a Greek word meaning management of a household. Housewives are managers, so why shouldn't they use the techniques of management accounting?

Let's turn now to the business world. There are many different sorts of businesses. One way of classifying them is according to how they are owned. Among the most numerous are sole traders, who are also known as sole proprietors or sole owners. Here one person owns the business. Other types include partnerships, limited companies, co-operatives and public corporations.

In Part I of this book we will be concerned only with the accounts of businesses owned by one person.

A typical example of such an organisation is the building and decorating business owned by Henry Plunkett. Besides general repairs and decorating he also does quite a number of extensions. He employs six people. Try to acquaint yourself with the administration of this sort of business by attempting the following.

Activity

Make a list of different sorts of information that such a business will need to record.

I would expect him to keep records or accounts of purchases of materials, payments made to suppliers of materials and services, invoices sent to customers, money received from customers, possessions of the business such as cash, premises, equipment and vehicles, money owed to creditors, e.g. the bank, wages paid to employees, income tax and national insurance deducted from employees' wages and value added tax paid on purchases or charged to customers.

Your list may be longer than mine but even if it only contains a few items it is still clear that records will need to be kept. Therefore book-keeping is essential.

Financial accounting is also of vital importance to Henry's firm. He will need to know how successful he is. This can be shown best by preparing a profit and loss account, which measures the amount of profit or less made in a particular period of time, usually a year. Henry is not the only one who will be interested in what it reveals. The Inspector of Taxes (Inland Revenue) will want to know. People who own businesses do not pay tax weekly or monthly as do employees under the 'pay-as-you-earn' scheme. Their tax is assessed according to the amount of profit earned each year.

Henry would also like to know how much his business is worth. One way of showing this is by preparing a balance sheet. This shows the financial position of the business at a particular moment of time. In this respect it differs from the profit and loss account which covers a period of time.

Exercise 1.2

Ginger Jenkins has started a business similar to that of Henry. He does not keep proper records but reckons that, as long as he has plenty of cash coming in, he must be doing all right and therefore has no need of financial accounts or accountants. Who will dispute Ginger's freedom to run his business this way?

To be successful, Henry Plunkett will also find management accounting a great help as decision making is important in all businesses. Some people have a knack for making the right decisions, relying mainly on intuition.

Others frequently choose incorrectly. However lucky a businessman may be, decisions made with knowledge of all relevant facts, including financial information, have most chance of being right in the long run.

The decisions Henry will have to make will be many and varied. Consider just one. Henry has been invited to submit an estimate to convert a farmer's barn into a home for his son and daughter-in-law. How will Henry go about this task? To begin he will need to know what the end product is to be like and what materials are to be used in its construction. An architect's drawing will provide much of the information he needs.

Given this, he will be able to calculate the amount of materials needed and the number of hours he thinks it will take to complete. He can then work out the cost of these materials and the amount of wages he will have to pay his men while they are working on this job. Information on the cost of materials will come from catalogues and recent invoices received for similar materials. For the wages cost he will be able to consult records of the various wage rates paid to his men, some of whom will be skilled and others unskilled. He will, of course, want to earn a profit for himself in return for taking on the risk involved in carrying out the job. Other considerations that might affect the final toal figure he gives for the job include how badly he needs the work and whether it is likely that other firms will be able to give an estimate below his. Henry's experience will be invaluable in drafting the estimate for the farmer. Without the facts provided by his accounting records, however, it is clear that the preparation of the estimate would be much more of a hit-or-miss affair.

Activity

Think of some other decisions that Henry might have to make in managing his business. Consider if accounting would help him in making them.

Decisions you could mention include: should he take on extra staff when trade is booming or rely on subcontracting some of the work to other firms? Should he purchase or lease the new equipment if needed? If he decides to purchase, what is the best way of paying for it? Should he expand with money that will have to be borrowed? What is the best way of persuading his customers to pay him more promptly? Which is better, buying materials for cash to obtain lower prices or on credit to give him time to pay? Of course there are many more, but whatever management decision you thought of it is inevitable that it would best be made by reference to book-keeping records and the financial accounts. In larger businesses management accountants would probably draft individual statements to assist in making each such decision. In smaller businesses this is less likely.

Having seen the use of accounting to all of us as individuals and to business owners like Henry, it should not be too difficult for you to look further afield for other examples of its use. For instance many businesses are much larger than Henry's and are involved in different activities. Many employees in such businesses will be working with accounts and not all of them will be in the financial department. They may well be employed in marketing, production or personnel departments.

There are other forms of business ownership. Partnerships need accounts to satisfy each partner that the profits are being fairly divided and companies are accountable to their shareholders. Local and central government provide a variety of services and will need accounts, not least for keeping a check on the money they receive from ratepayers and taxpayers.

Exercise 1.3

3.1 Complete the following sentences:
- (a) Recording transactions is known as ________________ because at one time most accounts were kept in ________________.
- (b) Reporting on the state of a business by means of statements such as ________________ and ________________ accounts and balance sheets is known as ________________.
- (c) Using accounts as an aid in controlling and managing a business is known as ________________.
- (d) The above activities together make up the subject matter of ________________.

3.2 What sort of business, from the point of view of ownership, is that of Henry Plunkett?

3.3 Give three examples of information that a business like Henry's would need to record. In each case say why this information should be recorded.

3.4 Which of the following is unlikely to be involved in any way with accounting: business owner, salesman, wages clerk, personnel manager, marketing director, inspector of taxes, treasurer of a tennis club, housewife?

1.2 STARTING A BUSINESS

When Bill Turner was made redundant he decided that he would never again work for someone else. He wanted to be his own boss! After thinking over a number of ideas he decided that he would like to purchase a shop. The sort of shop he had in mind was a general store which sold a variety of things but which concentrated on food and groceries. He reasoned that these were items which everybody needed and would give his business a reasonable amount of safety. Bill's wife, Joan, had been complaining for several years about the dirtiness of the town in which they lived - buying a shop in a Devon village seemed a good way of satisfying both his wife's and his own ambitions.

Selling their semi-detached house realised £72,000 after the mortgage had been repaid to their building society. This, together with Bill's redundancy payment of £10,000, meant that they had a total of £82,000 of their own money to invest in a business.

Many people would have spent a great deal of time talking to shopkeepers, bank managers and business agents before making a decision to spend their £82,000. Not Bill! He had always been quick at making decisions and this time proved to be no exception. He spent one weekend in Devon, looked at five properties and agreed to buy one of them for £96,000. Only then did he approach his bank manager and ask for a loan of £14,000 to meet the difference between the buying price and their available capital.

After listening to Bill rave about the potential of the business, the bank manager looked carefully at a copy of the accounts and agreed to advance the loan. This was made subject to a favourable report from a representative of the bank, which would be completed after visiting the premises.

The business which Bill purchased had been run unsuccessfully for several years. Because of this he had been able to buy it for an amount which just equalled the value of the premises, fixtures and fittings and stock-in-trade. These are called the assets of a business. Assets are basically the possessions of the business on which a money value can be placed. If the business had been more successful the sellers might have been able to demand a price higher than the value of the assets purchased. This would have been to buy something called the goodwill of the business. Goodwill is the benefit obtained from buying a business which has good connections and a good reputation. As the previous owner had not been successful, little or no goodwill existed. Hence Bill was able to buy the business for the agreed value of the assets.

When a new business starts it is a good idea to draw up a statement showing its financial position. One way of doing this is in the form of a balance sheet. Look carefully at the following statement.

Balance sheet of Valuemart as at 1 July 1990

	£		£
Assets		*Sources of finance*	
Premises	84,000	*Proprietor's capital*	82,000
Fixtures and fittings	7,000		
Stock	5,000	*Liabilities*	
Cash at bank	1,900	Bank loan	16,000
Cash in hand	100		
	98,000		98,000

From this we can derive a definition of a balance sheet. It is a statement drawn up at a particular date (in this case 1 July 1990) to show the value of the assets of the business (which Bill had decided to call Valuemart) and how the finance for these assets was obtained.

'Assets' are those possessions or advantages a business has on which a money value can be placed. There are, of course, some advantages on which it is not possible to place a definite money value; for instance the effort that Bill expects to put into the business or the hard work he expects from Joan. 'Stock' is the name given to any item which is bought and sold with the intention of making a profit.

Examples of items which might count as 'fixtures and fittings' in a general store are: shelving, counters, displays, fridge and the till.

The sources of finance may be divided into two types: first the finance provided by the owner, which is called the proprietor's capital or sometimes simply the capital. In this case the proprietor is Bill Turner himself. His wife Joan was prepared to help him but did not want to be considered as an owner of the business. The second source of finance is called liabilities. This is the money owing to people outside the business which has been used to finance some of the assets of the business. In this case the only liability is to the bank which agreed to lend Bill some of the money he needed to buy the business. People, or other organisations like the bank, to whom money is owed are called the creditors of the business.

You may have remembered that Bill needed a loan of only £14,000 to top up his own capital of £82,000 by enough to buy the business for £96,000 (see page 8). The loan in the balance sheet is £2,000 greater than he originally requested. If you look carefully at the balance sheet you will see that there are two assets which together are worth £2,000 and which were not actually purchased by Bill. These are cash in hand and cash at bank. All businesses need both very ready money (cash in hand) and money which can be obtained fairly quickly (cash in the bank). It is likely that Bill will have realised that and returned to his bank manager with a request for a further loan. It is also possible that the bank manager himself will have suggested Bill should have the extra finance which should be kept readily available. In any case it is clearly necessary for a business to have some money for use when needed. For example more stock may be required from the local cash-and-carry or a broken window might have to be repaired.

The balance sheet on page 8 is only one style of layout. Those of you who have seen a balance sheet before might be surprised by it for one of two possible reasons.

- You could be used to seeing the assets to the right of the sources of finance. That is the traditional style of a horizontal balance sheet and is still occasionally found today.
- You might be used to seeing the balance sheet displayed vertically down the page. This style will be introduced later.

We will use the horizontal method in this chapter because of its value in emphasising the relationship between assets and their sources of finance. In any business the value of assets equals the value of capital and liabilities that make up the sources of finance. This known as the book-keeping equation and we can use it to reduce Bill Turner's opening balance sheet to the simple form of;

assets 98,000 = *capital* (82,000) + *liabilities* (16,000)

If we know the value of two items in this equation it is always possible to calculate the third. The equation can be turned around to read:

assets less *liabilities* = *capital*
or *assets* less *capital* = *liabilities.*

Exercise 1.4

To make sure you understand this equation complete the table below by filling in the missing figure for each of the four separate businesses.

	Business	*Capital* £	*Liabilities* £	*Assets* £
(a)		10,000	5,000	
(b)			16,000	30,000
(c)		12,000		37,000
(d)			60,000	50,000

The first three calculations should have presented no problems. If you had difficulty reread the section about the book-keeping equation. The fourth calculation perhaps required a little more thought. What has happened here is that the business concerned has been so unsuccessful that its assets are not sufficient to pay off all the liabilities. Thus if the assets were sold for £50,000 some of the creditors of the business would not receive the money that was due to them. £10,000 would be left unpaid and the owner of the business would be responsible for meeting these extra debts himself. The 'negative capital' is called a deficiency of capital.

If you are not happy working with negative figures you could rewrite the book-keeping equation to read:

assets + *deficiency* = *liabilities.*

But remember, this only applies when the liabilities are greater than the assets.

A firm which has liabilities greater than its assets is said to be insolvent. Naturally this sort of position would not be allowed to continue for very long. Once the creditors knew about it they would be afraid things would become worse and that they might lose even more of what was owed to them. The bankruptcy court is only a small step away for a businessman who finds himself in such a difficult financial position.

1.3 THE BALANCE SHEET

The balance sheet below relates to one of the businesses Bill Turner looked at but did not buy. Compare it with the opening balance sheet of Valuemart on page 8.

Balance sheet of Rivendale General Store as at 31 May 1990

	£	£		£
Assets			***Sources of finance***	
Fixed assets			*Proprietor's capital*	85,000
Premises	80,000			
Furniture and fittings	6,000		*Long-term liabilities*	
			Mortgage on premises	10,000
		86,000	*Current liabilities*	
			Trade creditors	1,500
Current assets				
Stock-in-trade	7,000			
Debtors	2,000			
Bank	1,000			
Cash	500			
		10,500		
		96,500		96,500

First, concentrate on the assets side of the balance sheets.

You will notice that the assets in the second balance sheet are grouped into two sections: fixed assets and current assets. **Fixed assets** are those possessions which are relatively permanent. They are used over a reasonable amount of time and are not constantly changing in value. Fixed assets are needed to enable the business to operate and make a profit, but they are not kept with the set purpose of making a profit on them.

Other typical fixed assets include vehicles, machinery, and equipment such as a computer or word-processor.

Current assets are also sometimes known as 'circulating' assets. They are the assets which are constantly changing in value and it is through the movement of these that the proprietor of a business intends to make a profit. As more stock is bought so this asset increases in value. If it is sold then it decreases in value. At the same time, either the amount of cash in hand or cash at bank will be changing as the business receives money or makes payments.

One new asset appears in the Rivendale balance sheet. This is debtors. Clearly debtors are not a possession in the same sense as property or cash but it is an advantage on which a money value may be placed. It is an advantage because the majority of debtors do pay their debts. Since businesses normally expect their debtors to pay them relatively soon, it is regarded as a current rather than a fixed asset.

You should beware of thinking that all assets can be classified as either fixed or current and remain the same whatever business is involved. It is the *use* to which the asset is put which determines whether it should be regarded as fixed or current.

Exercise 1.5

Where would you place motorcars in the balance sheet of the following businesses? Are they fixed or current assets?

(a) The cars used by the salesmen of a confectionery firm.
(b) The cars on the forecourt of a garage with 'for sale' on each windscreen.

The assets in the balance sheet of Rivendale have been displayed in order of permanence. The fixed assets are followed by the current assets. Property, which probably takes longer to turn into cash than any other asset, is shown first and cash comes last. This is the normal practice in the UK, though in some other countries the assets are shown in order of liquidity. Then cash comes first and those assets which can be turned into cash follow in the order of how quickly they can be turned into cash

Now compare the finance side of Rivendale's balance sheet with that of Bill Turner. You will see that the former contains two types of liabilities: long-term and current. Liabilities are finance provided by people or other organisations who are not owners of the business. The money has to be repaid at some time. The distinction between long-term and current is usually made on the basis of the amount of time allowed to repay the amount due. **Current liabilities** are due to be repaid within one year. Trade creditors are the suppliers from whom Rivendale has purchased its stock-in-trade on credit. Usually suppliers will allow a maximum of only one or two months' credit before payment is demanded. Trade creditors must therefore be regarded as current liabilities. **Long-term liabilities** are those which are not expected to be repaid during the current year, e.g. a mortgage.

In the absence of information abut the date of repayment you should assume that a loan is a long-term liability and a creditor is a current liability.

Confusion often arises over bank overdrafts. Clearly this is money which the business owes to the bank. Should it be regarded as a long-term or current liability? The correct answer is current because a bank may recall this money on demand at any time. It is true that many firms are sometimes allowed by banks to keep their overdrafts over a relatively long period. This does not make them a long-term liability, however, because the owner of the business can never be *sure* that the bank might not demand immediate repayment.

Before attempting the next exercise, make certain that you understand each of the following: balance sheet, the book-keeping equation, proprietor's capital, long-term liabilities, current liabilities, fixed assets and current assets. Are you happy? If so, you should be able to answer the following.

Exercise 1.6

The information that follows refers to the business of Peter Bright on 31 January 1990: freehold property £40,000, debts due to suppliers £2,350, stock £6,800, cash £180, bank overdraft £1,000, debts due from customers £1,900, furniture and fittings £3,000, delivery vehicle £2,000, mortgage on property (10 years) £5,000, loan from ABC Finance Limited (5 years) £3,000.

Draft a balance sheet for Peter Bright on the date given. *Advice:* take care to divide your assets and liabilities as you have been shown on page 11. To complete the balance sheet, you will need to calculate one piece of information which has been left out. Refer to the book-keeping equation for help.

1.4 THE BALANCE SHEET IN ACTION

Now that you understand what a balance sheet is, we are going to look at how it changes once a business begins operating.

Remind yourself of the position of Bill Turner's Valuemart (page 8) before he began trading. He has made at least two transactions already. First, he purchased the premises, fixtures and stock from the previous owner. Second, he borrowed £16,000 from the bank. Once trading begins the number of transactions will increase.

Activity

Make a list of transactions that Bill will be undertaking regularly from now on.

Our list includes selling his stock to customers, purchasing more stock from suppliers, making payments for insurances, heating, lighting and rates. He might purchase new equipment and perhaps negotiate for a further loan to pay for it.

There are many more and it is important to realise that the people involved in successful businesses will be busy. They will be dealing with a variety of different transactions. Each time a transaction is made it will affect the business. Let's see how. To simplify things imagine that Bill begins very slowly making only one transaction a day at first. We will also omit the subheadings in the balance sheet.

On 2 July Bill purchased a new fridge for £300, paying for it by cheque. After this transaction his balance sheet would have looked like this:

Balance sheet of Valuemart as at 2 July 1990

	£		£
Premises	84,000	Owner's capital	82,000
Furniture and fittings	7,300	Bank loan	16,000
Stock	5,000		
Bank	1,600		
Cash	100		
	98,000		98,000

One asset, furniture and fittings, has increased in value by £300 while another, bank, has been reduced by the same amount. The balance sheet still balances and the totals are the same as at 1 July. Note, this balance sheet and the ones that follow have been simplified by omitting the division of assets into fixed and current and liabilities into long-term and current.

On 3 July, Bill purchased £500 worth of stock on credit from a supplier. His balance sheet again changed.

Balance sheet of Valuemart as at 3 July 1990

	£		£
Premises	84,000	Owner's capital	82,000
Furniture and fittings	7,300	Bank loan	16,000
Stock	5,500	Trade creditor	500
Bank	1,600		
Cash	100		
	98,500		98,500

This time an asset, stock, has increased by £500 while a new liability, trade creditor, has been increased by the same amount. The balance sheet still balances but this time with totals £500 more than on 2 July.

On 4 July, Bill sold an old fridge, which had been valued at £100 when he bought the business, to a friend for £100. His friend paid £50 in cash and agreed to pay the rest later. Bill's balance sheet then looked like this.

Balance sheet of Valuemart as at 4 July 1990

	£		£
Premises	84,000	Owner's capital	82,000
Furniture and fittings	7,200	Bank loan	16,000
Stock	5,500	Trade creditor	500
Debtor	50		
Bank	1,600		
Cash	150		
	98,500		98,500

On this occasion one asset, furniture and fittings, has been reduced by £100 while there has been an increase in cash of £50 and a new asset, debtor £50, is included. The net effect is that the assets are still worth what they were before the transaction and the balance sheet totals are unchanged.

On 5 July, Bill saw an electronic till reduced to £500 in a sale. The seller would not allow credit and Bill did not want to use any of the money he had available. He managed to persuade his bank manager to lend him the £500 which he used at once to buy the till.

Balance sheet of Valuemart as at 5 July 1990

	£		£
Premises	84,000	Owner's capital	82,000
Furniture and fittings	7,700	Bank loan	16,500
Stock	5,500	Trade creditors	500
Debtor	50		
Bank	1,600		
Cash	150		
	99,000		99,000

His furniture and fittings have increased in value by £500, the value of the till, and the amount he owes to the bank has increased by the same amount. Thus the balance sheet totals £500 more on each side.

On 6 July, Bill started selling and that day he did very well. He sold £300 worth of stock for £400 cash. How did this affect his balance sheet? His stock was reduced in value by £300 but his cash increased by £400. It seems, on first thought, that the balance sheet would not then balance because the assets had increased by £100. However, it must be realised that this £100 represents Bill's profit to date. It is shown in the balance sheet by adding it to his capital. It is extra finance for him to use as he wishes. The balance sheet would now look like this:

Balance sheet of Valuemart as at 6 July 1990

	£		£
Premises	84,000	Owner's capital	82,000
Furniture and fittings	7,700	*add* Profit	100
Stock	5,200		
Debtor	50		82,100
Bank	1,600	Bank loan	16,500
Cash	550	Trade creditors	500
	99,100		99,100

To see if you can keep track of the changes resulting from a series of transactions, attempt the following:

Exercise 1.7

On 1 February 1990 Tom Spear decided to start a mobile greengrocery business. He opened a business bank account with £2,000 of his own money and his balance sheet looked like this:

Balance sheet of Tom Spear as at 1 Feb. 1990

	£		£
Bank	2,000	Capital	2,000

During the next week he made the following transactions:

2 Feb. Negotiated a loan of £500 with his bank manager which was paid into his bank account.
3 Feb. Purchased a motor vehicle for £2,200 from ACE Motors. He paid £1,600 by cheque and agreed to pay the balance within three months.
4 Feb. Withdrew £50 from the bank for use as cash.
5 Feb. Purchased £200 worth of fruit and vegetables, paying for them by cheque.
6 Feb. On his first day of selling he received £120 cash for the sale of £80 worth of fruit and vegetables.

Show his balance sheet on 6 Feb. after all these transactions had taken place. It may help you to do a balance sheet after each transaction.

Of course in most businesses transactions will be taking place with much greater frequency than in the above exercise. There will also be a much greater variety of transactions. This variety will be most evident in businesses which are expanding or already have interests in a range of different activities. Reflect for a moment on this question. How suitable is the balance sheet as a means of recording the large number of different transactions that are taking place continuously?

Some thought should lead you to the conclusion that it is not at all suitable. For a businessman to rewrite his balance sheet after each transaction or even after each week's transactions would be quite time-consuming. In addition it would not provide enough information about the actual transactions. Some other method is needed, therefore, and this will form the subject-matter of the next chapter.

If the balance sheet is so unsuited to reflecting day-to-day changes, why have we used it in that way in this chapter? The answer to my question is that it is an excellent way of learning that:

- every transaction affects a business by altering either the assets or sources of finance or both, while

- the fundamental relationship between sources of finance and assets does not alter.

Understanding these points is central to understanding accounting.

Exercise 1.8

8.1 Complete the following statement. Any transaction causes at least ______ changes within the balance sheet. As a result of these changes the total value of the ________ will still equal the value of ________ ____________ of ________ .

8.2 Write down the book-keeping equation on which the balance sheet is based.

8.3 Explain what happens to the items in the book-keeping equation when £200 worth of unfashionable stock is reduced and sold for £120 cash.

8.4 Look back at the balance sheet of Valuemart as at 6 July on page 15 and rewrite it in good style. Assume that the bank loan does not have to be repaid for five years.

CHAPTER 2

DOUBLE ENTRY BOOK-KEEPING

The last chapter demonstrated how any transaction will have two effects on a balance sheet. You should now be able to identify which assets and/or sources of finance are affected by different transactions. In this chapter we will introduce a more efficient way of recording transactions than redrafting a balance sheet after each one. This will be done by means of ledger accounts. You will learn the principles of double entry book-keeping which will enable you to keep a simple set of ledger accounts.

2.1 THE LEDGER

Book-keeping is the part of accounting concerned with recording transactions. The main book used to record these transactions is known as the ledger. At one time all ledgers were bound volumes. Today loose-leaf paper, ledger cards and computer-based systems are also used. Whatever the means used to record transactions, the principles and methods are basically the same.

The ledger contains accounts of each asset and liability of the business as well as the capital of the owner. It also contains other types of account which will be introduced in the next chapter. The word 'account' is usually abbreviated to 'a/c' and means 'a record of'. Each account contains a record of changes in one particular asset, liability or in the capital. The traditional layout of a page in the ledger is shown on page 19.

Note:

- Each page in the ledger is divided clearly into two sides.
- The left-hand side is known as the debit side but is usually abbreviated to 'Dr'. This abbreviation derives from 'Debtor'. a term still used in some texts to describe the left-hand side of the page.
- The right-hand side is known as the credit side and is abbreviated to 'Cr'. The word 'credit' has different meansings in other contexts. When referring to ledger accounts, though it is simply the right-hand side of the account.

Dr			Cash account				4	Cr
date	details	folio	£	p	date	details	folio	£	p

- The name of the account is written at the top of the page, which is numbered for reference purposes. The cash a/c above is on page 4 of the ledger. Some accounts will require more pages than others. The loose-leaf system provides useful flexibility in such circumstances.
- The columns on the debit side are the same as on the credit side. There is space to record the date, brief details and the amount of money involved in a transaction. The folio column is used mainly to provide a cross-reference system. This will be demonstrated later.

Ledger paper and books can be purchased from all good stationers.

Let's turn now to the principles and practice of keeping a ledger. Suppose that Bill Turner, to whom we referred in Chapter 1 decided when he started the business that he would keep a set of ledger accounts. How should he begin? One way is to write down the state of the business on the date he decides to begin his ledger. The easiest way of showing this clearly is by means of a balance sheet. Bill's balance sheet of 1 July 1990 is repeated here for ease of reference.

Balance sheet of Valuemart as at 1 July 1990

	£		£
Assets		*Sources of finance*	
Premises	84,000	Owner's capital	82,000
Furniture and fittings	7,000		
Stock	5,000	*Liabilities*	
Bank	1,900	Bank loan	16,000
Cash	100		
	98,000		98,000

2.2 OPENING AN ACCOUNT

The first step is to open a ledger account for each item in the balance sheet. The value of each asset is placed on the debit side of its own account, while the values of capital and any liabilities are placed on the credit side of their accounts. The date will be that of the balance sheet from which we have taken the figures and in the details column each entry can be described by the term 'balance'. For the time being we will not bother giving each account a page number as the use of the folio column for cross-referencing will be dealt with later. Apart from the fact that they wouldn't be condensed together on one page, the ledger accounts will then appear as below.

Dr — Premises account — Cr

1990		£			£
1 July	Balance	84,000.00			

Furniture and fittings account

1 July	Balance	7,000.00			

Stock account

1 July	Balance	5,000.00			

Bank account

1 July	Balance	1,900.00			

Cash account

1 July	Balance	100.00			

Capital account

			1 July	Balance	82,000.00

Bank loan account

			1 July	Balance	16,000.00

In Chapter 1 you learnt that a balance sheet was a reflection of the book-keeping equation: assets = capital + liabilities. If all the assets are now entered on the debit side of their ledger accounts while the capital and liabilities are placed on the credit side of their accounts, it follows that the total value of all the debit balances must equal the total value of all the credit balances.

It is important, however, that you do not confuse balance sheets with ledger accounts. Use the terms debit and credit to refer to the left and right hand side of ledger accounts. Do not use these terms when referring to a balance sheet. A balance sheet is an accounting statement not a ledger account.

2.3 ENTERING TRANSACTIONS

The next step in keeping a ledger is to enter transactions in the accounts. We will consider the assets first and then the sources of finance. An asset is represented in its own account by a debit balance. If something happens to increase the value of this asset, we show it by making another debit entry. If the asset is reduced in value a credit entry is made in that account.

For example, on 1 May, Tom Smith possessed two delivery vehicles worth £4,000 and £2,000. On 2 May he purchased another for £1,000 and 3 May he sold his most valuable vehicle for £4,000, exactly what it was worth. These events would be recorded as follows.

Dr — Delivery vehicles account — Cr

		£			£
1 May	Balance	6,000	3 May		4,000
2 May		1,000			

Sources of finance, whether owner's capital or liabilities to outsiders, are shown in their own accounts by credit balances. If something happens to increase the value of one of these, we show it by making another credit entry. If the source of finance is reduced in value a debit entry is made in that account.

For example, on 1 May, Tom Smith owed Busifinance Co. £4,000, which had been borrowed to enable him to start his business. On 4 May he negotiated a further loan of £3,000 but on 8 May an early and successful conclusion of a deal enabled him to repay £2,000. These events in the account of this liability will be recorded as follows.

Dr — Busifinance Co. account — Cr

		£			£
8 May		2,000	1 May	Balance	4,000
			4 May		3,000

What has been learnt so far about entries in ledger accounts can be summarised for easy reference.

Debit	Any asset account — Credit
1 Opening value of that asset. 2 Increases in value of that asset.	Deductions in value of that asset.

Debit	Any source of finance account — Credit
Deductions in value of that source of finance.	1 Opening value of that source of finance. 2 Increase in value of that source of finance.

The amount that any asset is worth can be calculated at any time. If the original value of an asset together with any additions to it are on the debit side and deductions are on the credit side, the difference between the two sides on a certain date will tell us what the asset is then worth. Similarly, the amount of a liability or the owner's capital can be calculated. If the original value of a source of finance together with any additions to it are on the credit side and deductions are on the debit side, the difference between the two sides at a particular time will tell us the amount of the liability or capital at that time.

The difference in value between the two sides of an account is known as the balance of the account.

2.4 DOUBLE ENTRY

When considering the effect of transactions on the balance sheet in Section 1.4 we saw how every transaction caused two changes in the assets and/or sources of finance of the business. This is shown in the ledger by making two entries, one in each account affected. Double entry book-keeping is the name given to this system of recording transactions in the ledger. It is important that you learn how to operate it.

As an example, look back at Tom Smith's delivery vehicles account on page 21. Neither the transaction of 2 May nor that of 3 May have any description in the 'details' column. This is because we did not give enough information for it to be completed. Take the transaction of 2 May - Tom purchased a vehicle for £1,000. How did he purchase it? There two possibilities. First he could have paid for it at the time of purchase. If he did this, besides showing an increase in his delivery vehicles by debiting this account, we should also show a reduction in one of his money accounts for the same amount. Whether this would involve an entry in the cash account or the bank account would depend on whether he paid by cash or by cheque. Let's assume he paid such a large sum by cheque. What kind of entry would you have to make in the bank account?

If you said credit, good. If not look at the summary on page 21 again. A deduction from an asset is shown by a credit entry in that account. Clearly the money in Tom's bank account would go down as a result of paying £1,000 by cheque for a vehicle. Therefore the bank account should be credited. (Those readers with current bank accounts who receive bank statements might find this confusing. When you pay £1,000 for, say, a vehicle, the bank will debit your account. This is because they are looking at the transaction from their point of view, not yours. If you have money in a current bank account, the bank owes you the money. From their point of view this is a liability. When you use £1,000 of it to pay someone, the bank owes you less. They show this reduction of the liability by a debit entry. We will look at this in more detail in Chapter 7.)

In double entry book-keeping each entry is described by the name of the account affected. The description in the details column of Tom's delivery vehicles account would therefore be 'bank'. In his bank account the description would be 'delivery vehicles'.

A second possibility is that Tom did not pay for the vehicle at the time of purchase but agreed to pay at a later date. This is known as a credit purchase. In this case the other effect of the purchase is that he owes £1,000 to the seller. This is a liability to Tom. The seller was Ted's Garage. An account would have to be opened for this company if one did not already exist. What kind of entry would it be? If you said credit, good. If not, look again at the summary on page 21. An increase or the start of a liability is shown by a credit entry in that account. Clearly Tom owes £1,000 to Ted's Garage as a result of this transaction, therefore the account for Ted's Garage should be credited.

In the delivery vehicles account the description would be 'Ted's Garage' and in the account for Ted's Garage the description would be 'delivery vehicles'. Remember, in double-entry book-keeping an entry is described by the name of the other account affected.

Of course, it is also possible that Tom might have combined the above two methods of purchase. He could have paid a deposit of, say, £400 by cheque and agreed to pay the outstanding £600 at a later date. If this was the case there would be a credit entry of only £400 in the bank account showing a reduction in this asset by that amount. There would also be a credit entry of £600 in the account for Ted's Garage, showing a liability of that amount. How would this be shown in the delivery vehicles account? The easiest way is to make two debit entries on the same date - one for £400 described as 'bank' and the other for £600 described as 'Ted's Garage'.

Tom's transaction of 2 May, however it was financed, illustrates the most important principle of double-entry book-keeping:

- *Every transaction involves a debit entry in one account and a corresponding credit entry in another account.*

If a transaction is more complicated it may involve two debit entries in one account and two separate credit entries in different accounts. The value of the debit entry or entries for each transaction, however, must equal the value of the credit entry or entries. This is how we express in the ledger what was learnt earlier when observing the effect of transactions on the balance sheet. Every transaction has two effects on the assets and/or sources of finance. In the ledger every transaction involves a debit entry in one account and a corresponding credit entry in another account.

Exercise 2.1

Look again at Tom's delivery vehicles account on page 21.
Referring to Tom's transaction of 3 May draft ledger accounts and complete the entries for each of the following *separate* possibilities:

(a) Tom sold the vehicle for £4,000 cash.
(b) Tom sold the vehicle to Parkhill Motors on credit.
(c) Parkhill Motors paid £1,000 by cheque and agreed to pay the outstanding £3,000 at a later date.

Note that whichever of the above circumstances applies there is a debit entry for each credit entry. Also the description of each account is the name of the other account affected by the transaction.

Understanding double-entry book-keeping is important. If you follow what we have done in this chapter so far, fine. If not, you should look through it again before attempting the following exercise. Practising it is the best way to master double-entry book-keeping.

Exercise 2.2

On page 20 in this chapter we opened a set of ledger accounts for Bill Turner's Valuemart, which began business on July 1990. Copy out these accounts leaving space to enter these transactions;

2 July Bill purchased a new fridge for £300, by cheque.
3 July He purchased £500 worth of stock on credit from a supplier called JLK Foods.
4 July He sold an old fridge worth £100 to a friend, Sally Moore, for that amount. She paid £50 in cash and agreed to pay the rest later.
5 July He borrowed a further £500 from his bank and used it to buy an electronic till.
6 July He sold £300 worth of stock for £400 cash.

These are the transactions we used in Section 1.4. They have been repeated for your convenience. Complete the entries for each of the transactions, opening new accounts where necessary. Make certain that every transaction has a debit entry to correspond to each credit entry.

2.5 VERTICAL LEDGER ACCOUNTS

In this chapter and the remainder of the book the style of ledger account layout is of the traditional horizontal sort. Descriptions for debit entries appear to the left of descriptions for credit entries. When accounting machines or computers are used a vertical style is normal with all descriptions in the same column. The furniture and fittings account on page 273 would look like this in vertical style:

Furniture and fittings

Date	*Description*	*Dr.*	*Cr.*	*Balance*
1 July	Balance			7000 dr
2 July	Bank	300		7300 dr
4 July	S. Moore		50	7250 dr
4 July	Cash		50	7200 dr
5 July	Bank loan	500		7700 dr

The only other occasion you will see a vertical ledger account in this book will be when we look at bank statements in Chapter 7. Banks are large organisations that have computerised their accounting systems.

One obvious advantage of this method is the automatic balancing that takes place after each entry. This is done speedily by a computer or machine. Usually its importance is not thought sufficient to calculate it after each entry when the accounts are hand-written.

Exercise 2.3

Complete the following sentences:

(a) A ________ ________ is a statement of the assets and sources of finance of a business at a particular date.
(b) A ________ ________ is an individual record of transactions affecting one aspect of the business.
(c) An asset is represented in its own account by a ________ ________.
(d) Increases in the value of an asset require a ________ entry in that account while decreases in value require a ________ entry.
(e) ______ ______ book-keeping is the name given to the system whereby the dual effects of each transaction are recorded in the ledger.
(f) A source of finance is represented in its own account by a ________ balance.
(g) Increases in the value of a source of finance require a ________ entry in that account while decreases in value require a ________ entry.

Exercise 2.4

State the accounts to be debited and credited for each of the following *separate* transactions:

(a) Purchased equipment by cheque £600.
(b) Sold motor vehicle by cheque £300.
(c) Purchased stock by cash £150.
(d) Paid £400 cash into bank.
(e) Withdrew £300 from the bank for use as cash.
(f) Paid trade creditors £50 cash.
(g) Paid trade creditors £450 by cheque.
(h) Paid £250 cash into the bank.
(i) Received £250 from debtors in cash.

Exercise 2.5

From the following information open ledger accounts. Then enter the transactions, opening new accounts when necessary.

Balance sheet of Jill Evans as at 1 May 1990

	£		£
Premises	33,000	Capital	65,000
Equipment	15,000	Trade creditors	6,750
Debtors	5,500		
Stock	17,000		
Cash	1,250		
	71,750		71,750

2 May Purchased equipment for £500 by cash.
3 May Purchased £950 stock from AJK on credit.
4 May Sold £2,000 of old equipment at book value for cash.
5 May Opened a bank account by paying in £500 cash.
6 May Paid £300 of amount owing to trade creditors by cheque.
7 May Sold £300 worth of stock for £500 cash.

CHAPTER 3

EXPANDING THE LEDGER

The last chapter introduced the principles of double-entry book-keeping and applied them to assets and sources of finance. In this chapter we will apply these rules to the asset, stock. Then we will consider how to deal with transactions involving expenses and incomes.

Many businesses are involved in buying and selling. The stock accounts of these businesses are therefore going to be very busy indeed, with large numbers of transactions to be entered. To keep things simple, four additional accounts are used to record the different events that change the amount of stock. These are: purchases account, purchases returns account, sales account and sales returns account. They may be thought of as subdivisions of the stock account.

3.1 PURCHASES

Purchases of stock increase the value of this asset. What kind of entry in the stock account shows this? If you have mastered the rules in the last chapter, you should have said 'debit'. Instead of making the debit entries in the stock account, we are going to enter all such debits in a purchases of stock account, which for convenience will be called the purchases account.

In which account will the corresponding credit entry be found? This will depend on the method of payment. If payment is made immediately the credit will be entered in the cash or bank accounts, showing the reduction of an asset. If the goods (as stock is sometimes called) are bought on credit then the credit will be entered in the account of the supplier, who is a creditor to the purchaser. This shows the increase of a liability.

For example, on 1 April a greengrocer bought £150 of fruit on credit from Fruitgrowers Ltd. The entries in the greengrocer's ledger accounts would be as follows:

Dr Purchases

		£	
1 April	Fruitgrowers	150	

Fruitgrowers Ltd					Cr
					£
			1 April	Purchaser	150

3.2 PURCHASES RETURNS

Sometimes goods which have been bought are later returned by the purchaser. This usually happens when something is found to be wrong with them. These purchases returns are also known as returns outward because they are being sent out from the firm which bought them. Sometimes, therefore, the account is called the returns outward account.

Let's see how such events are recorded in the purchaser's accounts. Suppose that the greengrocer mentioned above discovered that £20 worth of the fruit he had purchased was rotten. On 2 April he sent it back to the supplier. The real value of his purchases on 1 April is now £130 (£150 less £20 returned). Also he owes Fruitgrowers Ltd only £130. We can show the reduction of the liability by making a debit entry in the supplier's account, following the rules of the last chapter. The credit entry could be made in the purchase account as this would achieve the desired effect of reducing the purchases figure to the right amount. To avoid complicating the purchases account, however, we make the credit entry in the purchases returns account. The accounts will now look like this:

Fruitgrowers Ltd

2 April	Purchases returns	20	1 April	Purchases	150

Dr		Purchases			Cr
		£			£
1 April	Fruitgrowers	150			

Purchases returns

			2 April	Fruitgrowers	20

The account for Fruitgrowers shows that £130 is now owing. To obtain the real value of the purchases we have to look at both the purchases account and the purchases returns account. Together they show that the net value of purchases is £130 (£150 less £20).

If all purchases and returns of goods bought were entered in the stock account the type of entries would be the same, i.e. a debit entry to record an increase of stock when goods are bought and a credit entry to show a reduction of stock when goods are returned. Putting all purchases account and purchases returns in a separate account helps keep things simple.

3.3 **SALES**

Sales of stock decrease the value of this asset. What kind of entry in the stock account would show this? Knowledge of the rules of entry introduced in Chapter 2 should have enabled you to say 'credit', which is the correct answer. Instead of making the credit entries in the stock account, however, we are going to make all such entries in the sales of stock account.

In which account will the corresponding debit entry be made? This will depend on how the stock was sold. If sold for money, it will be in either the cash or bank account, showing an increase in the value of one of these assets. If the goods were sold on credit then the person to whom they were sold owes that sum to the business. A debit entry in the customer's account will represent an asset because we assume that debtors will pay their debts.

For example, on 1 June a wholesaler sold £90 worth of tinned peas to Les Solt, a retailer who was allowed monthly credit. The entries in the wholesaler's accounts will be as follows:

Sales		Cr
		£
	1 June L. Solt	90

Dr	Les Solt	
	£	
1 June Sales	90	

3.4 **SALES RETURNS**

When goods which have been sold are returned later for a valid reason, entries must be made to record the event. These sales returns are called returns inward because they are being returned back into stock by a customer. Sometimes, therefore, the account is known as the returns inward account.

Let's see how such a transaction is recorded in the seller's books. Suppose that, on checking the peas he had purchased, Mr Solt found that £10 worth of them were beans. As he had more than enough of these already he returned them to his supplier on 2 June. The wholesaler will have to reduce the amount of Solt's debt by £10. A credit entry will be made in Solt's account, following the rules in the last chapter. Remember, a debtor's account represents an asset and an asset is reduced by a credit entry. The corresponding debit entry for £10 could be made in the sales account, as this would have the desired effect of reducing the sales to its true figure. To avoid complicating the sales account, however, we make the debit entry in the sales returns account instead. The accounts will now look like this:

Les Solt

1 June	Sales	90	2 June	Sales returns	10

Dr		Sales			Cr
		£			£
			1 June	L. Solt	90

	Sales returns				
2 June	L. Solt	10			

The account for Les Solt shows that £80 is now owed by him to the wholesaler. To obtain the real value of sales we have to look at both the sales account and the sales returns account. Together they show that the net value of the sales is £80 (£90 less £10).

If all sales and sales returns were entered in the stock account, the type of entries would be the same, i.e. a credit entry to record a decrease of stock when goods are sold and a debit entry to show an increase when goods are returned. Using a sales account to record all the sales and a separate sales returns account for all such returns helps to keep matters simple.

Correctly used the four accounts we have just considered enable the stock account to be reserved for the valuation of stock which is made at stocktaking time.

Exercise 3.1

1 State whether the entries in the following accounts will be debit or credit: (a) purchases, (b) purchases returns, (c) sales, (d) sales returns.
2 Give the alternative names for: (a) purchases returns, (b) sales returns.

Exercise 3.2

Powa Electrics is a wholesaler which has Jim Hogg, a DIY retailer, as one of its customers. On 1 March, Jim owed £160 from the previous month. The following transactions then took place. On 2 March, Powa Electrics supplied Jim with £170 worth of materials on credit. On 3 March, Jim returned materials worth £40 because they were not of the type he had ordered.

Show how the above would be recorded in the ledger of (a) Powa Electrics and (b) Jim Hogg.

Note: when you do this kind of exercise it is important to be absolutely clear from whose point of view you are considering the transaction. Begin by labelling clearly for (a) *Powa Electrics books*. Then consider the transactions *solely* from this company's point of view. When you have done this put a new heading and consider the transactions from Jim Hogg's viewpoint.

3.5 **EXPENSES**

All businesses will have to make payments for a number of benefits and services they receive but which do not directly provide an asset owned by the business. These are known as expenses. For example the owner may employ people to work for him. In return for their services he will pay them wages or salaries depending on their conditions of service. He will need to open an account to record the amount they are paid. This will be called the wages or salaries account. Of course some employees may be wage earners and others salaried. In this case the business will usually have two separate accounts.

Activity

Make a list of some services required and expenses incurred by any business known to you.

Services required by different businesses will vary but many will be the same. Some of the most common are: the use of another's property, for which rent will be paid; use of local authority services such as refuse collection for which rates will be paid; the use of the Royal Mail, for which postage will be paid; and the use of a loan from someone else, on which interest will be paid. Each of these will be given its own account with a name which concisely explains its function. Accounts for the above services would be entitled 'rent', 'rates', 'postage' and 'interest on loan'. Other expenses you might have mentioned include: lighting and heating, advertising, repairs, insurance, telephone, carriage inwards (the delivery charge on goods coming into the firm, i.e. purchases) and carriage outwards (the delivery charge paid to have goods going out of the firm, i.e. sales).

The actual name given sometimes varies. For example, 'electricity account' may be preferred to 'lighting and heating account'. Some firms join similar expenses together such as rent and rates or postage and telephone. Small items may be put together under the heading 'sundry expenses', particularly if they do not occur often.

You may be able to work out what sort of entry will be needed in an expense account. Assume that a businessman who rents his premises makes his payments in cash. What sort of entry will he make in his cash account? Credit is the correct answer because this reduces the value of an asset. Each time the rent is paid, cash is reduced.

What sort of entry must be made, therefore, in the rent account? The answer must be debit because each transaction needs a debit and a credit entry. This does not give a reasoned expanation, but of course there is one. Expenses have been defined earlier as payments for services that do not directly provide an asset owned by the business. These services are advantages to the business, however, and very similar to assets in that respect.

Therefore the rules for their entry are the same as for assets - a debit entry to record an increase and a credit entry to record a reduction in its own account. In the above example, each time the rent is paid the total amount paid is increased and therefore a debit entry is needed in the rent account.

We can summarise the rules for making entries in expense accounts as follows:

Debit	Any expense account	Credit
Increase of the expense		Decrease of the expense

The double entry will normally be completed by an entry in the cash or bank account. There are three main exceptions to this.

Exercise 3.3

Complete the following table:

Transaction	Account to be debited	Account to be credited
(a) Paid wages by cash		
(b) Paid insurance by cheque		
(c) Received by cheque rebate of insurance previously paid		

3.6 DISCOUNT ALLOWED

This is an expense which many firms incur in order to encouage prompt payment from their debtors. For example, a retailer called Ben Wilson owed a wholesaler £200 for a purchase made on 18 May. In the wholesaler's books the debt will appear like this:

Dr		B. Wilson	Cr
		£	
18 May	Sales	200	

The wholesaler has a policy of allowing debtors to deduct a discount of 3% for settlement within seven days of a statement being sent. This was done on 31 May and Wilson paid by cheque on 4 June. How much did he pay?

Wilson's cheque would have been for £194 as he is entitled to deduct £6 discount from the £200 due. Being able to calculate percentages is essential. We will explain the basic method in case you have forgotten it.

'Per cent' means per hundred. Whatever percentage is involved is written as a fraction of 100. Three per cent is therefore written $^3/_{100}$. The next step is to multiply this figure by the amount you are calculating the percentage of. In the above example this will be:

$$\frac{3}{100} \times \frac{200}{1} = £6.$$

Let's now return to the question of how the discount allowed to B. Wilson will be shown in the wholesaler's ledger. On 4 June two separate credit entries will be made in Wilson's account to show howsettlement of the £200 due has been made. First, an entry for £194 with a corresponding debit entry in the bank account for the amount of the cheque. Second, an entry for £6 with a corresponding debit entry for the discount allowed. The accounts will then look like this:

Dr B. Wilson Cr

		£			£
18 May	Sales	200	4 June	Bank	194
			4 June	Discount allowed	6

Discount allowed

4 June	B. Wilson	6			

Bank

4 June	B. Wilson	194			

3.1 BAD DEBTS

This is the expense incurred when debtors fail to pay their debts. In the balance sheet, debtors appear as an asset because it is assumed that anyone to whom credit has been allowed will pay what they owe. Once it is known that a debt is never going to be collected this fact must be shown in the accounts. If it were not then the accounts would not be giving a fair picture of the assets of the business. For example, Ron Evans, who for a short and unsuccessful time was a retailer, owes a wholesaler £180. The wholesaler has been unable to collect his money and has just heard that there is no likelihood that he ever will. He must remove the asset by making a credit entry in the debtor's account. The corresponding debit entry will be in an account termed 'bad debts'. The accounts will look like this:

Dr Ron Evans Cr

		£			£
6 Jan.	Sales	180	10 Oct.	Bad debts	180

Bad debts

10 Oct.	R. Evans	180			

In effect an asset has been converted into an expense. Naturally any firm allowing credit to another takes all reasonable precautions to make certain that this kind of thing does not happen too often. It is accepted, however, that 'writing off' a bad debt, as this process is called, is an occasional and inevitable part of allowing credit to others.

Activity

Put yourself in the position of a wholesaler who has just received a request from a retailer that he should be allowed to make use of the monthly credit terms allowed to other retailers. What steps would you take to minimise the possibility of bad debts?

There are a number of possibilities. References could be requested from other firms with which the retailer has been dealing. You might give monthly credit only when he has proved to be a reliable payer on a weekly basis. Perhaps a maximum credit limit could be set for a trial period to reduce the risk of large debts not being paid.

Whatever you do, the risk of non-payment by some debtors always exists. It is important, therefore, to act quickly when a slow or bad payer is identified and try to prevent the loss involved being too great. This might involve correspondence from yourself or even a solicitor. In the case of larger debts you will have to decide whether legal action, which can sometimes be very costly, is worthwhile. If all this fails the value of the asset, debtor, must be reduced in the manner described.

3.8 **DEPRECIATION**

This is the expense incurred when one of the fixed assets owned by a business falls in value. Just as 'debtors' cannot be allowed to include any amounts which it is known will not be collected, so it would be wrong to allow an asset, such as motor vehicles, equipment, machinery or furniture and fittings, to be valued at a figure greater than its true worth.

By now you should have grasped what kind of entry in an asset account is needed to reduce the value of that asset: a credit entry. Refer back to page 21 if you thought otherwise. The corresponding debit entry will be in an account named 'depreciation on . . .' (the name of the fixed asset involved).

For example, B. Wilson purchased a delivery van on 27 April for £1,500. By 31 December of that year it was worth only £1,100. Its value had fallen or depreciated by £400. This would be shown in the accounts like this:

Dr		Delivery vehicle			Cr
		£			£
27 April	Bank	1,500	31 Dec.	Depreciation	400

Depreciation on delivery vehicle			
31 Dec.	Delivery vehicle	400	

Discount allowed, bad debts and depreciation are all expenses commonly incurred in running a business. The difference between them and other expenses like rent, rates and insurance is that, instead of a direct money payment being made, an asset other than bank or cash is reduced in value.

Exercise 3.4

Which asset is reduced in value under the following circumstances?

(a) Rent is paid by cheque.
(b) A customer is allowed 3% discount for prompt payment.
(c) Wages are paid in cash.
(d) A customer unable to pay an amount owed.
(e) It is discovered that machinery purchased for £1,000 is now worth £800.

3.9 INCOMES

While all businesses will have to pay for a variety of expenses to enable them to operate, some will also receive income for the services they provide for others. For many businesses the major receipt of money will come from sales of their stock, an item dealt with at the beginning of this chapter. Here we are concerned with those receipts of money which come from sources other than sales of stock. For example, a business may own property which it does not need for its own use but which it does not wish to sell. Renting this property to another firm will enable it to gain useful income. Similarly one firm may provide a service for another and charge commission. Care is needed in the accounts to distinguish such receipts from payments. It is usual to label an account for income received from letting out property 'rent received account' to avoid confusion with the rent account which is for the expense involved when another's property is used by the firm itself. Similarly, commission account will be for the expense, and commission received account for the income.

The entries to be made in accounts recording incomes will be opposite to those demonstrated for expenses. When the money is received an asset account such as bank is increased by a debit entry. At the same time a compensating credit entry is made in the income account.

For example, a retailer lets the flat above his shop for £80 a month. This is paid in cash on the first of each month. The relevant entries for March in the retailer's accounts will be:

Dr		Cash			Cr
		£			£
1 March	Rent received	80			

Rent received

			1 March	Cash	80

3.10 DISCOUNT RECEIVED

An income which many businesses enjoy comes from settling the amounts due to their suppliers promptly. This is known as discount received. It takes the form of a reduction in the amount that has to be paid rather than an actual physical receipt of money. Thus the debit entry corresponding to the credit entry in the discount received account will be in the creditor's account, showing the reduction of a liability. For example, a retailer purchases goods for £400 from Western Suppliers on 3 July. A discount of 2% is offered for settlement received by 31 July so the retailer pays by cheque on 30 July. Relevant entries in the accounts of the retailer follow.

Dr		Western Suppliers			Cr
		£			£
30 July	Bank	392	3 July	Purchases	400
30 July	Discount received	8			

Bank

			30 July	Western Suppliers	392

Discount received

			30 July	Western Suppliers	8

It is important to make the two debit entries in the account for Western Suppliers simultaneously. Otherwise it might seem that £8 was still owing at the end of the month and a payment might be made.

3.11 SUMMARY

It is possible to summarise all the reason for making a debit or credit entry in the form of a ledger account.

Reasons for making an entry in its own account	
Debit	*Credit*
1 An opening asset value	1 Opening value of a source of finance
2 Increasing asset value	2 Increase of a source of finance
3 An expense	3 An income
4 Increase in an expense	4 Increase in an income
5 Reduction of a source of finance	5 Reduction of an asset
6 Reduction of an income	6 Reduction of an expense

You can use this as a quick means of reference when in doubt about whether a credit or debit entry is needed. Remember, sources of finance include capital and liabilities. Try it now if you need to.

Exercise 3.5

Complete the table below to show the entries need to record the transactions.

Transaction	*Account to be debited*	*Account to be credited*
(a) Payment of rates by cheque.		
(b) Purchase of goods for resale on credit from Asta Suppliers.		
(c) Purchase of office desk for cash.		
(d) Commission received by cheque for services rendered.		
(e) Deducted discount for prompt settlement of amount owing to Asta Suppliers.		
(f) Discovery of error resulting in repayment by cheque of part of the commission received.		

Exercise 3.6

John Dean has £1,560 in his business bank account on 1 April. Open a ledger account with this balance and then enter the following transactions, completing all the entries in the other accounts you will need to open.

2 April	Paid rates by cheque £250
3 April	Paid employees' wages by cheque £620
4 April	Received £60 rent from a tenant by cheque.
5 April	Paid insurance £120
6 April	Paid tenant rent rebate of £10.
7 April	Received insurance rebate of £12.
8 April	Withdrew £100 from bank for private use.

Exercise 3.7

Food Supplies is a wholesaler which has Jim Turner, a retailer, as one of its customers. On 1 June Jim owed £250 from the previous month. The following transactions then took place:

3 June Jim purchased £458 of materials from Food Supplies on credit.
6 June Jim returned materials worth £75 because they were unsuitable.
9 June Jim settled the amount due on 1June. He was entitled to 4% cash discount.

Show how the above would be recorded in the ledger of: (a) Food Supplies, (b) Jim Turner.

Exercise 3.8

Prepare accounts to show the following information in (a) the ledger of Zoe Clough, (b) the ledger of Peter Blake.

1 April Zoe Clough owed Peter Blake £450.
3 April Zoe purchased £356 of goods on credit from Blake.
5 April Zoe paid the amount due on 1 April by cheque and was prompt enough to deduct the 2% discount that applied.
6 April Zoe returned £20 worth of wrongly-sized goods to Blake.

Exercise 3.9

Helen Berry started a retail business on 1 March 1989 with £3,000 in the bank, furniture and fittings worth £3,000 and premises valued at £15,000. She had borrowed £2,000 from Busifinance Ltd for six months.

Draft a balance sheet and open ledger accounts for all the items included. Enter the following transactions in the ledger, opening new accounts where necessary.

2 March Purchased on credit £1,000 stock from Northern Foods and £500 stock from AKJ.
3 March Sales for cash £50.
4 March Sales for cash £100.
5 March Paid £80 cash into bank.
6 March Returned £100 of goods to AKJ.
7 March Paid amount owing to Northern Foods by cheque less 2% discount.
8 March Sold goods for £100 to N. Timms on credit.
9 March Paid insurance £25 by cheque.
10 March Received £20 cash for letting the flat above the shop.

Note that you have to calculate the owner's capital on 1 March yourself.

CHAPTER 4

THE TRIAL BALANCE

The last two chapters concerned the rules of double-entry book-keeping and the application of these rules to a variety of transactions. In this chapter we are going to look at a simple way of making a preliminary check on the accuracy of the entries made in the ledger. We will do this by balancing the accounts and then drafting a trial balance. We will start, however, by demonstrating how the folio column in the ledger can be used to provide a reference system for all the double entries. Such a system helps to speed up the process of checking that all the double entries have been completed correctly.

4.1 THE FOLIO COLUMN

The folio column in the ledger is the only one we have not used so far. Remind yourself of its position by looking back at the diagram on page 19. You will remember that a folio is a page or leaf of a book and that all pages in the ledger will be numbered. We can use these numbers to provide us with our reference system. An example should make this clear. This a/c appears in the ledger of a wholesaler.

Dr Tom Paxton 44 Cr

			£ p				£ p
1 Aug.	Sales	26	100.00	2 Aug.	Returns in	32	25.00
4 Aug.	Sales	26	8.00	5 Aug.	Bank	12	70.00
				5 Aug.	Discount allowed	38	5.00

Tom's account is on page 44 of the ledger (or on a ledger card numbered 44). The entry in the folio column for each transaction tells us on which page of the ledger the other entry can be found. From this you can deduce that the account for sales is on page 26, returns inward on page 32, bank on page 12 and discount allowed on page 38. Looking for a numbered page or card is much quicker than looking for the name of an account when you are checking to make certain that all entries have been completed correctly.

4.2 BALANCING ACCOUNTS

Let's turn now to checking the accuracy of transactions made in the ledger. To do this, you must learn the technique of balancing the ledger accounts. The balance of an account is the difference between the two sides. This is the most significant figure in the account because it tells us the value of the asset, liability, expense or income of which the account is a record. When the debit side is greater it is termed a debit balance. Conversely, credit balance indicates the difference when that side of the account is greater.

To illustrate this, look at the solution to Exercise 3.9 on page 278. The ledger accounts there contain the following balances:

Premises £15,000 dr balance; furniture and fittings £3,000 dr balance; bank £2,075 dr balance; capital £19,000 cr balance; Busifinance £2,000 cr balance; purchases £1,500 dr balance; AKJ £400 cr balance; sales £250 cr balance; cash £90 dr balance; purchases returns £100 cr balance; discount recd. £20 cr balance; N. Timms £100 dr balance; insurance £25 dr balance; rent received £20 cr balance.

In many of the accounts there was only one entry on one side. In some of these, e.g. premises and capital, that one entry was described as balance in the details column. This was because that opening entry had come directly from the list of balances in the balance sheet.

We can now proceed to the method used to show what the balance is at a particular time. This is known as balancing the accounts. Let's assume that Helen Berry's accounts in Exercise 3.9 are to be balanced on 10 March. This is what her bank account will look like after it has been balanced:

Dr | Bank account | Cr

		£			£
1 March	Balance	3,000	7 March	Northern Foods	980
5 March	Cash	80	9 March	Insurance	25
			10 March	Balance c/d	2,075
		3,080			3,080
11 March	Balance b/d	2,075			

This, in stages, is how it is done:

1 Find the difference between the two sides.
2 Place this figure on the side of the account that is smaller. It is described as balance c/d which means that the balance is to be carried down. The date is that on which the account is being balanced.
3 Total the two sides, drawing the lines carefully so that the two totals are level with each other. As the difference between the two sides has been added to the smaller side both sides will now be equal.

4 Enter the balance on to the side to which it really belongs, describing it as the balance b/d which means that the balance has been brought down. It is dated one day after that of the balance carried down figure. The folio column is used for c/d and b/d.

In the above account we can now tell at a glance that, when business starts on 11 March, Helen Berry has £2,075 in her bank account. The significance of dating the balance to be carried down one day earlier than the balance which has been brought down is that account is shown as being temporarily closed at the end of business on one day and then reopened, with the same amount, when business begins next day.

Where there is only one entry in an account, that is the balance or difference between the two sides. It perhaps seems unnecessary to go through the process of balancing such an account. However this is still done by some people and it does serve as a means of showing that all the accounts have been looked at and brought up to date at the same time. For example, it is not likely that the premises account will contain many new entries from one year to the next. Suppose Helen Berry decides to balance it at the end of her current financial year which will be on 28 February 1990. This is how it will look:

Dr Premises account Cr

1989		£	*1990*		£
1 March	Balance	15,000	28 February	Balance c/d	15,000
1990					
1 March	Balance b/d	15,000			

The procedure is the same as above except that there is no need to total the two sides. When the balance to be carried down is inserted on the smaller, credit, side both sides are immediately equal. Underlining the two figures is enough to show they are the totals.

When should accounts be balanced? There is no hard and fast rule. Occasions when it is often done include: the need for a new page of an account when the existing page is full and at the end of a firm's financial year. There is in fact nothing to prevent an account being balanced at any time when it is felt that the information it reveals will be useful. One such occasion might be when a check is to be made on the accuracy of entries made in the ledger accounts. It is to this that we will now turn.

A brief summary of what has been learnt so far about double entry book-keeping will help to show how the balances in the accounts can be used as a means of checking the accuracy of the entries within. The following diagram is virtually self-explanatory.

	BALANCE SHEET	
Assets	=	Capital and Liabilities
	LEDGER	
Dr balances	=	Cr balances
	Transactions	
Dr entry £X	1	Cr entry £X
Dr entry £Y	2	Cr entry £Y
Dr entry £Z	3	Cr entry £Z
Dr balances	=	Cr balances

We begin with the balance sheet which reflected the book-keeping equation, i.e. *assets* must equal the *sources of finance (capital* and *liabilities)*. In the ledger each asset was shown as a debit balance in its own account and each source of finance as a credit balance. Therefore the debit balances will equal the credit balances. When transactions are entered in the ledger additional accounts may be opened but whatever the transaction it will involve a debit entry of the same amount as the corresponding credit entry. Therefore after any number of transactions the total value of the debit balances *should* still equal the total value of the credit balances.

Checking that the debit balances do in fact equal the credit balances is done by making a list of all the balances. This is known as a trial balance and usually takes the following form.

Trial balance of Helen Berry as at 10 March 1989

Accounts	*Dr balances* £	*Cr balances* £
Premises	15,000	
Furniture and fittings	3,000	
Bank	2,075	
Capital		19,000
Busifinance		2,000
Purchases	1,500	
Northern Foods	–	–
AKJ		400
Sales		250
Cash	90	
Purchases returns		100
Discount received		20
N. Timms	100	
Insurance	25	
Rent received		20
	21,790	21,790

The figures contained in the above trial balance have been obtained from the accounts of Helen Berry in Exercise 3.9. Note that, as there is no balance at present in the Northern Foods account, it is not essential to show that account in the trial balance. The fact that the total debit balances equals the total of the credit balances is sufficient evidence to prove that the transactions have been entered correctly in the ledger. To give you practice in entering transactions and checking their accuracy by drafting a trial balance, work through the following exercise.

Exercise 4.1

Mike Bishop opened his petrol service station on 1 May 1989. He had £1,000 in the bank,£200 in cash, £8,000 worth of stock and machinery and equipment worth £12,000. He had borrowed £4,000 from Petrofinance Ltd for nine months and provided the rest of the finance himself.

1 Draft a balance sheet to show Mike's position on 1 May 1989, taking care to calculate the figure for owner's capital.
2 Open a ledger account for each item and enter the opening balances.
3 Enter the following transactions in the ledger, opening new accounts where necessary. Then extract a trial balance on 7 May to check the accuracy of your entries.

   2 May Cash sales £600.
   3 May Cash sales £550; purchases £1,200 on credit from PB Ltd.
   4 May Cash sales £720; paid £1,500 cash into bank.
   5 May Cash sales £680; paid rent £160 by cheque.
   6 May Cash sales £540; purchases £200 on credit from Greasoils Ltd.
   7 May Paid amount owing to PB Ltd, less 3% discount by cheque.

The following procedure is recommended if your trial balance totals do not agree:

1 Make certain that you calculated the owner's capital correctly and that the balance sheet balanced with the same totals as mine.
2 Check that the assets and sources of finance were entered on the correct side of their accounts. The opening debit balances (assets) should, of course, equal the total credit balances (capital and liabilities).
3 Go through each transaction following the rules on page 37. Make sure that for each debit entry there is a corresponding credit entry of the same value.
4 Check that you have calculated the balances on each account accurately, paying particular attention to those accounts with most entries. Remember the balance of an account is the difference between the two sides. It is described as a debit balance when the total value of debit entries is greater than the credits. If the credit side is greater than the debit the difference is a credit balance.
5 Make certain that you have put the balances in the right column of the trial balance.

4.3 DEALING WITH ERRORS

Practice helps to eliminte mistakes and aids in finding them more quickly when they do occur. Sometimes, though, finding why the trial balance does not agree proves to be very difficult, especially in a large firm where hundreds of transactions are being recorded in a single day. There may simply not be enough time available to look for the errors. What can be done? One way round this problem is to invent an account and debit or credit it with the amount needed to make the trial balance agree. This account is called a suspense account. When the error is discovered the suspense account can be closed.

For example, on 30 April the debit balances in our firm's trial balance total £100 more than the credit balances and a suspense account is opened.

Dr Suspense account Cr

					£
			30 April	Difference in books	100

If this credit balance is added to the trial balance the debits will now equal the credits. They have been made to be equal.

Suppose that on 27 May Mr Chandler writes to complain that the statement we have sent him shows that he owes £450 when in fact he owes £350 because he paid £100 by cheque on 28 April. When this is checked we discover that a debit entry has been made in our bank account to record the money received but no credit entry has been made in Mr Chandler's account to reduce the amount he owes. We can put matters right by debiting the suspense account and crediting the account of Mr Chandler. We should also apologise to him of course! The accounts will then look like this:

Dr Suspense account Cr

		£			£
27 May	Chandler	100	30 April	Difference in books	100

M. Chandler

		£			£
1 May	Balance	450	27 May	Suspense account	100

The suspense account is closed until it is needed again and Mr Chandler's account is reduced by £100 to a debit balance of £350. Provided no other errors have been made in the meantime a trial balance extracted now would agree.

Although useful as a means of checking the accuracy of transactions recorded in the ledger, the trial balance is not foolproof. There are some errors which it will not reveal. These are often grouped into five types:

- *Errors of omission* – omitted from both debit and credit sides of the accounts – will leave the trial balance unaffected.
- *Errors of commission* – this means that something has been done but has been done incorrectly. A common example is when M. B. Brown's account is debited with £10 instead of that of, say, M. R. Brown. As long as the credit entry has been made such an error will not show up in the trial balance.
- *Errors of principle* – these are errors which offend against a basic rule of book-keeping. For example, earlier you learnt that purchases of stock for resale should be entered in the purchases account while the purchase of any other asset should be entered in its own account. A garage which purchases a breakdown vehicle for £4,000 and records this in the purchases account containing cars bought for resale would be making an error of principle. Such an error would not affect the trial balance.
- *Compensation errors* – if the sales account is overcast by, say, £150 and the wages account is overcast by the same amount the trial balance will not be affected. The extra £150 credit in the sales account will have been compensated by the extra £150 debit in the wages account.
- *Original errors* – these are made when copying figures from the documents from which the entries are made. For example if an invoice for £110 received from R. Evans, a supplier, is entered in the supplier's account and the purchases account as £11, the trial balance will not show us that an error has been made.

All such errors must be corrected when they are discovered.

- *Errors of omission* can be put right by making the entries which have been omitted.

Here is how the other errors mentioned above would be corrected when discovered:

- *Errors of commission*

M. B. Brown

	£		£
		M. R. Brown	10

M. R. Brown

M. B. Brown	10		

The credit entry in the account of M. B. Brown removes the mistake and the debit entry in M. R. Brown's account places the £10 where it really belongs.

- *Errors of principle*

Purchases

	£		£
		Motor vehicles	4,000

Motor vehicles

Purchases	4,000		

This is similar to Brown's case as it involves removing an amount from an account (purchases) where it had been placed incorrectly and entering it where it should have been from the beginning (motor vehicles).

- *Compensating errors* can be corrected by repeating the addition of sales and wages accounts and amending the totals.
- *Original errors*

Purchases

	£		£
R. Evans	99		

R. Evans

		Purchases	99

The £99 debited to purchases account and credited to Evans' account raises the £11 to £110.

Exercise 4.2

Imagine your trial balance of 30 June shows that the credit balances are £50 greater than the debits. £50 discount received for promptly settling an amount owing to K. Bryant has been entered on the credit side of the discount received account but has not been debited to Bryant's account.

First open a suspense account to record the difference in the books on 30 June. Then show the double entries which would be made to correct the error.

Exercise 4.3

Study the account of B. John, which has been extracted from the ledger of G. Edwards, and answer the questions which follow it.

B. John						39	
1989			£	1989			£
1 May	Balance	b/d	150	8 May	Bank	6	140
17 May	Sales	21	250	8 May	Discount allowed	12	10
27 May	Sales	21	130				

(a) Define the term 'balance' and explain what it means on 1 May in the above account.
(b) Explain the two entries of 8 May. To what do '6' and '12' refer?
(c) Balance the account correctly on 31 May.

Exercise 4.4

What is a trial balance and why is it used?

Exercise 4.5

An inexperienced book-keeper has drafted the following trial balance. He has made some basic errors which you should be able to correct. The totals of the trial balance will then agree.

Trial balance of John Williams as at 30 April 1990

	£ dr	£ cr
Capital		20,000
Premises	12,000	
Equipment	4,000	
Debtors		2,000
Creditors	1,000	
Stock	5,000	
Rent and rates	1,000	
Insurance	400	
Wages		8,600
Sales	40,000	
Purchases		25,000
Cash in bank	3,000	
	66,400	55,600

Exercise 4.6

Name the types of error which will not be revealed by drafting a trial balance.

Exercise 4.7

A cheque for £60 received from M. Smith has been incorrectly credited to the account of M. J. K. Smith. Show the entries needed to correct the error.

CHAPTER 5

THE CASH BOOK

In this chapter we will see how the contents of a ledger can be subdivided into a number of sections. We will then deal in some detail with one of these subdivisions - the cash book.

5.1 DIVISIONS OF THE LEDGER

So far, we have been thinking of the ledger as one book containing all the accounts. This has one obvious disadvantage. Only one person may use it at any one time. This might not matter in a small business where there are only a few transactions each day. In a larger business, however, where there may be many different transactions, and more than one accounts clerk employed, real difficulties will be encountered. The idea of subdividing the ledger to enable the work of recording transactions to be shared and carried out more efficiently appealed to many businesses. The diagram below summarises the main ways in which this was done.

Divisions of the ledger

<table>
<tr><td>Stage</td><td colspan="7">General ledger</td></tr>
<tr><td>1</td><td colspan="6">General ledger</td><td>Cash book</td></tr>
<tr><td>2</td><td colspan="2">General ledger</td><td colspan="2">Debtors' ledger</td><td colspan="2">Creditors' ledger</td><td>Cash book</td></tr>
<tr><td>3</td><td>General ledger</td><td colspan="2">Private ledger</td><td colspan="2">Debtors' ledger</td><td>Creditors' ledger</td><td>Cash book</td></tr>
</table>

The first stage is to take out the two accounts which are most used - the cash account and bank account - and place them in a separate book, which becomes known as the cash book. All other accounts remain in the general ledger. The second stage involves extracting from the general ledger the debtors and creditors accounts. These are then kept in their own separate books. Note that the terms 'purchases ledger' and 'bought ledger' are sometimes used instead of creditors' ledger, and 'sales ledger' instead of debtors' ledger. Goods purchased on credit are bought from creditors. Sales on credit are made to debtors. Whichever terms you choose, it is best to use them consistently.

The names of the new divisions of the ledger are a good indication of the accounts contained within them. This is true also when the third stage is reached and some accounts are withdrawn and placed in the private ledger. Clearly such a book will contain any accounts which the owner wishes to keep private. The capital account is one example, and drawings account (which we will meet later) is another. Again all other accounts not withdrawn into a separate book remain in the general ledger.

It should not be thought that these stages have to occur in the order we have given. Some owners might have decided to extract their private accounts from the prying eyes of their clerk before even considering the practical advantages to be gained by putting the cash and bank accounts together in the cash book. Nor should it be thought that all businesses which open a debtors' ledger will automatically open a creditors' ledger. A business with a large number of customers, to whom it sells on credit, will probably find it advantageous to have a separate ledger to contain them. If, however, it purchases stock from only a few suppliers it might not be worth taking these accounts out of the general ledger. Further, there is nothing to prevent a business subdividing its accounts to an even greater extent than the diagram suggests. One common occurrence, for example, is for businesses with large numbers of debtors' accounts to have them entered on cards and kept in a filing system. These debtors might be filed alphabetically in a drawer with A-D kept separate from E-H, etc. The diagram does, however, give a general summary of how a ledger might be subdivided.

Exercise 5.1

EBA Ltd has a cash book, debtors' ledger and a general ledger. In which of these would you find the following accounts? (a) T. Smith, a customer, (b) wages account, (c) bank account, (d) A. Lindsay, a supplier.

5.2 TYPES OF ACCOUNT

It is also possible to classify ledger accounts into personal and impersonal accounts. The former comprises the accounts of people and other firms with which a business deals and the latter all other accounts. The impersonal accounts can be further subdivided into real accounts and nominal accounts. Real accounts are those in which a record is kept of the assets of a business. They are real in the sense that it is possible to touch them - for example, buildings, furniture, cash. Nominal accounts contain the records of income and expenses. Rent, rates and insurance are common examples of expenses while discount received and commission received are examples of incomes which we met earlier. Nominal means 'in name only'. The rent account may have a balance of £1,000 but the money will not really be there. Similarly, the commission received account may show that £200 was received last month but the money may now be spent. The following diagram summarises this classification.

Types of account

Personal (debtors and creditors)	Impersonal (all other accounts)	
Personal (debtors and creditors)	Real accounts (assets)	Nominal accounts (incomes and expenses)

Exercise 5.2

Classify the following accounts as real, nominal or personal. (a) Peter Finch, supplier, (b) wages, (c) stock, (d) Robin Withe, customer, (e) machinery, (f) bank, (g) rent received, (h) capital.

Placing accounts in separate sections in the ledger causes no major book-keeping problems, though some thought must be given to adapting the reference system used. The abbreviations GL (General Ledger), DL (Debtors' Ledger) CL (Creditors' Ledger), and CB (Cash Book) normally appear alongside the title of the account to show in which section of the ledger it is positioned. They also prefix the number of the double entry which is recorded in the folio column.

Some businesses keep a nominal ledger *instead* of a general ledger, in which case you would expect the business to have an assets ledger for the real accounts. This logic is not always followed, however, and you may sometimes come across a nominal ledger containing *all* the impersonal accounts, that is, real accounts and nominal accounts.

5.3 THE TWO-COLUMN CASH BOOK

In the cash book it is usual not just to keep a separate account for cash and bank records but also to combine the accounts together to form one unit. The rest of this chapter will be devoted to different ways of using the cash book. An example of a two-column cash book is shown on page 52.

From our earlier work, when the cash and bank accounts were kept separately in the ledger, you should have recalled that the debit entries record money received which increases the assets, cash or bank. Credit entries are used to record payments of money which decrease the assets, cash or bank. Although the accounts for cash and bank have been combined together they are still in reality separate. The debit entries for cash must be kept apart from the debit entries for bank and the credit entries must also be kept apart. It is very important, therefore, to label the columns clearly. By convention, the cash column appears to the left of the bank column.

You should be able to explain each of the entries in the cash book. Debit entries are receipts of cash or amounts paid into the bank. Credit entries are payments by cash or amounts paid out of the bank. The description gives the reason for the money received or paid.

Two transactions sometimes cause confusion. This is because both the debit and credit entries appear in the same book.

First, on 9 Feb., £750 cash was paid into the bank. The debit entry in the bank column shows that the money in the bank has increased by £750. The description 'cash' explains how. We know that the description given should be the name of the other account affected. The credit entry is to be found therefore in the cash column. As a credit entry in an asset account shows a reduction in the value of the asset, the cash has been reduced by £750. The description for the credit entry in the cash column is 'bank', the name of the other account affected.

Now look at the folio columns for the two entries of 9 Feb. The letter 'c' is short for *contra*, a Latin term for opposite or against. It is used here to indicate that the double entry is on the same page of the same book.

Second, on 13 Feb. £150 was withdrawn from the bank for use as cash. Note that this is the reverse of the transaction of 9 Feb. The debit entry in the cash column shows this asset increasing and the credit entry in the bank column shows that asset decreasing. A 'c' for *contra* again appears in the folio columns and each description gives the name of the other column affected. If you ever have an entry in the bank column described as 'bank' or in the cash column described as 'cash' you will know immediately that an error has been made.

Exercise 5.3

Rewrite the cash and bank accounts on page 280 as they would appear in a two-column cash book. It is possible to buy a variety of types of cash books or loose-leaf paper from good stationers but it is not difficult to rule your own. You need not complete the folio column unless there is a *contra* entry.

Dr | Cash book | Cr

Date	Details	F	Cash	Bank	Date	Details	F	Cash	Bank
1 Feb.	Balances	b/d	100.20	700.60	2 Feb.	Postage	GL 4	12.15	
3 Feb.	Sales	GL 6	220.60		3 Feb.	N. Keegan	CL 9		150.00
4 Feb.	C. Winston	DL 41		320.50	4 Feb.	Purchases	GL 12		260.00
5 Feb.	N. Jones	DL 20		110.90	6 Feb.	Rates	GL 15		79.00
8 Feb.	Sales	GL 6	600.20		7 Feb.	Wages	GL 19	60.00	
9 Feb.	Cash	c		750.00	9 Feb.	Bank	c	750.00	
11 Feb.	R. Starr	DL 31		140.30	10 Feb.	R. Willis	CL 10	60.00	
13 Feb.	Bank	c	150.00		12 Feb.	Insurance	GL 6	20.00	
					13 Feb.	Cash	c		150.00
					14 Feb.	Balances	c/d	168.85	1,383.30
			1,071.00	2,022.30				1,071.00	2,022.30
15 Feb.	Balances	b/d	168.85	1,383.30					

5.4 THE THREE-COLUMN CASH BOOK

Combining the cash and bank accounts together in one book, so that current transactions in cash and by cheque are recorded together, makes for far greater efficiency. This can be taken a step further. In many businesses payments to suppliers are timed to enable the business to receive a discount. At the same time money will be received from customers who will have deducted discount allowed in return for prompt settlement. There are thus going to be many entries for discount allowed associated with the money received from customers and many entries for discount received associated with money paid to suppliers. A simple way of recording these discounts in the cash book at the same time as the money is recorded will further increase efficiency. This can be done by extending the cash book into a three column cash book. See the example on page 54.

The only additions to the two-column cash book we looked at earlier are the columns for discount allowed to customers on the debit side and the column for discount received from suppliers on the credit side. We will concentrate here on these additions and the transactions involved.

On 3 May the supplier B. Thomas was paid £206.29 by cheque. The credit entry in the bank column shows this. We also see that £4.21 discount has been received for paying promptly. This is deducted when payment is made because it will be known then whether the discount can be claimed. This is preferable to paying the full amount due and then receiving a rebate later. The debit entries relating to both the cheque and the discount received will be in the account of B. Thomas.

There are three other transactions involving discount received on the credit side of the cash book and they are similar to the ones we have considered. Look now at the balancing of the accounts on 14 May. Cash and bank balances are obtained and brought down to continue these accounts. However, the column for discount received is totalled. This is because it is not a proper account but merely a memorandum or supplementary record. The total for the first fortnight in May is entered in the account proper for discount received. The reference beneath the total of £15.72 tells you that this account will be found on page 27 of the general ledger. The entry in that account will look like this:

Dr	Discount received	GL 27	Cr
			£
	14 May	Sundry creditors	15.72

The debits corresponding to this one total credit will be in the accounts of the various suppliers from whom discount was received from 1 to 14 May. These were Thomas, Rees, Robson, Blimp and Hazel. The end result is still the same in that the total value of the debits equals the total value of the credit entry in the discount received account.

Dr — Cash book — Cr

Date	Details	Fol.	Discount allowed	Cash	Bank	Date	Details	Fol.	Discount received	Cash	Bank
1 May	Balances	b/d		115.20	760.50	2 May	Wages			80.00	
2 May	Sales			120.80		3 May	B. Thomas		4.21		206.29
3 May	Sales			109.55		4 May	J. Rees		2.00		98.00
4 May	R. Evans		12.00		388.00	5 May	W. Jones			88.47	
5 May	Sales			96.47		6 May	B. Robson		3.01		147.49
6 May	Sales			80.21		7 May	Bank	c		190.00	
7 May	Cash	c			190.00	7 May	Rent				45.00
8 May	J. Morris		1.77		86.73	9 May	C. Blimp		5.00		205.00
9 May	Sales			95.60		9 May	Wages			80.00	
10 May	N. Smith		4.15		220.50	10 May	A. Hazel		1.50		75.50
11 May	D. Baker		1.87		84.62	11 May	Rates				86.25
12 May	Sales			221.40		12 may	Insurance				42.60
13 May	W. Bolton		4.20		195.80	14 May	Postage			20.14	
14 May	Sales			262.30		14 May	Balances			642.92	1,020.02
			23.99	1,101.53	1,926.15				15.72	1,101.53	1,926.15
15 May	Balances	b/d	GL 21	642.92	1,020.02				GL 27		

The method of keeping a note of discounts received in a column of the cash book and then entering a total at regular intervals in the discount received account in the ledger has an additional advantage. It keeps the discount received account shorter.

If you have followed the explanation of the use of the discount received column you should be able to work out for yourself how the discount allowed column is used on the debit side of the cash book. Look first at one transaction involving discount allowed - that of 4 May. A cheque for £388 has been received from R. Evans who has paid promptly enough to claim a discount of £12. This has been deducted by him from the full amount owing before he makes out the cheque. There are four other similar transactions.

The discount allowed column is also a memorandum and not a proper account. At the end of the period the total for all discounts allowed is added and this total is entered in the account proper.

Exercise 5.4

Show the entry in the discount allowed account relating to the transactions from 1 to 14 May. Put as much information in it as you can.

5.5 **TRADE DISCOUNT**

The discounts we have been referring to so far are known fully as cash discounts in order to distinguish them from trade discounts. The latter is a discount that is allowed by a supplier and received by a customer when they are both involved in the same trade. For example, when I buy materials from the local builders' merchant I pay a higher price than would a builder who was a regular customer. He would receive trade discount whereas I would not. Many such merchants even have separate counters to deal with their two categories of customer. The amount of trade discount given will vary according to the trade. As far as the accounts are concerned it does not concern us. The amount of trade discount is taken off *before* any entries are made.

For example, the catalogue or list price of a bag of cement might be £5.00. A builder receiving 10% trade discount will be charged only £4.50, the 50p trade discount being 10% of £5.00. The merchant will make a credit entry of £4.50 in his sales account and debit the builder's account with the £4.50 due from him. The builder would debit his purchases account and credit the account of the merchant with the amount owed to him. Again only the £4.50 would be shown in the accounts. Trade discount is deducted *before* any entries are made.

Of course this does not mean that there will be no cash discount to be shown in the accounts. The merchant may well allow a small discount of, say, 2% to encourage his customers to pay within a certain time period. If he does then this amount will be recorded in the accounts.

Exercise 5.5

ACE Motors, a small garage, purchases on credit an exhaust from Spare-parts plc on 25 May. The catalogue price is £80 but all garages are allowed trade discount of 10%. ACE Motors pay the amount due by cheque on 31 May, which is prompt enough to allow them to deduct a cash discount of 3%. Show the accounts in the books of ACE Motors.

5.6 **THE PETTY CASH BOOK**

Some firms keep another cash book in addition to either a two- or three-column cash book. It is called the **petty cash book**. It is used for recording small (petty comes from the French 'petit') Payments for such items as postage, taxi fares and window cleaning. It may also include receipts of cash – for example when someone uses the business telephone and pays for it. The rule for entering transactions are the same as for any other cash account, that is, debit receipts of cash and credit payments.

The petty cash book is usually operated on the imprest system. An **imprest** is a sum of money advanced to the cashier or clerk in charge of the petty cash. This is used to make payments for those items mentioned above. It is often called a float. At the end of a short period a senior clerk will check that the amount of the cash left is in agreement with the amount

The petty cash book

Dr	*Date*	*Details*	*PCV*	*Total*	*Postage*	*Canteen*	*Travel*	*Stationery*
30.00	1 May	Imprest	CB 6					
	2 May	Stamps	1	4.50	4.50			
	3 May	Teas	2	1.05		1.05		
	4 May	Taxi	3	2.25			2.25	
	4 May	Envelopes	4	1.50				1.50
	5 May	Coffees	5	0.75		0.75		
	6 May	Stamps	6	3.75	3.75			
	6 May	Bus fares	7	0.95			0.95	
	9 May	Lunch	8	1.20		1.20		
	10 May	A4 Paper	9	2.54				2.54
	11 May	Taxi	10	1.35			1.35	
	12 May	Petrol	11	1.95			1.95	
	13 May	Stamps	12	2.50	2.50			
				24.29	10.75	3.00	6.50	4.04
	14 May	Balance c/d		5.71	GL 27	GL 41	GL 29	GL 30
30.00			30.00					
5.71	15 May	Balance b/d						
24.29	15 May	Imprest						

shown in the book. As with all transactions involving cash it is necessary to obtain a receipt. Such receipts for items in the petty cash book are known as vouchers. They are a means of checking that the cashier has indeed spent the money in the manner described in the book. The imprest will then be restored to its starting level. The table on page 56 shows a typical example of a petty cash book.

The types of expenditure which occur most frequently will be given an analysis column of their own, in this case postage, canteen, travel and stationery. Some firms keep one column for items which cannot be placed in a specific category - this is usually headed 'sundries'. If each expense payment is then written in the total column as well as on one of the analysis columns it will be possible to check that the total column is correct by 'cross-totting' the totals of each of the analysis columns. The imprest in the above example is £30. Thus when the account is balanced on 14 May and it is discovered that £24.29 has been spent, there should be £5.71 left in the petty cash box. To restore the imprest to £30.00 the cashier will have to be given an additional £24.29p. The total of each individual column will be posted to the ledger account for that expense. For example, the stationery paid for by petty cash will be posted to the stationery account which will be found on page 30 of the general ledger.

5.7 SINGLE ENTRY CASH BOOK

So far we have assumed that businesses will have their accounts kept on a double-entry basis. This is not done, however, by many small businesses where it is felt that the effort involved is not sufficiently rewarded by the advantages gained. These businesses will normally keep only a record of money received and paid in a cash book of one kind or another. Such a system is known as single entry because only one entry is made for each transaction. Where this is done, the cash book becomes of even greater importance because it contains the only record of a transaction. It is possible to gain some of the advantages of a double-entry system while keeping only a cash book if the number of columns is expanded and the receipts and payments of money analysed.

For example the cash book on page 58 is used by a trader who makes all his payments by cheque and who banks all receipts of money each day. As he is liable to the government for VAT he uses two columns for this. The first contains the amounts of VAT he has charged customers to whom he has sold goods. The second contains the amounts he has paid the suppliers who have charged him VAT. Wages are the only other expense regular enough to deserve its own column so all the other expenses are classified as sundries. There is nothing to prevent a larger number of columns being used if there are sufficient items which are regular enough to make this worthwhile.

Cash book

Receipts	Sales	VAT	Date	Details	Payments	Purchases	Wages	Sundries	VAT
500.00			1 Mar.	Balance b/d					
151.80	132.00	19.80	1 Mar.	J. Smith					
			2 Mar.	B. Jones	115.00	100.00			15.00
			3 Mar.	R. Evans	75.50		75.50		
			4 Mar.	British Rail	24.00			24.00	
193.20	168.00	25.20	4 Mar.	W. Toms					
			5 Mar.	M. Morgan	312.80	272.00			40.80
103.73	90.20	13.53	6 Mar.	T. Lewis					
			7 Mar.	Balance c/d	421.43				
948.73	390.20	58.53			948.73	372.00	75.50	24.00	55.80
421.43			8 Mar.	Balance b/d					

What you have learnt about the cash book so far should enable you to follow the organisation of the one on page 58 if you take it one item at a time. It has been assumed that the rate of VAT is 15%.

Exercise 5.6

Enter the following transactions in the three-column cash book of J. Harris and balance it on 14 April.

1 April	Cash balance £67.23; bank balance £191.20.
2 April	Cash sales £138.00.
3 April	Paid £100 cash into bank.
4 April	Paid Bentley £120 by cheque, receiving discount of £3.
5 April	Paid Royce £94 by cheque in full settlement of an amount owing of £100 (balance is discount).
6 April	Cash sales £97.24.
7 April	Received a cheque from W. Barnes for £169.50 to settle an amount due of £178.50 (balance is discount).
8 April	Paid wages in cash £120.80.
9 April	Paid T. Ford £98.00 in cash, having deducted a discount of £4.
10 April	Withdrew £75 from bank for use as cash.
11 April	R. Hewitt paid £95 in cash, having deducted a discount of £5.
12 April	Paid insurance on car by cheque £78.90.
13 April	Cash sales £120.62.

Exercise 5.7

Enter the following transactions in the three-column cash book of B. Finn and balance it on 14 May.

1 May	Cash balance £47.53; bank balance £449.52.
2 May	Cash sales £313.56.
3 May	Paid £250.00 cash into the bank.
4 May	Paid Bennett £152.00 by cheque, receiving discount of £13.00.
5 May	Paid Johns £47.00 by cheque in full settlement of an amount owing of £50.00 (balance is discount).
6 May	Cash sales £297.54.
7 May	Received a cheque from R. Robbins for £369.50 in full settlement of an amount due of £378.50 (balance is discount).
8 May	Paid wages in cash £92.80.
9 May	Paid G. Edwards £132.00 by cheque, having deducted a discount of £14.00.
10 May	Withdrew £75.00 from the bank for use as cash.
11 May	R. Hewitt paid Sawyer £105.00 in cash, having deducted a discount of £5.00.
12 May	Paid insurance on car by cheque £97.39.
14 May	Sawyer withdrew £100.00 cash and £200.00 by cheque for private use.

CHAPTER 6

DOCUMENTS AND JOURNALS

In this chapter we are going to look at the main sources of information from which entries are made in the ledger and cash book. Then we will examine the way in which some details may be kept in subsidiary books known as journals. These help to reduce the amount of detail needed in the ledger.

6.1 BUSINESS DOCUMENTS

The information from which transactions are entered in a trader's personal accounts is obtained from two main documents - invoices and credit notes. An example of an invoice is shown below.

Invoice

Western Electrical Factors
2 Croft Road
Newton Abbot
Devon Tel. (096) 613412

Invoice to:
RKL Electrics
6 High Street
Torquay

Date: 8.7.1989

Invoice No. 1693

Quantity	*Description*	*Unit price*	*Total* £ p
160 metres		30p	48.00
850 metres		40p	340.00
			388.00

Terms: 5% cash discount if payment made within 28 days.

An invoice is basically a bill sent to a purchaser of goods by the seller.

The purchaser (RKL Electrics), who has received the invoice, will use it to make a record of the transaction in his acocunts. The seller (Western Electrical Factors), who has sent the invoice, will retain a duplicate copy for the same reason. RKL will debit its purchases account and credit an account for WEF to show that it owes the supplier £388. In the books of WEF, the sales account will be credited and an account for RKL debited to show that the customer owes £388.

Activity

Invoices come in a variety of forms. Try to obtain some for comparison. You will find they will have a number of features in common - the most important of which is that one business is telling one of its customers that a certain amount of money is owed to them.

The second important document which relates to buying and selling is the credit note, an example of which is shown below.

Credit notes are frequently printed in red to distinguish them from invoices. They are sent to the purchaser by the seller when goods which have been invoiced are returned. The seller will keep a duplicate copy of the credit note for his own records.

Credit note

Western Electrical Factors
2 Croft Road
Newton Abbot
Devon Tel. (096) 613412
Date: 15.7.1989
Credit note No. 312

To:
RKL Electrics
6 High Street
Torquay

Quantity	*Description*	*Unit price*	*Total*
			£ p
160 metres		30p	48.00
			48.00

This credit note has been sent by Western Electrical Factors to RKL Electrics because the latter has returned £48 worth of goods. Western Electrical Factors will debit its sales returns account and credit the account of RKL. The term 'credit note' comes from the fact that the seller is telling the buyer that the buyer's account has been credited with the value of the goods returned.

RKL will debit the account of Western Electrical Factors and credit the purchases returns account.

Another document connected with buying and selling is the statement. This is a summary of the amounts on all invoices and credit notes sent during a period - normally a month. It shows the purchaser the total amount due from him as a result of all the transactions made. It should be possible for you to obtain a copy of such a document. If you have difficulty refer to a commerce textbook, where you should be able to find a specimen.

When money is paid or received different documents are involved. Payments made by cheque will be entered on the credit side of the cash book from the cheque counterfoils which should be completed each time a cheque is written. Money received by cheque will be entered on the debit side of the cash book using the cheque itself as the document. When payment is made in cash a receipt should be obtained by the payer from which an entry on the credit side of the cash book is made. A business receiving cash should keep a duplicate of the receipt given to the payer, from which debit entries can be made in the cash book.

Exercise 6.1

1 Which of the following documents are used to record transactions by (a) the purchaser and (b) the seller? Invoice; duplicate copy of an invoice; credit note; duplicate copy of a credit note.
2 Which of these documents is used to record transactions by (a) the receiver of money and (b) the payer? Cheque; cheque counterfoil; receipt; copy of receipt.

6.2 **SUBSIDIARY BOOKS**

We will now consider the use of journals – a term meaning a daily record. At one time all transactions were entered in detail in a journal before being posted to the ledger and because of this journals were frequently referred to as the books of original entry. 'Posting to the ledger' is a phrase used to describe the process of making entries in the ledger and does not involve the post office!

The journals are also known as subsidiary books. This is because they are subsidiary or secondary to the ledger. In other words they supplement the ledger. They are not part of the double-entry system itself but relieve the ledger of much unnecessary detail. We have already come across an occasion on which two ledger accounts can be saved too much detail. Do you remember? If not turn to page 54 and look at the three-column cash book. The columns for discount allowed and discount received were used as memorandum records and were not in themselves part of the double-entry system. At the end of a certain period the columns were added and the totals entered in their respective ledger accounts. This considerably reduced the information contained in the accounts for discount allowed and received.

Today few firms would consider it worthwhile to enter all transactions in a journal before making the ledger entries. Journals are still used, however, to keep detailed records of some transactions. The five main ones are:

- The sales journal.
- The sales returns or returns inward journal.
- The purchases journal.
- The purchases returns or returns outward journal.
- The journal.

The first four are kept for credit transactions involving sales, purchases and returns. You should note that 'day book' or 'book' often replaces 'journal', so do not be confused if you encounter a sales day book or returns outward book. The fifth - *the* journal - is often pronounced with emphasis on the first word to distinguish it from other journals. It is sometimes referred to as 'the journal proper' for the same reason. It is used for a number of different transactions when it is felt that extra detail needs to be recorded.

We will now consider each of the journals in turn. WEF, the electrical wholesalers used as an illustration earlier, can be used again here.

6.3 THE SALES BOOK

All credit sales will be entered here from the duplicate copies of the invoices sent to customers. WEF's sales book could look like this:

Sales book 28

Date	Customer	Invoice	Folio	£ p
1 July	Robinsons	1690	DL 147	77.50
4 July	Carter and Son	1691	DL 12	31.20
5 July	Allens DIY	1692	DL 6	80.80
6 July	RKL Electrics	1693	DL 152	388.00
7 July	Electroshop	1694	DL 21	163.12
7 July	Transferred to sales a/c		GL 21	740.62

You might be able to follow this but, if not, some explanation will help. Each customer to whom WEF sells will have his own personal account in the debtors' ledger. This assumes that WEF subdivides its ledger. If not the folio reference of DL will be replaced by GL for general ledger or perhaps simply L for ledger. The debit entries are made in each customer's personal account from the duplicate of the invoice as soon as the invoice is sent. Instead of making a credit entry each time in the sales account, the entries are saved up and one entry is made at a convenient time to correspond to the total number of debits which have been made in the customers' accounts. In the above example one credit entry for £740.62 on 7 July will be the double entry corresponding to the five debits from 1 July to 7 July in the customers' accounts. The sales account will look like this:

	Sales account	GL 21	Cr
			£
	7 July Sundry debtors	SB 28	740.62

Note the cross-reference to the sales book and the description which indicates that several different debtors' accounts are involved.

The delay in posting the credit entry to the sales account means that a trial balance extracted between 1 July and 6 July will not agree. This is because debit entries have been made without a corresponding credit entry. Book-keepers must be aware of the effect of keeping subsidiary books on the accuracy of a trial balance. They should choose carefully the date on which they draft it.

6.4 THE RETURNS INWARD BOOK

This can take the same form as the sales book. The example below has been prepared from the following list of credit sales returns received by WEF during July.

6 July	Robinsons	£50.12
15 July	RKL	£48.00
24 July	Evans DIY	£6.54
30 July	Walters	£22.12

Returns inward book 3

1989	Customer	Credit note	Folio	£ p
6 July	Robinsons	217	DL 147	50.12
15 July	RKL	218	DL 152	48.00
24 July	Evans DIY	219	DL 24	6.54
30 July	Walters	220	DL 189	22.12
31 July	Transferred to returns inward a/c		GL 22	126.78

Dr	Returns inward account		GL 22
		£	
31 July	Sundry debtors RIB 3	126.78	

6.5 THE PURCHASES BOOK

This contains all the credit purchases. It will be made up from the invoices received from suppliers. WEF's purchases book might look like this:

Purchases book 8

1986	Supplier	Invoice	Folio	£ p
3 July	Wireplies	82/101	CL 29	289.50
16 July	UVC	82/101	CL 17	341.38
17 July	Plugplies	82/103	CL 22	429.17
24 July	Jones	82/104	CL 14	121.12
29 July	Electose	82/105	CL 7	321.03
31 July	Transferred to purchases a/c		GL 16	1,502.20

Each of WEF's suppliers has a personal account in the creditors' ledger. The credit entries are made in each of these accounts from an invoice as soon as it is received. The debit entries are saved up and one entry is made to correspond to the total number of credits which will have been made already in the suppliers' accounts. In the above example one debit entry of £1,502.20 is made on 31 July in the purchases account which will look like this:

Dr Purchases account GL 16

			£	
31 July	Sundry creditors	PB 8	1,502.20	

Note that the invoices received from suppliers will have a variety of reference numbers. To aid filing, WEF has stamped each one with its own number which is used in the purchases book.

6.6 THE RETURNS OUTWARD BOOK

This can take the same form as the others and you should be able to draft your own.

Exercise 6.2

The following is a list of the credit notes received by WEF during July:

		£ p
8 July	EQP Ltd	38.29
10 July	Electose	49.54
23 July	Plugplies	56.20
28 July	Jones	17.47
29 July	Wilsons	38.25

Enter these in a returns outward book and show the transfer to the ledger account on 31 July. Invent suitable details.

To save space the examples used have been fairly brief. The real value of removing much of the detail from ledger accounts like sales, purchases, returns inward and returns outward into journals is seen when the number of entries is very large. Not all firms, however large, will keep separate day books. A good filing system for copies of invoices sent (sales), invoices received (purchases), copies of credit notes sent (returns inward) and credit notes received (returns outward) may well suffice. It will still enable total entries for sales, purchases, returns inward and returns outward to be made at regular intervals while the entries in the personal accounts are made as the transactions occur.

6.7 THE JOURNAL

At one time this was used to record transactions that did not have their own book of original entry. As well as the four books we have just dealt with the cash book is also considered to be a book of original entry in this context because entries are made in it directly from documents such as cheques. The cash book differs, however, in that it is also part of the ledger as it contains two ledger accounts - cash and bank.

Today the journal is usually reserved for those transactions that need extra explanation. Its form is the same as the day books we have just examined bu the columns are used differently. The standard layout is like this:

Journal

Date		*Folio*	*£ dr*	*£ cr*
	Name of the a/c to be debited. Name of the a/c to be credited. The narrative or explanation.			

Let's see how some transactions that might be entered in the journal would fit into this layout.

6.7.1 The purchase or sale of a fixed asset on credit

On 28 January, WEF purchased a Mini-van registration no. OAF 691D on credit from Apex Garages for £2,500.

Journal

			£ *dr*	£ *cr*
28 Jan.	Motor vehicle a/c	GL 9	2,500	
	Apex Garages a/c	GL 22		2,500
	Purchase of mini-van reg. no. OAF 691D			

6.7.2 Opening a set of ledger accounts

On 1 May, N. Couch started in business with capital of £2,000 consisting of £1,800 in the bank and £200 cash.

Journal

			£ dr	£ cr
1 May	Cash a/c	CB 1	200	
	Bank a/c	CB 1	1,800	
	Capital a/c	GL 1		2,000
	Assets and capital at the start of business			
			2,000	2,000

In this case, because there is more than one debit, the entries have been totalled. This was not done in the first example because it can be seen immediately that the value of one debit entry equals the value of the other credit entry. Entries in the journal cover a great variety of transactions and it is necessary only to draw a line beneath one before writing the next. Of course the entries must still be made in the ledger accounts themselves.

6.7.3 **Writing off a bad debt**

On 12 April, G. Thomas died owing £12 to WEF. The firm wrote off the debt when it was discovered that he died penniless.

Journal

			£ dr	£ cr
26 April	Bad debts a/c	GL 28	12	
	G. Thomas a/c	DL 13		12
	Debt written off owing to death of G. Thomas			

As you can see, there is nothing difficult about doing the journal entries. Provided that you understand the rules of double-entry book-keeping it is merely a question of fitting the information into the right boxes. The advantage is that more information can be given in the journal narrative than in the details column of the ledger. Remember, however, that the entries must still be made in the ledger accounts themselves.

Exercise 6.3

Enter the following transaction in the journal to make certain you have grasped the layout.

9 May, WEF sold an electronic typewriter (serial no. 68/54321) valued in the books at £600 for this amount to Southern Electrical Factors on credit.

Exercise 6.4

(a) Are journals part of the double-entry system of book-keeping?
(b) What descriptive term indicates that details were recorded in journals before entries were made in the ledger?

(c) What term is used to describe the process of making entries in ledger accounts from the journals?
(d) State two other possible names for the sales day book.
(e) State five other possible names for the purchases returns book.

Exercise 6.5

State the daybook associated with the following business documents:

(a) invoice received
(b) credit note received
(c) copy of invoice sent
(d) copy of credit note sent.

Exercise 6.6

A trader sent the following invoices during July:

		£ p
4 July	Baxter	218.35
14 July	Carter	134.43
16 July	Davies	223.26
24 July	Evans	212.52
27 July	Fearns	132.73

Enter them in the relevant journal and show all relevant ledger account entries.

Exercise 6.7

A trader sent the following credit notes during July:

		£ p
6 July	Gregg	28.79
14 July	Hector	79.78
21 July	Inder	59.86
26 July	Jones	16.97
29 July	Kelly	76.85

Enter them in the relevant journal and show all relevant ledger account entries.

Exercise 6.8

State the journal entries needed in the following cases:

(a) Purchase of motor vehicle on credit from Abbot Motors for £5,000.
(b) Transfer sales total of £30,000 to the trading account.

(c) Sale of delivery vehicle, book value £1,000, on credit to T. Hall for £1,200.
(d) Bad debts of £58 written off sundry debtors.
(e) Sale of equipment, book value £450, on credit to R. Bly for £390.

CHAPTER 7

INTRODUCING CONTROL

In the chapter we are going to examine two very important matters. The first involves the money in the bank and the second concerns the personal accounts of debtors and creditors. Control is really a function of management aacounting and as such might seem beyond the scope of this book. Our task here, therefore, will be to take an introductory look at the idea of control. It is assumed you are fully acquainted with the cash book and the divisions of the ledger which were looked at in Chapter 5.

7.1 BANK RECONCILIATION STATEMENTS

If you have a current account with a bank, you may have received a statement showing a balance in the bank considerably different to what you expected it to be. Your delight or dismay (depending on the nature of the difference) at the amount shown will probably have disappeared once you sat down and worked out the reasons for the difference. If you write up a cash book yourself in order to keep a check on your spending (and by this stage in the book it is to be hoped that you do!) then accounting for the difference should not be too difficult. In a big business where there have been a large number of entries to record money received and paid it may take a little longer. The principles are the same however detailed the account. Once mastered you should have no problems explaining or 'reconciling' (the technical term) the differences between your record and that of the bank.

In reconciling the bank balance in the cash book with the balance in the bank statement, it is possible that you will uncover errors made by either yourself or the bank. This is the main object in drafting a bank reconciliation statement. Correcting such errors when they are discovered is essential.

For the sake of those readers who do not have a current account we will begin by looking at the bank statement on page 71 which is a fairly typical specimen.

Lloyds Bank *Torre branch* *A/c No: 4623610* *Valuemart*	*Description of entries* BGC Bank giro credit DIV Dividend D/D Direct debit S/O Standing order Cheques are designated by the serial

Date	Particulars	Payments	Receipts	Balance
1989	Opening balance			146.12
14 May	Sundry credit		200.60	346.72
17 May	004520	21.98		
	004521	100.26		224.48
18 May	Sundry credit		300.25	
	004524	19.90		
	004526	44.20		460.63
20 May	Bank giro credit		280.62	
	004522	20.62		
	004527	220.14		
	004529	16.21		484.28
21 May	Sundry credit		461.90	
	Alpha Insurance S/O	46.80		
	004528	315.20		
	004530	16.29		567.89

Activity

Make sure you are fully conversant with the terms used in the bank statement.

If you were uncertain of any of these terms, e.g. the difference between bank giro credit and sundry credit, you could have inquired at your local bank.

You should be able to give a good account of what has been happening in Valuemart's current account in the week covered by the account. For example you can state that the balance *before* business began on 14 May was £146.12 and that as a result of £200.60 being put into the account the balance grew to £346.72. After two cheques had been cleared for payment on 17 May the balance fell to £224.48. It is impossible to give any more detail about the transactions. For instance you cannot say to whom cheque no. 004520 was paid. To obtain this kind of information you would need access to Valuemart's cash book or the documents, such as cheque counterfoils, from which it is prepared. To assist you the relevant parts of the cash book have been reproduced overleaf. To simplify matters the columns for cash and discounts have been omitted. The owner uses the folio column on the credit side to record the reference numbers of the cheques he has written.

Dr — Cash book — Cr

Date			£ p	Date		Ch. no.	£ p
14 May	Balance	b/d	146.12	14 May	Health Foods Ltd	4520	21.98
14 May	Cash sales		200.60	14 May	Tresco C&C	4521	100.26
18 May	Cash sales		300.25	15 May	Electricity Board	4522	20.62
19 May	Cash sales		280.62	15 May	Advertising – *Echo*	4523	18.50
21 May	Cash sales		461.90	16 May	Vehicle expenses	4524	19.90
				16 May	Rates	4525	105.25
				16 May	Johnsons	4526	44.20
				17 May	Tresco C&C	4527	220.14
				17 May	Bilby Vintners	4528	315.20
				17 May	Evans	4529	16.21
				17 May	Sibsons	4530	16.29
				20 May	Yeos	4531	10.80
				21 May	Balance	c/d	480.14
			1,389.49				1,389.49
22 May	Balance	b/d	480.14				

Spend some time comparing the structure of the statement kept by the bank with that of the cash book kept by the owner of Valuemart. Do not concern yourself with each individual entry but concentrate on obtaining a general picture of the differences between them.

You should have noticed the following:

- Only one date and one details column are used in the bank statement.
- In the bank statement the receipts column containing amounts deposited into the bank is to the right of the payments column which contains the amounts paid by cheque, standing orders, etc. In the cash book the receipts are shown as debits and the payments as credits, exactly the other way around. This was explained in Chapter 22, page 50, and it may help you to refer back to it now.
- In the bank statement a running balance is shown after each days' transactions. This is easy for them as their records are computerised.
- Although the opening balance is the same in each account the balance differs on 21 May.

We will now turn to reconciling or explaining the different balances which exist on 21 May. If the records of the two parties to the current account - the bank and the owner of Valuemart - result in a different balance being shown there are two reasons why this may have happened.

First, and most likely, one party may not know what the other party has done, or possibly it was known but has been forgotten. The most common example of this surrounds the writing of cheques. The account holder is able to record a payment by cheque in the cash book on the day he writes the cheque. His bank will learn of this only when the cheque is presented for payment. This will take a few days even when the receiver pays it into his own bank immediately. If he holds on to it for a while, this increases the time that the bank will be out of step with the client's cash book. It is also possible that the account holder will lack knowledge of a transaction completed by his bank. For example, it is normal practice not to invoice clients for the charges due for operating the account. A deduction is made from the account and the client learns of this only when he receives his next statement. In addition many people forget that they have completed a form permitting their bank to make payments for them by standing order or direct debit. The arrival of the statement serves as a timely reminder.

The second reason for a discrepancy in the balances is that an error has been made by either one party or the other.

The sooner errors are discovered, the sooner they can be corrected. This is why bank reconciliation is so important. To illustrate the best way of approaching it, we will reconcile Valuemart's cash book balance in the bank statement on 21 May. There are three main steps:

1 Compare the cash book with the bank statement, noting any differences. It is useful to tick each entry in the cash book that is also in the statement and each entry in the statement that is also in the cash book. The entries not ticked will help to explain why the balances are different.

In the cash book the payments by cheques numbered 4523, 4525 and 4531 will not be ticked and in the bank statement the payment to Alpha Insurance by standing order. It is advisable to write down these differences clearly:

In the cash book but not in the statement
15 May £18.50 paid for advertising by cheque no. 4523.
16 May £105.25 paid for rates by cheque no. 4525.
20 May £10.80 paid to Yeos by cheque no. 4531.

In the statement but not in the cash book
22 May £46.80 paid to Alpha Insurance by standing order.

2 The next step is to **bring the cash book up to date** by entering any items which are not yet included but which are in the statement

Cash book

					£
22 May	Balance b/d	480.14	22 May	Alpha Insurance	46.80

The entry for the payment to Alpha Insurance by standing order must be made on the credit side of the cash book. Remember, from Valuemart's point of view this shows the reduction of an asset. You are now able to tick this entry in both cash book and bank statement. The bank balance as shown in the cash book now stands at £433.34, i.e. £480.14 less £46.80. Sometimes this is all that has to be done to reconcile it with the bank statement. We know that on this occasion there is still more to be done.

3 The final step is to **draft a brief statement** to reconcile the differences which remain. Here is the normal method:

Bank reconciliations statement 22 May 1989

		£	£
Balance (amended) as per cash book			433.34
add back cheques not presented	4523	18.50	
	4525	105.25	
	4531	10.80	
			134.55
Balance as per bank statement			567.89

The cheques are added back to the cash book balance because the bank statement will be that much *greater* because they have not yet been deducted from Valuemart's account. The above statement achieves its purpose in that it successfully accounts for the differences between the two balances. If the two balances had not been reconciled by this process, the errors would have to be located and corrected. Bank reconciliation statemens are usually filed with the bank statements for future reference.

Example

A trader checked his cash book against the bank statement dated 31 July. He listed the following discrepancies:

- Balance as per CB £456.71; balance as per BS £182.78.
- Cheques written by him but not yet presented for payment: no. 2179 for £20.50; no. 2181 for £5.32; no. 2184 for £65.74.
- His takings of £300 on 31 July had been banked late in the day and were not shown in the statement.
- Payment had been made to Grampian Insurance for £48.25 by direct debit.
- Bank charges £17.24.

First he brought the cash book balance up to date by entering those transactions which would be in the statement but not yet included in the cash book. Then he drafted a bank reconciliation statement to account for the remaining differences between the bank statement balance and the amended cash book balance.

Dr		Cash book			Cr
		£			£
31 July	Balance b/d	456.71	31 July	Bank charges	17.24
			31 July	Grampian Insurance	48.25
			31 July	Balance c/d	391.22
		456.71			456.71
1 Aug	Balance b/d	391.22			

The trader would not have known the amount of the bank charges until he received his statement. He should have known that he had completed a direct debit form for payments to be made to Grampian Insurance but it is the type of transaction often overlooked. In addition, the amount to be paid could vary and he would know this only when receiving the statement. The amended cash book balance will therefore now be £391.22.

Bank reconciliations statement 31 July 1989

		£	£
Balance (amended) as per cash book			391.22
add back cheques not presented	2179	20.50	
	2181	5.32	
	2184	65.74	
			91.56
			482.78
deduct cash takings not yet entered by the bank			300.00
Balance as per bank statement			182.78

The only difference between this and the other example we looked at is the cash takings. Since the trader has entered this in his cash book but the bank has not done so in its records the statement balance will be that much *less* than the cash book balance. Deducting this amount from the trader's amended cash book balance should therefore give us the same balance as in the bank statement. As it does, we can assume there are no errors.

Exercise 7.1

Jane Morgan received the following bank statement for March:

Date	*Particulars*	*Cheque no*	*Payments*	*Receipts*	*Balance*
1 Mar	Balance				150.25
4 Mar	Sundry credit			150.33	300.58
7 Mar		2961	41.36		259.22
		2962	92.75		166.47
10 Mar	Sundry credit			135.60	302.07
		2964	69.49		
		2965	28.45		204.13
17 Mar	BGC			73.40	277.53
24 Mar		2963	76.25		
		2966	94.00		
25 Mar	Direct debit		45.00		62.28
27 Mar	Div			95.25	157.53
31 Mar	Bank charges		22.25		135.28

On 31 March the bank columns of her cash book looked like this:

Cash book

1 Mar	Balance b/d	£150.25	3 Mar	Advertising	£19.67
4 Mar	Sales	150.33	5 Mar	T. Keith	92.75
10 Mar	B. White	135.60	7 Mar	B. Brain	69.49
17 Mar	D. Flyte	73.40	8 Mar	W. Tang	28.45
31 Mar	Cash	120.00	18 Mar	Rates	76.25
			19 Mar	T. Rice	94.00
			27 Mar	R & G Ltd	45.25
			28 Mar	K. Simms	56.30
			31 Mar	Balance c/d	147.42
		629.58			629.58
1 April	Balance b/d	147.42			

Bring the cash book up to date and then prepare a bank reconciliation statement.

7.2 SALES LEDGER AND PURCHASES LEDGER CONTROL ACCOUNTS

In Chapter 4 we saw how a trial balance could be used to check the accuracy of transactions made in the ledger. This process can be extended by checking individual sections of the ledger, such as the sales or debtors' ledger and purchases or creditors' ledger. It is especially useful for firms with large numbers of debtors and creditors, where the chances of error are greater. In such firms it is likely that the sales and purchases ledgers will be sectionalised.

As an illustration we will assume that Jill is responsible for a firm's sales ledger containing the accounts of customers with names in the range A–D. She will have to make a large number of debit entries for sales and credits for payments received, discounts allowed, returns accepted and perhaps bad debts written off. Look at one of the debtor accounts earlier in the book to remind you of what would be included. At the end of April the debit balances in her customers' accounts totalled £12,984. We can tell if this is correct by obtaining all the information referring to her customers and entering it into one account as follows.

Dr — Sales ledger (A–D) control account — Cr

		£			£
1 April	Balances b/d	13,621	1–30 April	Cash	465
1–30 April	Sales	16,200	1–30 April	Bank	15,000
			1–30 April	Discount allowed	324
			1–30 April	Returns in	944
			1–30 April	Bad debts	104
			30 April	Balances c/d	12,984
		29,821			29,821
1 May	Balance b/d	12,984			

This account could also be known as the total debtors (A–D) control account. This is because it contains as totals all the entries referring to debtors (A–D). It is not part of the double-entry system but is kept outside it as a memorandum account.

You can see that when Jill's balances from her sales ledger are inserted on to the credit side (ready to be brought down to the debit side where they belong), the totals of the account £29,821 agree. This would be accepted as sufficient proof that there are no errors in Jill's section of the sales ledger. Suppose, however, the balances in her section totalled £12,274 on 30 April. The control account with this inserted would be as follows.

Dr	Sales ledger (A–D) control account				Cr
		£			£
1 April	Balances b/d	13,621	1–30 April	Cash	465
1–30 April	Sales	16,200	1–30 April	Bank	15,000
			1–30 April	Discounts allowed	324
			1–30 April	Returns inward	944
			1–30 April	Bad debts	104
			30 April	Balances c/d	12,274
		29,821			29,111

Clearly something is wrong in this section of the sales ledger. The error(s) will have to be traced and corrected as soon as possible. If this control account had not been kept the error(s) would not have been revealed until the trial balance was prepared. This would give no guidance as to which accounts in it were at fault.

The figures for the sales ledger control account should be obtained from original entries. To do this easily the sales book and returns inward book should have analysis columns to match the sections of the ledger covered by the individual clerks. It will help also if the cash book is analysed in this way as the entries for cash and cheques received as well as discounts allowed will be obtained from that source. Entries for bad debts will be obtained from the journal which is not analysed. However, as such entries are comparatively few, it should not take too long to go through this book and extract the entries relevant to each of the sections of the sales ledger.

Exercise 7.2

From the following information about the sales ledger (E–H) prepare a control account on 30 April and state whether it reveals any errors.

		£
1 April	Debit balances	15,321
1–30 April	Total credit sales	18,640
1–30 April	Total cash received	720
1–30 April	Total cheques received	12,930
1–30 April	Total discounts allowed	380
1–30 April	Bad debts	206
1–30 April	Total returns inward	621
30 April	Debit balances obtained from sales ledger	19,104

The purchases ledger can be controlled in a similar manner. It will, of course, differ because it contains the accounts of suppliers. In these accounts the balances will be credit balances and there will be credit entries for goods bought on credit. The debit entries in these accounts will be for amounts paid by cash or cheque, discounts received and returns outward.

The principles involved in constructing a purchases ledger control account are the same as for the sales ledger. Similarly, it may be known as the total creditors' control account.

The purchases ledger (A-M) control account below has been constructed from the following information about the purchases ledger (A-M).

		£
1 April	Credit balances	27,431
1-30 April	Total goods bought on credit	82,500
1-30 April	Total cash paid	462
1-30 April	Total cheques paid	84,160
1-30 April	Total goods returned	468
1-30 April	Total discounts received	1,605
30 April	Credit balances obtained from purchases ledger	23,236

Dr Purchases ledger (A-M) control account Cr

		£			£
1-30 April	Cash	462	1 April	Balances b/d	27,431
1-30 April	Bank	84,160	1-30 April	Purchases	82,500
1-30 April	Discounts rec.	1,605			
1-30 April	Returns outward	468			
30 April	Balances c/d	23,236			
		109,931			109,931
			1 May	Balances b/d	23,236

To obtain information easily the books of original entry should be analysed in the same manner in which the purchases ledger is subdivided. This will involve the purchases book, returns outward book and the credit side of the cash book.

As the purchases ledger control account contains total figures covering all the accounts in the purchases ledger it is possible that there will be some debit balances included. How can a ledger containing the accounts of suppliers to whom money is owed contain debit balances? The answer is that it is possible for returns to be made *after* goods have been paid for. Thus, for a short time, the suppliers will owe the purchaser for the amount of the returns. Such accounts will be relatively small, as can be seen from the following example.

Dr Purchases ledger control account Cr

		£			£
1 May	Balances b/d	200	1 May	Balances b/d	20,600
1-31 May	Bank	68,720	1-31 May	Purchases	72,000
1-31 May	Discounts rec.	14,830	1-31 May	Balances c/d	180
1-31 May	Returns outward	641			
31 May	Balances c/d	8,389			
		92,780			92,780
1 June	Balances b/d	180	1 June	Balances b/d	8,389

At both the beginning and end of the month the credit balances are much bigger than the debit balances, as you would expect in a ledger containing the accounts of suppliers.

It is common also for the sales ledger to have a number of accounts with temporary credit balances. These will be the accounts of customers who have returned goods after having paid for them. Eventually they will purchase more goods and the credit balances will be set off against these purchases. The majority of the accounts in the sales ledger will, of course, have debit balances.

Exercise 7.3

Write up a sales ledger control account from the following information.

		£
1 May	Debit balances in sales ledger	24,860
1 May	Credit balances in sales ledger	190
31 May	Debit balances in sales ledger	28,140
31 May	Credit balances in sales ledger	240
1–31 May	Cheques received from customers	86,420
1–31 May	Discount allowed to customers	1,730
1–31 May	Returns inward	960
1–31 May	Sales on credit	92,340

In this chapter we have assumed that the sales ledger and purchases ledger control accounts are being kept outside the double-entry system. It is possible for them to become an integral part of that system. However, if this is done the personal accounts must be regarded as outside the system otherwise some entries would be appearing twice.

Exercise 7.4

(a) Give reasons why the bank balance in the cash book may differ from that in the bank statement at the same date.
(b) Give the three stages involved in reconciling the bank balance as per the cash book with that in the bank statement.
(c) State the sources from which entries will be made in (i) the sales ledger control account; (ii) the purchases ledger control account.

Exercise 7.5

A trader checked his cash book against the bank statement dated 30 June and noted the following discrepancies:

(i) Balance as per cash book £156.37; balance as per statement £167.91.
(ii) Cheques written by him but not yet presented for payment: No. 1545 £15.21; No. 1546 £14.28; No. 1547 £7.30.
(iii) His takings of £20.00 on 30 June had been banked late in the day and were not shown in the statement.

(iv) Payment had been made for £45.00 rates by standing order.
(v) Bank charges £15.50.

Bring the cash book up to date and prepare a bank reconciliation statement.

Exercise 7.6

From the following information about the sales ledger (K–R) prepare a control account on 31 May and state whether it reveals any errors.

		£
1 May	Debit balances	14,000
1–31 May	Total credit sales	19,364
1–31 May	Total cash received	1,326
1–31 May	Total cheques received	17,693
1–31 May	Total discounts allowed	648
1–31 May	Bad debts	396
1–31 May	Total returns inward	672
31 May	Debit balances in sales ledger	12,692

Exercise 7.7

From the following information about the purchases ledger prepare a control account on 31 May and state whether it reveals any errors.

		£
1 Jan	Debit balances	234
1 Jan	Credit balances	18,657
1–31 Jan	Total cheques paid	55,876
1–31 Jan	Returns outward	1,378
1–31 Jan	Discounts received	6,876
1–31 Jan	Purchases	63,143
31 Jan	Debit balances in purchases ledger	235
31 Jan	Credit balances in purchases ledger	15,671

CHAPTER 8

MEASURING AND ACCOUNTING FOR PROFIT

The main theme of the remainder of this book can be summed up by one word: profit. It is something of vital importance to all businesses. In this chapter we will examine concepts which are essential to understanding how to measure profit and we will deal with the method of measurement. In the remaining chapters with particular problems relating to its measurement.

8.1 **DEFINITION**

We will begin with a simple definition:

- *The profit made by a business is the difference between the total income or revenue earned and the total expenses incurred during a particular period of time.*

The trouble with a simple definition is that it often hides a number of difficulties, and this one is no exception. Let's explore some of them.

The actual period of time chosen is not a major problem. The owner may decide to see how much profit he has made in the last six months, three months, week, day or in any period that he chooses. However, in order to meet the requirements of the Inland Revenue, which assesses the tax that he has to pay on his profits, it is necessary for him to provide information on an annual basis. In fact most small businesses measure their profits at yearly or, at most, six-monthly intervals.

The calculation itself is not especially difficult - though the above definition does fail to make one thing absolutely clear. If earnings are less than expenses, profit is *negative*. In practice the term 'loss' is more frequently used.

The main problem is not, then, one of the time period chosen nor is it the actual calculation. It lies, rather, in the need to answer the questions: What counts as expenses incurred? And what counts as income or revenue earned? To answer the first question correctly it is necessary for you to understand the distinction between capital and revenue expenditure.

8.2 CAPITAL AND REVENUE EXPENDITURE

Capital expenditure is expenditure on acquiring fixed assets. These are those assets which are bought to last the business a long time and which help to make profits over that period. You should be able to list some examples of fixed assets as they were mentioned earlier in this volume. If you cannot remember, a glance at the balance sheet on page 11 should help. When you are happy that you can give some examples of fixed assets, consider this: would it be fair to take the cost of buying such an asset, which will last for several years, from the earnings of only one year? Clearly the answer is 'no'. Therefore it would be wrong to include the purchase of a fixed asset or capital expenditure in the calculation of one year's profit.

Revenue expenditure is the spending which relates to benefits which do not last for longer than one year. Expenditure on all items except the purchase of fixed assets can therefore be regarded as revenue expenditure. You should be able to think of some examples but if you find it difficult look back to Chapter 3, where we considered how such expenses should be entered in the ledger. Since expenditure of this nature is directly related to the earning of revenue it is quite correct that it should be deducted from revenue when calculating profit.

Exercise 8.1

Judy Brooks recently opened a restaurant. Some of her items of expenditure are listed below. Complete the table by putting a tick in those columns which are relevant to each item.

Items of expenditure	*Capital*	*Revenue*	*Used in measuring profit*
(a) Purchase of premises			
(b) Wages			
(c) Insurance			
(d) Purchase of equipment			
(e) Gas and electricity			
(f) Purchase of china			
(g) Advertising			
(h) Repairs to equipment			

You must not assume that the distinction between what counts as capital expenditure and as revenue expenditure is always clear cut. We referred earlier (page 34) to the concept of depreciation, which is the reduction in the value of a fixed asset resulting from its use. For example, some kitchen equipment bought by Judy for her restaurant might have an estimated working life of five years. She (or her accountant) might decide that, each year, one fifth of the cost of this equipment should be deducted from that year's profits to allow for its depreciation in value. One fifth of the asset's cost will be removed from the asset account and transferred to an account for depreciation. This depreciation will then be counted as one of the items of revenue expenditure for that year and deducted from the year's income in order to obtain the profit figure. We will consider this in more detail in Chapter 11. For now, it is enough if you recognise that even the purchase of a fixed asset, which counts as capital expenditure, may directly result in an expense which is included in the calculation of profit.

8.3 CAPITALISING A REVENUE EXPENSE

Sometimes an expenditure which is normally quite correctly classified as revenue, and recorded as such, is turned into capital expenditure. The most common example involves maintenance workers who spend most of their time repairing and maintaining fixed assets. Their earnings will normally be recorded in a wages account and quite correctly, as an item of revenue expenditure, deducted from each year's income to obtain profit. Occasionally, however, they might be employed to *improve* a fixed asset and not merely to restore its value. If this happens their earnings, while performing this task, should be removed from the wages account, which counts as revenue expenditure, and transferred to an account for the fixed asset which has increased in value.

An example will help to make this clear. The maintenance staff at Tom Brown's engineering works used waste material to build shelves in a storeroom. Their total wages for the period when the shelves were being erected amounted to £250. If this is allowed to remain in the wages account it will be deducted (as part of the total wages paid during the year) from income to obtain profit. Clearly this would not be fair as £250 of the expenditure on wages is resulting in an increase in the value of an asset which will last for some considerable time. The £250 should be transferred from the wages account to an account for fixtures and fittings. As it is a relatively unusual transaction it would probably be recorded in the journal before being posted to the ledger. It is known as the capitalisation of a revenue expense and the journal entry for it is shown below.

		F	dr	cr
28 Feb.	Fixtures and fittings		250	
	Wages account			250
	Being the capitalisation of revenue expenditure on improving the storeroom			

Having considered the distinction between the capital and revenue expenditure we can now turn to the second question posed earlier: what counts as income or revenue earned? The answer to this requires an understanding of the distinction between capital and revenue receipts.

8.4 CAPITAL AND REVENUE RECEIPTS

A capital receipt is finance invested in a business either by the owner or by an outside firm. Suppose that one year Judy Brooks decided to invest an additional £1,000 of her own money in her restaurant and paid this amount into the business bank account. Would it be fair to include this amount as income or revenue received for that year, from which expenses will be deducted to calculate profit? Clearly not, as the business is not *earning* any revenue but is being given additional finance to use. The entries to show this in the accounts would be: debit entry in the bank account to increase the value of the asset, and a credit entry in the capital account to increase the value of the finance invested by the owner.

Similarly, finance may be received by way of a loan from another person or firm. Suppose Judy borrowed £6,000 by means of a loan from Cityfinance plc. The assets of the business will increase by this amount. Such an increase is not income or revenue earned, however, but simply additional finance borrowed for use in the business. It is therefore regarded as a receipt of capital and not included as income from which expenses are to be deducted to arrive at profit.

A debit entry in the bank account (or bank column in the cash book) records the increase in the value of the assets and the credit entry in an account for Cityfinance creates a liability for that amount. The latter is a loan account recording finance invested by an outside firm and *not* an income account which would record revenue or income earned.

It is also possible that the capital of a business will increase as a result of the capitalisation of a revenue expense. Look again at the example on page 84. Suppose that the work of Tom Brown's maintenance men resulted in fixtures and fittings worth £550. This is £300 more than the value of the labour employed in the construction. This £300 is not regarded as income or revenue earned from the normal activities of the business because the maintenance men are really employed to carry out repairs to assets. It is considered to represent a direct increase in the value of the business to the owner by means of an increase in the capital of the business. The journal entry to record the capitalisation of the revenue expenditure under these circumstances would be as follows.

		F	dr	cr
Date	Furniture and fittings		550	
	Wages			250
	Capital			300
	Being capitalisation of revenue expenses on improving the storeroom			

Revenue or income is money received from the normal profit-making activities of a business. In a business which sells goods, the value of the sales will be the major item of income or revenue. Other business, such as accountants or lawyers, receive fees for their services rendered. Whatever the business, it is also possible that some additional income may be received which may be regarded as part of normal trading. For instance, the owner of a shop may let the flat above it and receive rent, or a service may be performed for which commission is received. Such additional income, however, will normally be relatively small in relation to the main profit-making activity of the business.

Having sorted out the meaning of the terms 'capital expenditure', 'revenue expenditure', 'capital receipts' and 'revenue receipts', you should now be quite clear on what to include and what to exclude when calculating profit. Let's see how well you have grasped the points made.

Exercise 8.2

First write down the definition of 'profit' with which we started this chapter. Try to do it without looking back. Then say whether each of the following statements is true or false.

(a) Both capital and revenue expenditure must be included in the calculation of a firm's profit.
(b) Neither receipts of capital nor receipts of income should be included in the calculation of a firm's profit.
(c) The purchase of fixtures and fittings is an example of capital expenditure.
(d) Wages paid to employees are an example of revenue expenditure.
(e) Repairs to a damaged machine are an example of capital expenditure.
(f) A legacy received by the owner of a business and invested in the business is an example of a receipt of revenue or income.
(g) The sale of a car by a car dealer results in the receipt of revenue.

It is worth summarising the main points of the chapter so far. In measuring profit the emphasis is on income or revenue earned (i.e. revenue receipts) and expenses incurred (i.e. revenue expenditure) during the period for which profit is being measured. In fact our definition of profit could be abbreviated to:

- *revenue receipts* less *revenue expenditure*.

The purchase of a fixed asset - capital expenditure - must not be included because the value will last for longer than one year. The receipt of capital must not be included because it is not derived from the profit-making activity of the business. It is likely that such a receipt is a loan to the business from an outside firm or a further investment of finance in the business by the owner.

8.5 DRAWINGS

Another transaction which occurs frequently and which must not be allowed to affect the calculation of profit is the withdrawal of any of the assets from the business by the owner for his private use. Such a withdrawal is known as 'drawings'. The assets most usually affected are cash or bank. The entries to record such a withdrawal are: credit the asset account and debit the capital account. The credit entry in the asset account has the effect of reducing the value of that asset while the debit entry in the capital account reduces the owner's investment in the business by the value of the asset withdrawn.

When an owner makes fairly frequent withdrawals from the business for his private use, it is likely that an extra account will be introduced. This will be called the drawings account and it will be debited instead of the capital account. At the end of the financial year the total debit balance in this account can then be transferred into the capital account. An example will help to make this clear.

On the first day of March, June, September and December last year Judy Brooks withdrew £500 from the business bank account for private use. On 31 December she transferred the total amount withdrawn from drawings account to the capital account. The entries recording this were as follows.

Dr — Bank account — Cr

			1 March	Drawings	500
			1 June	Drawings	500
			1 Sept.	Drawings	500
			1 Dec.	Drawings	500

Drawings account

		£			
1 March	Bank	500	31 Dec.	Transferred to capital account	2,000
1 June	Bank	500			
1 Sept.	Bank	500			
1 Dec.	Bank	500			
		2,000			2,000

Capital account

31 Dec.	Drawings	2,000			

Note the technique of transferring an amount from one account to another. An entry is made on the smaller side of the account from which the transfer is to be made. This account is totalled and then closed. The double entry is completed by an entry on the other side of the account to which the transfer is being made. You are still following, therefore, the rules of double-entry book-keeping, because such a transfer requires one debit entry and one credit entry.

The end result is that the debit entry for £2,000 in the capital account reduces the owner's capital by that amount. The four credit entries in the bank account or cash book remove the £2,000 from the assets of the business. Using a drawings account does not hide the fact that assets taken out of a business by the owner for his private use reduce his capital investment in the business. It must not therefore be allowed to affect the calculation of profit.

Exercise 8.3

If you have understood this chapter you should be able to calculate Judy Brooks's profit for the year to 31 December 1989 from the information which follows. Take care - some information has been listed which is not needed. Provided you understand the difference between capital and revenue expenditure, and capital and revenue receipts, you should not find it too difficult.

Year ended 31 December 1989

	£
Sales revenue – meals and drinks	20,000
Cost of food and drinks sold	7,000
Purchase of equipment	2,000
Rent and rates	500
Depreciation on fixed assets	500
Loan from bank	1,000
Additional finance invested by owner	4,000
Insurances	200
Waiters' wages	4,000
Drawings	2,000
Gas and electricity	800

8.6 ACCOUNTING FOR PROFIT

The last exercise tested your ability to calculate the profit of Judy Brooks's restaurant. In this section we are going to break down the concept of profit into two parts: gross profit and net profit. We will then consider how to prepare the accounts in which these profits will be measured. To do this we will need to return to the ledger account balances for information. Finally we will look once more at the balance sheet to see how making a profit (or loss) affects this statement of the financial affairs of a business.

First refer back to the answer to the last exercise which you will find on page 290. You will see that the total amount of profit earned by Judy in 1989 was £7,000. This, in fact, is more correctly known as the net profit. Most businesses, however, do not calculate this figure by deducting total revenue expenditure from total sales revenue in one single calculation as we did. They introduce a preliminary stage in which gross profit is calculated.

Gross profit may be defined as the difference between the revenue earned from sales and the cost of the goods sold.

Self-check

Apply this definition to the information on page 88 and state Judy's gross profit for the year 1989.

ANSWER

	£
Revenue earned from sales of meals and drinks	20,000
Cost of goods (food and drinks) sold	7,000
Gross profit	13,000

As long as you understand the definition of gross profit you should not have found this difficult. Let's look at another example just in case. A friend of ours called Henry likes doing up motorcars in his spare time. He also enjoys wheeling and dealing. One day recently he bought an old Mini for £50 and was able to sell it within the week for £80. A very nice gross profit of £30 was made on that Mini.

On single deals like this it is not too difficult to state precisely the cost of the item sold and the revenue earned from selling it. When business becomes a little bigger, things become more complicated. Look at the following information for 1989 and you will see what we mean.

1 Jan.–31 Dec.	Vehicles bought by Henry for £9,000.
1 Jan.–31 Dec.	Revenue earned from sales £14,000.
1 Jan.	Henry's stock of vehicles: two Fords, cost price £500 each.
31 Dec.	Henry's stock of vehicles remaining: two Vauxhalls, cost price £750 each.

At first glance you might think that Henry's gross profit for 1989 was £5,000. This is calculated as the difference between revenue earned from sales (£14,000) and the cost of the vehicles bought (£9,000). Wait a minute, though, something is wrong here!

Gross profit is the difference between the revenue earned from sales and the cost of goods sold. While it is correct to state that £14,000 revenue was earned from sales it is incorrect to deduct £9,000 from it. The total cost of the cars *bought* during the year was £9,000 but this is not the same as the cost of the cars actually sold. There are two reasons for this. First, some of the cars sold in 1989 had been bought the previous year and would have already been part of his stock at the beginning of the year. Second, some of the cars bought in 1989 had not been sold by the end of the year and form the closing stock on 31 December. Cost of goods sold is not, therefore, the same as the cost of goods bought.

The above explanation is important so read it through again carefully. To find how much gross profit Henry really made in 1989 we will need to work out the actual cost of the cars sold. A simple formula can be applied: *add the cost of the stock purchased to the opening stock at cost price.* This gives us the cost of stock *available* for sale. If we deduct from this the cost of the stock not sold – i.e. the closing stock at cost price – we are left with the actual cost of stock sold.

This can be seen more clearly in the following form:

- *opening stock at cost price;*
- add *cost of stock purchased during the year = cost of stock (or goods) available for sale;*
- deduct *closing stock at cost price = cost of stock sold.*

If we apply this formula to the information given about Henry's dealings and calculate his cost of stock sold for 1989 we will then be able to state accurately his gross profit for 1989.

	£
Opening stock at cost price	1,000
add Cost of stock purchased during year	9,000
Cost of stock available for sale	10,000
less Closing stock at cost price	1,500
Cost of stock sold 1989	8,500
Revenue earned from sales 1989	14,000
less Cost of stock sold 1989	8,500
Gross profit for 1989	5,500

Henry's gross profit of £5,500 seems very good – especially as it is earned from an interest which only occupies his spare time. However it is not the same as his true or **net profit**, which is the total revenue received from business operations less the total revenue expenditure incurred. So far we have only deducted one item of revenue expenditure – the actual cost of the cars sold. To calculate net profit you will have to deduct all the other items of revenue expenditure from the gross profit.

For example, suppose Henry's other items of revenue expenditure were: lubricants £100, parts £700 and wages of a part time assistant £900. His net profit would be calculated as follows:

	£	£
Gross profit 1989		5,500
less Wages	900	
Lubricants	100	
Parts	700	
		1,700
Net profit for 1989		3,800

The account in which profit is measured is called the **trading and profit and loss account**. The example below contains the information relating to Henry's business for 1989.

Trading and profit and loss account of Henry Reeve for the year ended 31 December 1989.

	£	£
Sales		14,000
less *Cost of goods sold*		
Opening stock	1,000	
Purchases	9,000	
	10,000	
less Closing stock	1,500	
		8,500
Gross profit		5,500
less *Expenses*		
Wages	900	
Parts	700	
Lubricants	100	
		1,700
Net profit		3,800

Notes:

- The heading contains the name of the account, the name of the business or owner and the period for which profit is being measured.
- It is incorrect to date such an account 'as at 31 December' as you would a balance sheet, because it contains information relating to the measurement of profit over a particular time period. In the above example this period is a year, although of course there is nothing to prevent profit being measured for six months or any other time period.
- The section of the account in which gross profit is calculated is known as the trading section, while that in which net profit is measured is known as the profit and loss section. Sometimes these sections might appear as separate accounts, in which case gross profit is measured in the trading account and net profit in the profit and loss account.
- The style of the account shown above is one of a number that could be used. At one time the trading and profit and loss account was prepared like a ledger account with debits (expenses) on the left and credits (incomes) on the right. This practice is less common today but examples can still be seen in certain textbooks. It is important that, whatever layout is used, the contents should be easily understood. Practice this by attempting the following.

Exercise 8.4

Prepare a trading and profit and loss account from the following information relating to the business of Judy Brooks for the period from 1 Jan. 1990 to 30 June 1990.

	£
Sales of meals and drinks	16,000
Purchases of food and drinks	4,000
Returns outward	200
Stock of food and drink 1 Jan. 1990	400
Stock of food and drink 30 June 1990	600
Rent and rates	250
Depreciation on fixed assets	250
Insurance	100
Waiters' wages	3,000
Gas and electricity	500

8.7 BACK TO THE LEDGER

We must now look back to the ledger and see what happens to the accounts which contain the items appearing in the trading and profit and loss account. Taking the last exercise as an example, assume that, before Judy's trading and profit and loss account was prepared, the trial balance shown below was extracted from her ledger.

The balances in the accounts which are needed to calculate profit will be transferred to the trading and profit and loss account. The process of transferring an amount from one account to another was demonstrated in 8.5 when drawings were transferred from the drawings account to the capital account. We will remind you how to do it by showing the transfer of sales.

Trial balance of Judy Brooks as at 30 June 1990

Account	*£ dr*	*£ cr*
Capital (1 Jan. 1990)		3,300
Equipment	4,000	
Furniture and fittings	6,000	
China, linen and cutlery	800	
Stock (1 Jan. 1990)	400	
Debtors	100	
Cash at bank	400	
Trade creditors		300
Sales		16,000
Purchases	4,000	
Returns outward		200
Waiters' wages	3,000	
Rent and rates	250	
Depreciation on fixed assets	250	
Insurance	100	
Gas and electricity	500	
	19,800	19,800

Dr		Sales account			Cr
1990		£	1990		£
30 June	Transferred to trading a/c	16,000	31 Jan.	Cash	2,000
			28 Feb.	Cash	3,000
			31 Mar.	Cash	4,000
			30 Apr.	Cash	2,000
			31 May	Cash	3,000
			30 June	Cash	2,000
		16,000			16,000

Whatever the total, this amount is placed on the smaller side with the date of transfer and a suitable description. The account is then totalled and totals are underlined. The account is thus temporarily closed and will be opened again when the first sales are recorded in the next financial period.

Exercise 8.5

Show the transfer of purchases to Judy's trading account. You may assume that the purchases were made as follows: Jan.–May £600 each month by cheque and June £1,000 on credit.

The only account in which complications arise is the stock account. This is because two stock figures are needed in the trading account while at any one time there will be only one balance for stock shown in the trial balance. It is important to realise that, unless told otherwise, the stock balance in the trial balance will be the opening stock for the period. Stock will be valued at the end of the period and this figure will be entered in both the trading account and the stock account. Here is how the stock account will appear after the trading and profit and loss account has been prepared.

Dr		Stock account			Cr
		£			£
1 Jan.	Balance b/d	400	30 June	Transferred to trading a/c	400
30 June	Trading a/c	600			

Do not be confused by the two entries dated 30 June. Although the credit entry is dated 30 June it is, in fact, the opening stock of 1 Jan. which is being transferred to the trading account on 30 June. The closing stock at 30 June is shown by the debit entry for £600. The description 'trading account' is used because that is where the other double entry can be found. As mentioned earlier, the practice of showing the trading and profit and loss account as a ledger account with two distinct sides has been largely discontinued. Those readers interested in the theory of double-entry book-keeping might like to see how the trading section would have been shown. The one below makes use of the same figures for Judy Brooks as does the one on page 291.

Trading account of Judy Brooks for six months ended 30 June 1987

	£		£
Opening stock	400	Sales	16,000
Purchases	4,000	Returns outward	200
Balance (gross profit)	12,400	Closing stock	600
	16,800		16,800

The entries for opening stock, purchases, sales and returns outward appear on the same side as they would have done in their individual accounts. The credit entry for closing stock is the entry corresponding to the debit made in the stock account after the stocktaking at the end of the year. The balance of the account is the gross profit. This figure is exactly the same as arrived at earlier. We are sure you will agree that, while this method gives the same answer, the process of obtaining it is nothing like as clear.

8.8 THE BALANCE SHEET

We have looked at the process by which some ledger accounts balances are transferred to the trading and profit and loss account. Now we need to consider what happens to those balances which remain in the accounts after the profit has been calculated.

Look back to the trial balance on page 92 and identify those accounts which will still have balances in them because they will *not* have been transferred to the trading and profit and loss account. You should be able to identify the following accounts which will still have balances: capital, equipment, furniture and fittings, china, linen and cutlery, debtors, trade creditors, cash at bank and stock (for the closing balance). Can you see what they all have in common? A glance back to page 11 may remind you. They are all balance sheet items.

Having closed all the accounts involving revenue receipts and revenue expenditure, we are left only with balances in the accounts for assets and sources of finance. The balances in these accounts can now be placed in a balance sheet showing the position of Judy's business at the end of the financial period. Before we do this, there is one final double entry to be made. The net profit of £8,300 belongs to the owner. The entry for this amount in the profit and loss account must be accompanied by another in the account of the owner, which is, of course, the capital account.

Dr		Capital account			Cr
		£			£
30 June	Balance c/d	11,600	1 Jan.	Balance b/d	3,300
			30 June	Net profit	8,300
		11,600			11,600
			1 July	Balance b/d	11,600

The credit entry for net profit increases Judy's capital. If a loss has been made a debit entry would be needed in the capital account to reduce her capital balance.

When all the remaining accounts are balanced at the end of June, the balance sheet will look like this:

Balance sheet of Judy Brooks as at 30 June 1990

	£	£		£	£
Fixed assets			Owners' capital	3,300	
Furniture and fittings	6,000				
Equipment	4,000		add Net profit	8,300	
China, etc.	800				11,600
		10,800			
Current assets			*Current liabilities*		
Stock	600		Trade creditors		300
Debtors	100				
Cash at bank	400				
		1,100			
		11,900			11,900

As the balance sheet has not appeared since very early in the book, you may have to remind yourself of its presentation by looking back to Chapter 1. You might think that the owners' capital could have been shown by one figure for £11,600. This is, after all, the balance in the capital account and the balance sheet is a collection of all the balances remaining in the accounts after preparation of the trading and profit and loss account. It is normal practice, however, to show all the information in the capital account again in the form of a sum in the balance sheet. Thus if Judy had drawn any assets for her private use we would also show these drawings, as a reduction of her capital.

8.9 VERTICAL BALANCE SHEETS

The above balance sheet of Judy Brooks is horizontal in its style of layout just like those that you encountered in the early part of the book. Look again at the balance sheet of Rivendale General Stores as at 31 May 1990 which is on page 11. This is a good example of a balance sheet in the horizontal layout because it includes fixed assets, current assets, long-term liabilities, current liabilities and owner's capital.

The balance sheet has reflected the accounting equation:

Assets = capital + liabilities

It could be written in even more detail as:

Fixed assets + current assets =
capital + long-term liabilities + current liabilities

Now look at the balance sheet below which uses the same figures to obtain a slightly different result.

Balance sheet of Rivendale General Stores as at 31 May 1990

	£	£	£
Fixed assets			
Premises		80,000	
Furniture and fittings		6,000	
			86,000
Current assets			
Stock	7,000		
Debtors	2,000		
Bank	1,000		
Cash	500		
		10,500	
Less current liabilities			
Trade creditors		1,500	
Net current assets			9,000
Total assets less current liabilities			95,000
Financed by:			
Long-term liabilities			
Mortgage		10,000	
Owner's capital		85,000	
			95,000

This is an example of a vertical balance sheet. Compare it with the balance sheet on page 11 and see what differences you can spot. This is what you should notice:

1. Instead of the accounting equation being written horizontally across the page, it has been written down the page. The two totals are directly underneath each other instead of being side by side.
2. The totals are different. This is because the equation has been changed.

Fixed assets + current assets =
capital + long-term liabilities + current liabilities

has become

Fixed assets + current assets − current liabilities =
capital + long-term liabilities

Remember it is possible to change any item in an equation to the other side of the equation provided you remember to change the sign of the item that is changed. Thus when + current liabilities moves to the other side of the equation it becomes − current liabilities.

3. There is a new item within the balance sheet. The subtotal for current assets less current liabilities is here labelled *net current assets* because that is what the current assets are worth net when any outstanding current liabilities are settled. It is also sometimes known as working capital.

   You are probably already wondering why it is necessary to have more than one style of balance sheet layout. The answer to that is that we are currently in a state of transition from the horizontal style which predominated for many years and the vertical style which, though of more recent origin, has become more popular. You will therefore meet both types of layout and must be able to understand them. There are, indeed, variations on both the horizontal and vertical layouts. However, if you can understand the ones we have shown you then you should not have too much difficulty with any slight variations. The most likely of these variations you will find involves the horizontal balance sheet. Until comparatively recently many of these were written with the assets on the right of the finance. This makes no difference to the equation that it represents as you should realise and the information it provides is exactly the same.

Which type of layout should you adopt in your course work and examination? As far as course work is concerned you will obviously be guided by your teacher or lecturer. In examinations too sometimes guidance is given. For example, a question might tell you to prepare a balance sheet in vertical style. Here there is no problem deciding what is required. It might, however, be a little less direct and tell you to prepare a balance sheet which shows the total of working capital. This, of course, is an indirect way of telling you to use vertical layout since, as we have seen, only this layout includes a figure within the balance sheet for working capital or current assets less current liabilities. Often, however, no instructions are given as to the method you should use. The advice I would give you is the same as I give my own students. As the vertical layout has become the preferred layout in the accountancy profession then it is better to opt for that format. You will get lots of practice at preparing balance sheets in this book and this is a good place to start.

Exercise 8.6

Rewrite Judy Brooks's balance sheet (page 95) in vertical style.

Before we give a full example to review the contents of this chapter, a few points ought to be made about some accounts which often cause confusion (and are frequently included in examination questions, therefore).

8.9.1 **Carriage inwards and carriage outwards**

These are both expenses and therefore appear as debit balances in their ledger accounts. The first is the expense of paying for the transport of goods which have been bought for resale. The second describes the expense of transporting goods sold to the customers. They are treated slightly differently, however, in the trading and profit and loss account. Carriage inwards is added to the purchases in the trading section while carriage outwards is listed with all the other expenses in the profit and loss account.

8.9.2 **Discounts allowed and discounts received**

Discounts allowed to debtors for prompt payment are shown as an expense in the profit and loss section. Discount received from creditors are shown as income in the profit and loss account along with any other income such as rent received. Such incomes are usually positioned immediately below the gross profit.

It could be argued that, as discount allowed is an expense arising from the sale of goods, it should be shown in the trading section. Similarly it might be argued that discounts received arise from purchases and should be shown as income in the trading section. In practice this is not normally done.

8.10 **FINAL ACCOUNTS**

The trading and profit and loss account and the balance sheet are often known as the final accounts because they are drawn up at the end of the financial year. Technically the balance sheet is not an account but a financial statement. You can normally assume, however, that when you are asked to prepare final accounts, a balance sheet is to be prepared as well.

Example

The following trial balance was extracted from the ledger of Frank Holden, a retailer. You are asked to prepare his trading and profit and loss account for the year ended 31 August 1990 and a balance sheet as at that date.

	£ dr	£ cr
Capital (1 Sept. 1989)		30,400
Cash	150	
Bank	1,700	
Stock (1 Sept. 1989)	8,000	
Purchases and purchases returns	69,000	1,200
Sales and sales returns	260	96,400
Carriage inwards	940	
Carriage outwards	320	
Discount allowed and received	920	1,380
Wages	8,000	
Depreciation on fixed assets	1,000	
Drawings	9,000	
Rent received		630
Premises	25,000	
Fixtures and fittings	5,000	
Motor vehicles	1,500	
Trade debtors and creditors	480	3,620
Rates	520	
Insurance	490	
Heating and lighting	800	
Miscellaneous expenses	550	
	133,630	133,630

Note:

- Stock on 31 August 1990 was valued at £12,000.
- Some of the balances have been combined together, for example trade debtors and creditors. Your knowledge of balances in the ledger should enable you to decide which figure refers to which item.

Solution on next page

Trading and profit and loss account of Frank Holden for the year ended 31 August 1990

	£	£	£
Sales		96,400	
less Sales returns		260	
Net turnover			96,140
less *Cost of goods sold*			
Opening stock		8,000	
Purchases	69,000		
less Purchases returns	1,200		
	67,800		
Carriage inwards	940		
Net purchases		68,740	
		76,740	
less Closing stock		12,000	
			64,740
Gross profit			31,400
Discount received			1,380
Rent received			630
Total revenue			33,410
less *Expenses*			
Wages		8,000	
Insurance		490	
Heating and lighting		800	
Rates		520	
Depreciation		1,000	
Carriage outwards		320	
Discount allowed		920	
Miscellaneous		550	12,600
Net profit			20,810

Balance sheet of Frank Holden as at 31 August 1990

	£	£	£
Fixed assets			
Premises		25,000	
Fixtures and fittings		5,000	
Motor vehicle		1,500	
			31,500
Current assets			
Stock	12,000		
Debtors	480		
Bank	1,700		
Cash	150		
		14,330	
Less current liabilities			
Trade creditors		3,620	
Net current assets			10,710
Total assets less current liabilities			42,210
Financed by:			
Owner's capital		30,400	
Add Net Profit		20,810	
		51,210	
Less Drawings		9,000	
			42,210

Exercise 8.7

Select the information that is relevant and prepare a trading and profit and loss account for the period 1 July 1990 to 31 December 1990. The accounts are those of Tom Evans, grocer.

	£
Sales	34,000
Purchases	10,560
Stock at 1 July	2,300
Stock at 31 December	3,540
Rent and rates	750
Purchase of delivery vehicle	2,595
Depreciation on fixed assets	375
Insurance	250
Drawings	9,000
Electricity	950

Exercise 8.8

The following information relates to the business of A. Brown for the six months ended 31 October 1990: Opening stock £4,870; Purchases £23,450; Sales £46,920; Returns inward £980; Returns outward £689; Carriage inwards £667; Closing stock £6,870.

(a) Prepare a vertical trading account.
(b) Prepare a ledger-style horizontal trading account.
(c) Show the stock account as it would appear after a balance sheet had been prepared on 31 October.

Exercise 8.9

The following trial balance has been extracted from the accounts of F. Whitbread on 31 May 1990.

	£	£
Sales		85,453
Purchases	35,654	
Returns inward and returns outward	1,754	2,352
Stock (1 June 1989)	6,750	
Carriage inward	292	
Discount allowed and received	163	279
Salaries	22,456	
Rates	386	
Insurance	263	
Depreciation on fixed assets	545	
Premises	34,000	
Furniture and fittings	6,000	
Debtors and creditors	1,655	876
Drawings	6,500	
Capital (1 June 1989)		28,000
Bank	542	
	116,960	116,960

The stock was valued at £8,560 on 31 May 1990.
Prepare Whitbread's trading and profit and loss account for the year ended 31 May 1990 and a balance sheet as at that date.

Exercise 8.10

Analyse the following trial balance and then prepare final accounts for the financial year ended 31 May 1990.

Trial balance of B. White as at 31 May 1990

	£	£
Sales		79,700
Purchases	30,780	
Returns inward and returns outward	797	1,457
Stock (1 June 1989)	4,680	
Salaries	27,200	
Discount allowed and received	426	349
Rent received		655
Rates	526	
Insurance	315	
Carriage outwards	350	
Carriage inwards	198	
Premises	55,500	
Furniture and fittings	7,000	
Debtors and creditors	1,565	4,765
Drawings	7,000	
Capital (1 June 1989)		51,000
Bank	1,589	
	137,926	137,926

Note: Stock at 31 May was valued at £9,185.

CHAPTER 9

PREPAYMENTS AND ACCRUALS

We have now covered the whole process involved in keeping a set of financial accounts - from opening a ledger and keeping track of transactions there and in the journals to preparing the final accounts at the end of the period. In the remaining chapters we will consider the reasons why certain adjustments have to be made to the information recorded in our books. We will also see how these adjustments can be made. In addition we will take the opportunity of giving you some additional practice preparing the final accounts. This chapter will cover the adjustments which arise because payments and receipts of money do not always occur in the financial period to which the expenditure or income relates.

9.1 EXPENSES PREPAID

Consider the following facts about a new business which was established on 1 January 1989 and therefore has a financial year which is the same as the calendar year.

All insurances were negotiated with a broker and the premiums payable amounted to £400 per annum. The business negotiated terms which allowed this amount to be paid in four quarterly instalments of £100 each. These instalments were due on the first day of January, April, July and October. Assuming that the instalments were paid by cheque on the dates due, the insurance account will appear like this after preparation of the final accounts for the year:

Dr Insurance account Cr

1989		£	1989		£
1 Jan.	Bank	100	31 Dec.	Transferred to profit and loss account	400
1 Apr.	Bank	100			
1 July	Bank	100			
1 Oct.	Bank	100			
		400			400

Insurance is an expense and, as such, debit entries are used to record its payment in the insurance account. The credit entries will appear in the bank column of the cash book.

Suppose, however, that in 1990 the insurance account looked like this:

Dr Insurance account Cr

1990		£	
1 Jan.	Bank	100	
1 Apr.	Bank	100	
1 July	Bank	100	
1 Oct.	Bank	100	
20 Dec.	Bank	100	

You might think that the cost of insurance for this firm had increased from £400 per annum to £500 per annum. While that might be true, it is not the case here. The insurance premiums remained at £400 per annum. What, then, do you think explains the extra £100 recorded? The only logical answer is that the payment of £100 on 20 December 1990 was made early. It was really the amount due on 1 January 1991. This is an example of a prepaid expense, which is what this section of the chapter is about. A prepaid expense is one which is paid in the period prior to the one in which it is due.

You might wonder whether or not it is correct to record such a payment when it is made on 20 December 1990. After all, it is an amount which belongs to 1991 and it might be argued that it should not be recorded until that year has begun. It is in fact correct to record it on the date it was paid and thus the account is in perfect order, as it stands.

This does cause a problem, however. How much should be transferred to the profit and loss account of 1990 as the expense of insurance? The answer is £400, which is the true expense for 1990. The additional £100 is really an expense which relates to 1991 and will be included in that year's profit and loss account. The principle on which this is based is that costs or expenses should be counted when they are incurred and not when they are paid. Thus £400 is counted as the expense of insurance for 1990. The additional £100 will count as part of the insurance for 1991.

There remains the technique of transferring to the profit and loss account the correct amount of £400. This is what the insurance account will look like when it has been done:

Dr		Insurance a/c			Cr
1990		£	1990		£
1 Jan.	Bank	100	31 Dec.	Transferred to profit and loss account	400
1 Apr.	Bank	100	31 Dec.	Balance prepaid	100
1 July	Bank	100			
1 Oct.	Bank	100			
20 Dec.	Bank	100			
		500			500
1991					
1 Jan.	Balance prepaid b/d	100			

As you can see, the problem has been overcome by bringing down the amount prepaid as a balance for the start of the next financial year. This procedure is quite correct because, after preparation of the trading and profit and loss account, all ledger accounts having balances within them should be balanced. Can you remember what happens to all accounts which contain balances. If you thought 'they appear in the balance sheet', well done! Perhaps you can even work out where in the balance sheet the £100 insurance should appear. It is in fact an asset, one clue being that it is brought down as a debit balance. You should be able to recognise the logic of this as it is an asset to the firm in that it will receive insurance in 1991 for which payment has already been made in 1990. The fact that this benefit relates to such a short time period means that it is a current asset and not a fixed asset. The relevant balance sheet entry will look like this:

Balance sheet as at 31 Dec. 1990

	£
Current assets	
Stock	—
Debtors	—
Bank	—
Prepaid insurance	100

Some textbooks advise placing prepayments with, or next to, the debtors. This is acceptable as logically the benefit of insurance which is to be received is owed by the insurance company to the firm which has paid for it in advance. Others prefer to place it last on the grounds that it is more liquid than cash in that the money has already been spent. We leave the choice to you but would stress the value of consistency. Once you have decided where you are going to show prepaid expenses in the balance sheet, stick to it.

Exercise 9.1

Harry Wilson's financial year ends on 30 June. He rents his premises at £200 per quarter which is payable on 1 July, 1 October, 1 January and 1 April. In the year ended 30 June 1990, which was his first year of trading, he made the following payments by cheque: 1 July 1989, £200; 3 October 1989, £200; 1 January 1990, £200; 2 April 1990, £200; 4 June 1990, £200.

Write up Harry's ledger account for rent and show all entries relevant to the final accounts at the end of the year. Be especially careful with the dates. It is never as easy when the financial year differs from the calendar year.

In both the example and the exercise you knew the true cost of the expense for the year. Sometimes, however, you are told how much has been paid for an expense and how much of that is a prepayment. You then have to calaculate the correct amount to be transferred to the profit and loss account. This often happens in an examination when you are given a trial balance entry and told by how much it should be adjusted. For example, the following item appeared in Harry's trial balance at 30 June 1990.

A/cs	*dr*	*cr*
Rates	350	

You are then told that, of the rates, £50 has been paid in advance for the year ending 30 Jun 1991. Deducting this from the amount paid gives you the true value of rates for the year ended 30 June 1990. The accounts would look like this:

Dr — Rates account — Cr

1989/90		£	*1990*		£
	Bank	350	30 June	Profit and loss a/c	300
			30 June	Balance prepaid c/d	50
		350			350
1990					
1 July	Balance prepaid b/d	50			

Profit and loss account of Harry Wilson, year ended 30 June 1990

	£
Expenses	
Rates	300

Balance sheet of Harry Wilson as at 30 June 1990

Current assets	
Prepaid rates	50

Exercise 9.2

The following item appeared in the trial balance of a business at 31 October 1990

A/cs	*dr*	*cr*
Rent	944	

You are told that £68 of the rent has been paid in advance for the next financial year.

Show the rent account balanced at 31 October and the relevant entries in the final accounts.

In examination questions you are frequently asked only to prepare the final accounts. If this is the case you may still decide to prepare a ledger account for any trial balance items that need adjustments. It might help you to get the answer right but it is not essential. You can do the adjustment arithmetically and, if you wish, show it within the profit and loss account. For example the entry in the profit and loss account of the last exercise could have been shown like this:

	£	£
Expenses		
Rent	944	
less Prepayment	68	
		876

Exercise 9.3

Complete the following table in which (a) has been done for you.

	Trial balance 31.12.1990	*Prepaid at 31.12.1990*	*Profit and loss a/c yr ended 31.12.1990*	*Current asset in balance sheet as at 31.12.1990*
A/c	dr	£	£	£
(a) Rent	900	100	800	100 prepaid rent
(b) Rates	750	150		
(c) Insurance	620		480	
(d) Salaries		640	4,320	
(e) Fuel			1,600	300 prepaid fuel
(f) Wages	490			120 prepaid wages

9.2 EXPENSES ACCRUED

The word 'accrued' here means 'owing' or 'outstanding'. Thus an accrued expense is one which is owing for a financial period but which is not paid until a subsequent period.

For example, suppose that a business rents property for £1,200 per annum and that this sum is payable in four instalments on the first day of

January, April, July and October. In 1990 the rent account looked like this when the firm's financial year ended on 31 December:

Dr	Rent account			Cr
1990		£		
1 Jan.	Bank	300		
1 April	Bank	300		
1 Sept.	Bank	300		

Would it be correct to transfer the £900 contained in this account to the profit and loss account as the total expense of rent for the year ended 31 December 1990? The answer to this is No! This would not be in agreement with the principle we set out earlier in this chapter. This states that costs or expenses should be counted when they are incurred and not when they are paid. The cost incurred of renting premises in 1990 is £1,200. This amount, and not the amount paid, is the true expenses of rent for 1990 and must be shown therefore in the profit and loss account.

In order to transfer the correct amount to the profit and loss account the amount outstanding is inserted on the debit side as a balance accrued to carry down at the end of the year. It is then possible to transfer £1,200 to the profit and loss account. This amount is made up of £900 actually paid and £300 owing. Of course, it is necessary that any balance carried down is then brought down to the other side of the account. The balance is brought down to the credit side which indicates that it is a liability at the end of the year. As such it will appear in the balance sheet and, because it is likely that payment will have to be made very soon indeed, it will be placed next to the creditors in the current liabilities.

When completed, the rent account and the relevant entries in the final accounts will look like this:

Dr		Rent account			Cr
1990		£	*1990*		£
1 Jan.	Bank	300	31 Dec.	Profit and loss	1,200
1 Apr.	Bank	300			
1 Sept.	Bank	300			
31 Dec.	Balance accrued c/d	300			
		1,200			1,200
			1991		
			1 Jan.	Balance accrued b/d	300

Profit and loss account, year ended 31 Dec. 1990

	£
Expenses	
Rent	1,200

Balance sheet as at 31 Dec. 1990

	£
Current liabilities	
Accrued rent	300

Exercise 9.4

The trial balance of a firm whose financial year ends on 31 March 1990 contains the following item.

A/cs	*£ dr*	*£ cr*
Wages	30,000	

Because the weekly wages were last made up on 26 March the amount of £350 has accrued by 31 March. Make the necessary adjustments to the wages account and show the relevant entries in the final accounts for the year ended 31 March 1990.

Many examination questions require only the final accounts to be shown. While you may decide to complete the ledger account adjustment as an aid to obtaining the correct answer, it is not absolutely necessary. The adjustment in the last exercise could be shown in the profit and loss account like this:

Profit and loss account year ended 31 March 1990

	£	£
Expenses		
Wages	30,000	
add Accrual	350	
		30,350

The key point to keep in mind when deciding how the amount of an expense is to be shown in the profit and loss account is the date it is incurred. If the expense refers to, say, 1990, it must be included in that year's profit and loss account. If the full amount has not been paid in 1990 then the expense account must be adjusted to show the true expense for the period. Remember, however, to include any such adjustment for an expense outstanding in the balance sheet under the heading of current liabilities.

Exercise 9.5

Complete the following table, in which (a) has been done for you.

Trial balance 31.12.1990 A/c	dr	*Accrued at 31.12.1990* £	*Profit and loss a/c yr ended 31.12.1990* £	*Current liability in balance sheet as at 31.12.1990* £
(a) Rent	600	200	800	200 accrued rent
(b) Rates	400	300		
(c) Insurance	750		820	
(d) Wages		100	800	
(e) Salaries			900	300 accrued salary
(f) Fuel	420			90 accrued fuel

9.3 INCOME PREPAID

The rule to follow when allocating income to the correct accounting period is the same as the one we applied to costs. Income or revenue is counted when goods are sold or services provided, not when the money is received. We have dealt already with the sale of goods on credit. The amount of the sale is credited to the sales account and a debit entry is made in the account of the customer who is a debtor. The total sales will be transferred to the trading account at the end of the period whether or not the customer has paid for them. Similarly all other income must be shown in its correct period.

For example, suppose a restaurant owner rents out the flat above his business to earn extra profit. He charges £100 per month and his financial year ends on 31 December. In the year ended 31 December 1990 the tenant paid the amounts due on the first of each month and in December he made an additional payment of £100 for January 1991. The rent received account will have been credited with a total of £1,300 and in the trial balance it will look like this:

	£ dr	*£ cr*
Rent received		1,300

It would be wrong, however, to show the whole amount in the profit and loss account as income for the year ended 31 December 1990. Clearly £100 is income for 1991. This amount must therefore be deducted from the £1,300 to show the correct income relating to 1990 as £1,200. The ledger account and final accounts entries will look like this:

Dr	Rent received account				Cr
1990		£	*1990*		£
31 Dec.	Profit and loss a/c	1,200	1 Jan.–31 Dec.	Bank (total)	1,300
31 Dec.	Balance prepaid c/d	100			
		1,300			1,300
			1991		
			1 Jan.	Balance prepaid b/d	100

Profit and loss account year ended 31 Dec. 1990

	£
Gross profit	—
Rent received	1,200

Balance sheet as at 31 Dec. 1990

	£
Current liabilities	
Rent received in advance	100

As an income the £1,200 rent received is added to the gross profit. The £100 received in advance represents a liability to the owner of the restaurant. He owes this sum, or rather the use of the flat which is worth this amount, to his tenant. It therefore appears in the balance sheet as a current liability. Note that this is the exact opposite to an expense prepaid which counts as a current asset in the balance sheet.

Exercise 9.6

Show the final accounts' entries relating to the following.

A hotel allows local firms to advertise in the foyer for which it makes a charge. During the year ended 30 June 1990 it had received £250 income for this. However, one firm has paid £20 in June for an advertisement to be displayed in July 1990.

9.4 **INCOME ACCRUED**

Sometimes a business will not have received all the income to which it is entitled by the end of its financial year. When this happens, the amount owing or accrued must be added to what has been received to show the true income for the year. For example a retailer rents part of his store room to another firm and charges £50 per month. On 31 December 1990, when his financial year ends, only eleven months' rent has been received. The rent received account will appear in the trial balance like this:

	£ dr	£ cr
Rent received		550

It is necessary to adjust the rent received account so that the correct amount of £600 can be transferred to the profit and loss account. The ledger account and the final accounts' entries will look like this:

Dr		Rent received account			Cr
1990		£	*1990*		£
31 Dec.	Profit and loss a/c	600	1 Jan.–31 Dec.	Bank (total)	550
			31 Dec.	Balance accrued c/d	50
		600			600
1 Jan.	Balance accrued b/d	50			

Profit and loss account, year ended 31 Dec. 1990

Gross profit	—
Rent received	600

Balance sheet as at 31 Dec. 1990

	£
Current assets	
Rent due	50

The £50 due from the tenant is a debt which the retailer will count as a current asset. In practice it will probably be included with sundry debtors.

Exercise 9.7

Show the entries in the final accounts relating to the following.

In the year ended 31 October 1990 a hotel received £160 for allowing firms to advertise in its reception area. One firm, however, had not paid a bill of £40 for an advertisement displayed in September.

Exercise 9.8

Trial balance of the White Hart Hotel as at 31 October 1990

	£	£
Capital		85,800
Stocks (1 Nov. 1989)	2,250	
Loan from Busifinance		15,000
Leasehold premises	97,500	
Furniture and equipment	22,500	
Debtors	900	
Creditors		750

	£	£
Advertising and insurance	1,905	
Salaries and wages	16,500	
Rates	1,350	
Discount received		105
Discount allowed	300	
Purchases	37,500	
Rent received		1,800
Bank	1,500	
Heat and light	825	
Sundry expenses	675	
Cash	150	
Sales		84,000
Drawings	3,600	
	187,455	187,455

Taking into account the following matters, prepare a trading and profit and loss account for the year ended 31 October 1990 and a balance sheet at that date.

(a) Stocks at 31 October 1990 were valued at £3,000.
(b) Salaries outstanding amounted to £200 on 31 October 1990.
(c) Insurance paid in advance on 31 October 1990 was £30.
(d) The loan from Busifinance was made on 31 July at an agreed interest of 12% per annum. This had not been paid.
(e) The rent received of £1,800 included £200 in advance for November 1990.

Guidance

If you find this exercise difficult, don't be alarmed. It does contain a great deal of information. It is probable that any errors you made will have included the adjustments as these are the difficult parts. Look carefully at the items in the profit and loss account and use your reasoning powers to satisfy yourself that each one is correct. Very often students forget that an adjustment will also require an entry in the balance sheet and this will result in the totals of this statement not agreeing. It is worth remembering that any adjustment to be made to items contained in a trial balance will affect both profit and loss account *and* balance sheet. When a balance sheet does not agree, therefore, the first thing to do in an exercise like the one above is to check that you have accounted for each adjustment in both statements.

Take (d) for example. As the loan has only been in existence for 3 months then only one quarter of a year's interest is due by the date of this profit and loss account. The interest for a full year will be 12% of £15,000, i.e. £1,800. Therefore one quarter's interest is £450. This amount must be shown in the profit and loss account as an expense and in the balance sheet as a current liability.

CHAPTER 10

PROVIDING FOR BAD DEBTS

In this chapter we are going to look at an adjustment involving debtors. It will enable the true amount of bad debts for a period to be included in that period's profit and loss account. In addition the asset 'debtors' will be shown at its proper value in the balance sheet. There are two methods of book-keeping that can be used and both of these will be illustrated. When you have mastered the process of providing for bad debts and recording the recovery of debts previously written off as bad, there will be an opportunity to gain extra practice in the preparation of final accounts.

You are advised to reread the section on bad debts in Chapter 3 before you begin this chapter. Then attempt the following.

Exercise 10.1

Fill in the blanks:

(a) Bad debts are the ____________ incurred when debtors fail to pay their debts.
(b) In the balance sheet, debtors appear as an ____________ because it is assumed that anyone to whom credit has been allowed will pay what they owe.
(c) Once it is known that a debt is never going to be collected this fact must be shown in the accounts. If it were not, then the accounts would not be giving a ____________ ____________ of the assets of the business.
(d) It is accepted that ____________ ____________ a bad debt is an occasional and inevitable part of allowing credit to others.

10.1 CREATING A PROVISION FOR BAD DEBTS

We are going to learn about providing for bad debts by following a business which started on 1 January 1989. That was the day when A. Rowe began trading as a wholesaler.

The thought of his customers failing to pay their debts did not occur to him at first. He soon learnt! By the end of his first financial year he had written off £300 worth of bad debts. The bad debts account appeared like this after the expense had been transferred to the profit and loss account:

Dr | Bad debts account | Cr

1989		£	*1989*		£
1 Jan.–31 Dec.	Sundry debtors	300	31 Dec.	Transferred to profit and loss account	300
		300			300

At the same time the debit balance in his sundry debtors' account showed that customers owed him £4,000.

Sundry debtors account

1989		£	
31 Dec.	Balance	4,000	

Two thoughts occurred to him: first, that it was likely that some of this £4,000 would probably not be paid. In other words it included some debts that would prove to be bad. The figure in the profit and loss account was thus likely to be an understatement of the ***real*** amount of bad debts for the year. Second, if he showed the £4,000 in the balance sheet at 31 December as an asset, he would be overstating the value of this asset. He decided to take the advice of a friendly accountant and created a provision for bad debts. This was done in three steps and helped to overcome the problems mentioned above.

1 He estimated the amount of likely bad debts. In this case Rowe decided £200 was about the right amount to allow for.
2 This amount was entered in the profit and loss account as an expense, thus reducing the net profit by £200. The profit and loss account now included two amounts as an expense for bad debts: the actual bad debts written off for the year and an estimate of those likely to be written off – the provision.

Profit and loss account, year ended 31 December 1989

	£
Expenses	
Bad debts	300
Provision for bad debts	200

3 The double entry corresponding to this entry in the profit and loss account for estimated bad debts was made in a provision for bad debts account thus:

Dr	Provision for bad debts account		Cr
		1989 31 Dec. Profit and loss account	200

This is a credit balance at the end of the year and therefore appears in the balance sheet. As a credit balance it is technically a source of finance, i.e. finance taken out of profits to be used for writing off bad debts when they occur. Instead of showing this with the other finance, however, it is usual practice to show it as a deduction from the asset debtors.

Balance sheet of A. Rowe as at 31 Dec. 1989

	£
Current assets	
Debtors	4,000
less Provision, bad debts	200
	3,800

Thus the balance sheet now shows debtors at a more realistic valuation. The question arises as to how much should be provided for bad debts. Greatest accuracy would be achieved if all the debts in the accounts were analysed at the end of the year to decide which ones were most likely to prove uncollectable. In practice those debts which have been due longest will probably be the most suspect. This, however, is a time-consuming process and it is much simpler to allow a certain percentage for probable bad debts, as we did in the example above. Experience will show us how accurate the figure is and, if necessary, it can be adjusted upwards or downwards.

Exercise 10.2

Simon Robinson began trading as a retailer on 1 January 1989. By the end of his first year of trading he had written off a total of £140 worth of debts as irrecoverable. On 31 December 1989 his debts were valued in the books at £2,500. He decided to create a provision for bad debts which would allow for 5% of that amount to be irrecoverable. Show the bad debts account, provision for bad debts account and relevant entries in his final accounts.

It is very important when dealing with this matter to read the instructions of a question carefully. Sometimes you may be asked to write off the actual bad debts *before* creating a provision based on the figure remaining in the debtors' account. In this exercise the actual bad debts had already been written off. The provision therefore to be based on the £2,500 actually in the account on 31 December.

Note that both the bad debts account and the provision for bad debts account there is an entry relating to the profit and loss account. However, there is a difference. The entry in the bad debts account is made to transfer that debit balance to the profit and loss account. The entry in the provision account is a credit entry made to correspond to the entry in the profit and loss account which is made first. In effect finance is being taken from the profits and specifically earmarked to cover future bad debts. It is very important that you realise that this adjustment does not actually involve the movement of any cash.

Once a provision for bad debts has been created there are two methods by which you can proceed:

1 All entries relating to bad debts from now on can be made in the provision account.
2 Separate accounts are maintained for actual bad debts and the provision for bad debts.

We will consider each in turn using the business of A. Rowe as an illustration.

10.2 METHOD 1

Remind yourself of the position of A. Rowe at 31 December 1989. The two accounts with balances in them as at that date were debtors (debit balance £4,000) and provision for bad debts (credit balance £200). The debtors' account will be changing frequently during 1990. Whenever Rowe sells goods on credit he will debit this account and whenever the retailers pay him he will credit this account with the money received and any discount allowed. Also, at various dates during the year he may have to write off some of the debts as irrecoverable. This will require a credit entry in the debtors' account. The corresponding entry can now be made in the provision for bad debts account because it contains an amount earmarked specifically for this purpose.

Suppose that in 1990 Rowe wrote off £250 of debts as being irrecoverable. Before preparing the final accounts, the provision account will look like this:

Dr	Provision for bad debts account				Cr
1990		£	*1990*		£
1 Jan.–31 Dec.	Sundry debtors	250	1 Jan.	Balance b/d	200

Clearly the provision made at the end of 1989 is a slight underestimate. All the £200 has been used and an extra £50 is needed to make up the deficiency. In addition it will be necessary to provide for the fact that some debtors at the end of 1990 will probably fail to pay.

Assume that Rowe's debtors are valued at £6,000 on 31 December 1990 and that he decides a 5% provision for likely bad debts is still about right. He will need a provision balance of £300 to meet this requirement. In order to achieve this he will need to make a credit entry for £350. This is made up of the £300 needed *plus* the £50 required to make up the deficiency from last year. After the final accounts have been prepared the situation will be as follows.

Dr	Provision for bad debts account				Cr
1990		£	*1990*		£
1 Jan.–31 Dec.	Sundry debtors	250	1 Jan.	Balance b/d	200
31 Dec.	Balance c/d	300	31 Dec.	Profit and loss a/c	350
		550			550
			1991		
			1 Jan.	Balance b/d	300

Profit and loss account for A. Rowe for the year ended 31 Dec. 1990

	£
Expenses	
Provision for bad debts	350

Balance sheet of A. Rowe as at 31 December 1990

	£
Current assets	
Debtors	6,000
less Provision for bad debts	300
	5,700

Note that the balance sheet entry consists of the two balances in the relevant accounts at 31 December. The profit and loss account entry is the amount needed to be withdrawn from profit in order to provide a balance of £300. This section is important so reread method 1 before attempting the following.

Exercise 10.3

Remind yourself of Simon Robinson's position at 31 December 1989 in the last exercise.

During 1990, his second year of trading, he had written off debts to the value of £110 and at the end of the year his debtors amounted to £1,500. He decided to retain a provision of 5% of outstanding debtors to allow for bad debts. Show his provision for bad debts account and relevant entries in the final accounts at the end of 1990.

10.3 METHOD 2

This involves keeping separate accounts for bad debts and the provision. We will use the information relating to Rowe's accounts for 1990 so that we can compare the results with those obtained by using method 1.

Dr — Bad debts account — Cr

1990		£	*1990*		£
1 Jan.–31 Dec.	Sundry debtors	250	31 Dec.	Transferred to profit and loss account	250

Provision for bad debts account

1990		£	*1990*		£
	Balance c/d	300	1 Jan.	Balance b/d	200
			31 Dec.	Profit and loss account	100
		300			300
			1991		
			1 Jan.	Balance b/d	300

Profit and loss account of A. Rowe, year ended 31 December 1990

	£
Expenses	
Bad debts	250
Provision for bad debts	100

Balance sheet of A. Rowe, as at 31 Dec. 1990

	£
Current assets	6,000
Debtors	300
less Provision for bad debts	5,700

Let's summarise what has happened.

- The actual bad debts for 1990 have been written off debtors as they occurred and then transferred to the profit and loss account at the end of the year.
- It is calculated that a provision balance of £300 is needed at the end of the year, i.e. $^{5}/_{100}$ × £6,000.
- The balance in the provision account will not have altered since last year. A credit entry for £100 is made to adjust this balance to the £300 needed and the double entry completed in the profit and loss account.
- The balance sheet contains the £6,000 balance for debtors and the £300 provision balance. As before the provision balance is deducted from outstanding debtors so that a true value can be placed on the asset, debtors.

In comparing this with method 1 you will notice that the real difference concerns the profit and loss account. Instead of one entry for £350 we now have two entries - £250 for actual bad debts and £100 adjustment to the provision. The net result is, of course, the same; i.e. £350 is being counted as the expense relating to bad debts. While the entry in the provision account at the end of the year differs, the final balance is exactly the same as with method 1. A final difference concerns the number of accounts used. Method 2 required an account for bad debts whereas in method 1 the bad debts were written off in the provision account and no bad debts account was needed.

Reread the explanation of method 2 before attempting the following.

Exercise 10.4

Rewrite the relevant accounts of Simon Robinson at the end of 1990 using method 2.

10.4 BAD DEBTS RECOVERED

Sometimes businessmen receive a pleasant surprise in connection with bad debts. A debt that has been written off as irrecoverable is paid by the debtor. Suppose that on 7 May 1991 the wholesaler Rowe recovers a debt of £45 which he had written off in 1990. The cash book will be debited with the money received. The credit entry to be made varies according to which of the two methods of dealing with bad debts is used.

Method 1 The recovered debt will be credited to the provision for bad debts account where it will help to offset the bad debts written off in 1990.

Dr			Provision for bad debts		Cr
			1991		£
			1 Jan.	Balance b/d	300
			7 May	Cash book	45

Method 2 A separate account for bad debts recovered will be credited with the £45. This amount will be transferred to the profit and loss account at the end of the year along with any other recovered debts. For the sake of simplicity we will assume here that this was the only such recovery in 1991.

Dr		Bad debts recovered account			Cr
1991		£	*1991*		£
31 Dec.	Transferred to profit and loss account	45	7 May	Cash book	45
		—			—

Profit and loss account, year ended 31 December 1991

	£
Expenses	
less Bad debt recovered	(45)

The £45 is shown in brackets to indicate that it will be deducted from the expenses for 1991. Alternatively, the sum could be added to the gross profit and other incomes such as rent received.

Whichever method is being followed this transaction is of such an unusual nature that it would probably be journalised.

Exercise 10.5

During 1991, Simon Robinson's third year of trading, he wrote off debts to the value of £130 and on 8 June recovered one debt of £30 which he had written off in 1990. At the end of 1991 his debtors amounted to £1,600 and he decided to retain a provision of 5% of outstanding debtors to allow for bad debts. Show his accounts as they would appear using method 1 and method 2. Remember, he started 1991 with a provision balance of £75.

Exercise 10.6

Trial balance of A. Wilson as at 31 December 1989

	£ *dr*	£ *cr*
Capital (1 Jan.)		86,000
Stocks (1 Jan.)	60,000	
Leasehold premises	120,000	
Fixtures and fittings	10,000	
Motor vehicles	30,000	
Debtors	15,000	
Creditors		40,000
Advertising and insurance	2,000	
Salaries and wages	45,000	
Provision for bad debts (1 Jan.)		500
Rates	1,000	
Discount received		1,000
Discount allowed	2,000	
Purchases	80,000	
Sales		150,000
Heating and lighting	2,000	
Bank	8,500	
Sundry expenses	2,000	
Mortgage on premises		100,000
	377,500	377,500

Taking into account the following matters, prepare a trading and profit and loss account for the year ended 31 December 1989 and a balance sheet at that date.

(a) On 31 December, Wilson reviews his debtors and decides that £1,000 of the £15,000 due should be written off as bad debts. The provision is to be 5% of the outstanding debtors after bad debts have been written off.
(b) A bill for £500 electricity is outstanding on 31 December.
(c) Insurance prepaid on 31 December amounts to £200.
(d) Stocks at 31 December were valued at £70,000.

CHAPTER 11

ESTIMATING AND RECORDING DEPRECIATION

In this chapter we are going to look at the way in which capital expenditure on a fixed asset can be spread over the life of the asset. This is done so that a fair amount of the expense can be recorded each year in the profit and loss account and a truer, more up-to-date valuation of the asset can be shown in the balance sheet. Two methods of book-keeping will be considered because both are encountered in examination questions. Before you begin this chapter you are advised to reread section 3.8 on depreciation in Chapter 3 and section 8.2 on capital expenditure in Chapter 8.

11.1 ESTIMATING DEPRECIATION

Most fixed assets have a limited number of years of useful life. Depreciation is the name given to the process by which these assets decrease in value over their lifetime. The only way to be absolutely sure of the amount of depreciation that has taken place is to sell the asset. Thus if a motor vehicle cost £4,000 on 1 January 1989 and was sold for £3,000 on 31 December 1989 we can quite safely say that depreciation on that asset for the year 1989 amounted to £1,000.

People in business are not, however, in it to sell their fixed assets. To do so simply to know precisely how much depreciation has occurred is clearly out of the question. Therefore some means of estimating the amount of the depreciation is needed. The most accurate way would be to obtain a valuation, by someone qualified, of what each asset is worth at the end of every year of trading. Thus machinery valued at £1,800 at 31 December 1989 might be revalued at £1,600 on 31 December 1990. We could therefore state that £200 would be a reliable estimate of the depreciation on machinery for the year ended 31 December 1990. In a small business with few fixed assets revaluing the fixed assets each year might not be too difficult. The problems arise when you attempt to do this in larger businesses which posses a greater number and variety of fixed assets. Accountants attempt to overcome these problems by using one of the following methods to estimate depreciation.

11.2 EQUAL INSTALMENT METHOD

As its name suggests, this involves depreciating an asset by an equal amount throughout its useful life. For example, equipment purchased for £10,000 on 1 January 1989 might be expected to last for ten years. To depreciate this in equal instalments would require an amount of £1,000 to be written off the value of the asset each year. A simple formula can be applied to obtain the annual amount of depreciation:

$$\frac{\text{cost of asset}}{\text{estimated life in years}} = \frac{£10{,}000}{10} = £1{,}000 \text{ depreciation per annum}$$

Many fixed assets will have some value even when their working life is over. This is known as their scrap value. The above formula can be adapted to allow for an asset having some value as scrap:

$$\frac{\text{cost of asset less estimated scrap value}}{\text{estimated life in years}}.$$

Suppose that the equipment in the above example had an estimated scrap value of £500. The amount of depreciation to be written off each year for the next ten years would be:

$$\frac{£10{,}000 \text{ less } £500}{10 \text{ years}} = \frac{£9{,}500}{10} = £950 \text{ per annum.}$$

Exercise 11.1

A new company began trading on 1 January 1986. Its fixed assets included new machinery which it had purchased for £13,000. This machinery had a life expectancy of eight years with an estimated scrap value of £1,000 after that time.

(a) Calculate the amount of depreciation to be written off each year.
(b) State the value of this machinery at the end of 1989.

It is possible to obtain a valuation of an asset at any stage of its working life by referring to a schedule such as the one below. This relates to the machinery in Exercise 11.1.

Machinery X: cost £13,000

Year	Depn for the year ended 31 Dec.	Accumulated depn up to the year ended 31 Dec.	Asset value at 31 Dec.
	£	£	£
1986	1,500	1,500	11,500
1987	1,500	3,000	10,000
1988	1,500	4,500	8,500
1989	1,500	6,000	7,000
1990	1,500	7,500	5,500

Each year the same amount of depreciation is being written off the asset's value. The column for accumulated depreciation enables us to see at a glance the total amount of depreciation that has been written off to date. Deducting this figure from the cost of the machinery provides us with its value at the end of any year in the schedule. Thus by the end of December 1990 five years' depreciation, i.e. £7,500, will have been written off and the machinery will be worth £5,500.

This method is also known as straight-line depreciation because the amount is the same each year.

11.3 REDUCING INSTALMENT METHOD

This involves depreciating the asset by a fixed percentage each year based on the value of the asset at the beginning of that year.

Suppose, for example, that the company which purchased the machinery for £13,000 on 1 January 1989 decided to depreciate at 10% per annum by this method. At the end of 1989 which is its first year of trading, the depreciation to be written off will be

$$\frac{10}{100} \times £13{,}000 = £1{,}300.$$

At the beginning of 1990 the machinery will be valued at £11,700, i.e. its cost less depreciation to date, or £13,000 less £1,300. The rate of depreciation remains at 10% but the actual amount of depreciation to be written off for 1990 will be

$$\frac{10}{100} \times £11{,}700 = £1{,}170.$$

You can now see why this method is known as the reducing instalment method. Although the rate of depreciation stays the same it is being calculated on the diminishing asset value. Thus each year the actual amount of depreciation written off will be less.

Exercise 11.2

Complete the following depreciation schedule for machinery X, using the reducing instalment method with a fixed rate of 10%. Depreciation should be calculated to the nearest £1.

Machinery X: cost £13,000

Year	Depn for the year ended 31 Dec.	Accumulated depn up to the year ended 31 Dec.	Asset value at 31 Dec.
	£	£	£
1986	1,300	1,300	11,700
1987	1,170	2,470	
1988			9,477
1989			
1990			

We can now turn to recording depreciation in the ledger. There are two main methods used. One I shall call the simple method and the other the accumulated depreciation method.

11.4 RECORDING DEPRECIATION – THE SIMPLE METHOD

This is the method introduced in Chapter 3. Each asset which is to be depreciated has its own depreciation account. At the end of each financial year the asset account is credited with the amount of depreciation for that year and the depreciation account is debited. The entry in depreciation account is then transferred to the profit and loss account as the expense for the period. Finally the asset account is balanced and the balance sheet shows the final value of the asset by deducting the year's depreciation from the asset's value at the start of the year.

An example will help to make this clear. We will use the information provided by the depreciation schedule in the last exercise showing the accounts completed for the first two years. Trace the double entries as they occur in the ledger accounts and then look at the entries in the final accounts

Dr — Machinery account — Cr

1986		£	*1986*		£
1 Jan.	Bank	13,000	31 Dec.	Depreciation	1,300
			31 Dec.	Balance c/d	11,700
		13,000			13,000
1987			*1987*		
1 Jan.	Balance b/d	11,700	31 Dec.	Depreciation	1,170
			31 Dec.	Balance c/d	10,530
		11,700			11,700
1988					
1 Jan.	Balance b/d	10,530			

Depreciation on machinery account

1986		£	*1986*		£
31 Dec.	Machinery	1,300	31 Dec.	Transferred to profit and loss account	1,300
1987			*1987*		
31 Dec.	Machinery	1,170	1 Jan.	Transferred to profit and loss account	1,170

Profit and loss account, year ended 31 December 1986

	£
Expenses	
Depreciation on machinery	1,300

Balance sheet, as at 31 December 1986

	£	£
Fixed assets		
Machinery	13,000	
less Depn for year	1,300	
		11,700

Profit and loss account, year ended 31 December 1986

	£
Expenses	
Depreciation on machinery	1,170

Balance sheet as at 31 December 1986

	£	£
Fixed assets		
Machinery	11,700	
less Depn for year	1,170	
		10,530

Exercise 11.3

Complete the accounts relating to the machinery and its depreciation up to the end of December 1988.

11.5 RECORDING DEPRECIATION – THE ACCUMULATION METHOD

Compared with the method just discussed this method requires one additional account which is used to maintain a record of the depreciation accumulated to date. This account is usually called the provision for depreciation account though a more accurate title would be accumulated depreciation account.

This method involves a debit entry each year in the depreciation account for that year's depreciation. Instead of making the credit entry in the asset account, however, it is made in the provision for depreciation account. Using the example of the machinery being depreciated by reducing instalments the ledger accounts for the first two years will look like this:

Dr — Machinery account — Cr

1986		£	*1986*		£
1 Jan.	Bank	13,000	31 Dec.	Balance c/d	13,000
1987			*1987*		
1 Jan.	Balance b/d	13,000	31 Dec.	Balance c/d	13,000
1988					
1 Jan.	Balance b/d	13,000			

Dr — Provision for depreciation on machinery account — Cr

1986		£	*1986*		£
31 Dec.	Balance c/d	1,300	31 Dec.	Depreciation	1,300
1987			*1987*		
31 Dec.	Balance c/d	2,470	1 Jan.	Balance b/d	1,300
			31 Dec.	Depreciation	1,170
		2,470			2,470
			1988		
			1 Jan.	Balance b/d	2,470

Dr — Depreciation on machinery account — Cr

1986		£	*1986*		£
31 Dec.	Provision for depn	1,300	31 Dec.	Transferred to profit and loss account	1,300
1987			*1987*		
31 Dec.	Provision for depn	1,170	31 Dec.	Transferred to profit and loss account	1,170

As you can see, the depreciation account is substantially the same as in the simpler method - only the description has changed slightly. The real difference lies with the asset account. This now shows the value of the asset at cost with no depreciation being deducted from it within the account. You might argue, with good reason, that it is not worth balancing this account each year. It is, however, probably a good thing to continue to do so as it does indicate that the account has been looked at each year. To obtain the value of the asset at any date it is now necessary to combine the asset balance with the accumulated depreciation balance in the provision account. Thus the value of the machinery at 31 December 1987 will be £10,530, i.e.

	£	
Cost	13,000	(from the asset account)
less Depn to date	2,470	(from the provision account)
	10,530	

The profit and loss account entries will be exactly the same as they were when using the other method. The balance sheet entries will differ, however, because we will always be showing the value of the asset at cost less the accumulated depreciation to date. This difference will not be apparent in the first year because the accumulated depreciation is identical to the first year's depreciation. From the second year, however, you will notice the difference. It should be emphasised that the actual final value of the asset shown in the balance sheet will be the same whichever method is used. Prove this to yourself by comparing the two entries below with those on page 127.

Balance sheet as at 31 December 1986

	£	£
Fixed assets		
Machinery at cost	13,000	
less Depn to date	1,300	
		11,700

Balance sheet as at 31 December 1987

	£	£
Fixed assets		
Machinery at cost	13,000	
less Depn to date	2,470	
		10,530

Exercise 11.4

Complete the accounts relating to the machinery and its depreciation up to the end of December 1988. This time, use the provision for depreciation method.

One aspect of the second method of accounting for depreciation that often causes problems to students involves the name of the ledger account in which the aggregate depreciation is accumulated. The title 'provision for depreciation account' gives an impression that finance has actually been set aside which can be used to purchase a replacement for the fixed asset when its working life is over. This is a false impression. The provision for depreciation account is simply an account in which the aggregate or total depreciation written off an asset is accumulated each year. For this reason, the term 'accumulated' or 'aggregate depreciation account' would be a more accurate title. There is, of course, nothing to prevent a businessman from keeping back a greater amount of the net profit for use within the business to replace worn-out assets. This, however, is not automatic on creating a provision for depreciation account – a conscious policy decision would have to be made to retain or 'plough back' profits for this use.

11.6 **FURTHER CALCULATIONS**

Until now we have been concerned only with calculations of depreciation on fixed assets which have been in the business for a complete financial year. In practice there will be occasions when assets are bought part-way through the business's financial year. When this happens you would be expected to calculate the correct proportion of depreciation relating to that year for inclusion in the accounts.

For example the business whose accounts we have been showing in this chapter has a financial year which ends at 31 December. Suppose that it purchases equipment for £6,000 on 1 July 1989 and estimates that it will last for ten years and have a scrap value of £200 at the end of that time. Depreciation using the equal instalment method will be:

$$\frac{\text{cost of asset less estimated scrap value}}{\text{estimated life in years}} = \frac{\pounds 6{,}000 - \pounds 200}{10 \text{ years}} = \frac{\pounds 5{,}800}{10}$$

= £580 depreciation per annum.

In 1989, however, it would be wrong to depreciate the equipment by £580 because the asset has been in use for only six months. The correct amount of depreciation for 1989 is thus

$^6/_{12}$ or $^1/_2 \times$ £580 = £290.

Exercise 11.5

The same business bought a motor vehicle for £5,000 on 1 April 1989. It was decided to depreciate it by 30% per annum using the reducing instalment method. Calculate the amount of depreciation to be written off in the financial year ended 31 December 1989.

Take care when calculating these proportions. In most examination questions the asset is purchased at the beginning or the end of a month. While 1 April to 31 December will be counted as nine months, if the asset had been purchased on 30 April it will have been used for only eight months in 1986. Thus in the latter case the proportion would be

$^8/_{12}$ or $^2/_3$.

You might wonder how you would deal with the depreciation on an asset purchased on, say, 19 September. Should the proportion be calculated on the number of days the asset has been used during the year? The answer to this is 'no'. Depreciation is only an estimate. It is quite sufficient, therefore, to calculate it solely on the total number of complete months in which it is used in that first year. Thus in this case the proportionate amount of depreciation would be

$^3/_{12}$ or $^1/_4$

because the asset was in use for only the three whole months of October, November and December.

11.7 DISPOSAL OF ASSETS AND ADJUSTMENTS TO DEPRECIATION

When a fixed asset is sold it is very unlikely that it will realise a figure exactly equal to its value in the accounts. For this to happen the depreciation estimate would have had to have been 100% accurate!

If the asset sells for less than its book value we might say that we have made a loss on sale whereas in fact we have probably underestimated the amount of depreciation to be written off the value of the asset. If the asset sells for more than its book value we might say that we have made a profit on sale. Probably the truth is that we have overestimated the amount of depreciation to be written off. When either of these eventualities occurs, an adjustment must be made to the depreciation shown in the profit and loss account for the year in which the asset is sold.

For example, a motor vehicle which has a book value of £2,000 is sold for £1,800. The £200 loss on sale or under-provision of depreciation will be added to the expenses thus:

Profit and loss account

	£
Expenses	
Under-provision of depn on motor vehicle	200

If the vehicle has been sold for £2,300 when valued in the books at £2,000 the profit on sale or over-provision of depreciation could be shown thus:

Profit and loss account

	£
Expenses	
Over-provision of depn on motor vehicle	(300)

The brackets around the £300 indicate that this amount is deducted from the other expenses for the year.

Exercise 11.6

Examine the following trial balance of M. Trigg, retailer, taken from his books at 30 June 1990.

	£ *dr*	£ *cr*
Fixed assets (at cost)	40,000	
Provision for depn on fixed assets		4,000
Stock	8,000	
Debtors	1,500	
Provision for bad debts		100
Bank		100
Creditors		500
Cash	200	
Capital		26,000
Sales		90,000
Purchases	60,000	
Wages	4,000	
Drawings	1,000	
General expenses	6,000	
	120,700	120,700

Prepare a trading and profit and loss account for the year ended 30 June 1990 and a balance sheet at that date, taking into consideration the following:

(a) Stock at 30 June 1990, £10,000.
(b) Fixed assets are to be depreciated by 10% on cost.
(c) Bad debts of £80 are to be written off and the provision adjusted to 5% of outstanding debtors.
(d) General expenses include a prepayment of £200 rent for July 1990.

PART II

ACCOUNTING FOR DIFFERENT ORGANISATIONS

CHAPTER 12

PARTNERSHIP ACCOUNTS

12.1 JOHN JONES

John Jones started in business as a self-employed plumber five years ago after completing his apprenticeship. He began with a small amount of money which he had saved, and worked long hours to build up contacts and establish a very good reputation for high quality work. After three years he was doing very well, in fact too well! He was having difficulty coping with the number of jobs he was getting, never mind dealing with the paperwork and VAT and trying to spend some time with his family. So he employed Kevin Crane to help him with the practical work. Kevin was an excellent worker - bright, hardworking and easy to get on with. He was also an expert on central heating systems, an area in which John had not got involved. With Kevin's help, John's business had continued to grow steadily but now, two years later, Kevin tells John that he wants to leave to set up his own business.

Activity

Briefly list the options open to John and the effects which each option could have on his business.

Our list contains three options, though you may have thought of more. These are:

1 To replace Kevin with another employee. It may not, however, be easy to find someone as good and John's business would be likely to suffer in the short term.
2 To allow the business to return to the position it was in before Kevin was taken on. But John would not like to go back to his old working conditions and it would be a pity to see the last two years of expansion wasted.
3 To ask Kevin to become his partner in the business. At present John's business is that of a sole trader. It is possible, however, for a business

to have more than one owner. It then becomes a partnership in which the partners each provide capital for the business and are usually each liable for the debts of the business.

Activity

Let's just clarify that point about liability for debts. Imagine that you are in equal partnership with Dave, a friend. The business collapses with debts of £20,000 due to problems with a contract signed by Dave. From the assets of the business you are able to pay off £12,000. Where does the other £8,000 come from?

You and Dave *equally!* You will have to find £4,000 each from your own private assets. You might lose your savings, your car, even your home – whatever is necessary to pay off your share of the debts, even though the problems were caused by Dave. So a knowledge of partnerships could be very useful to you!

In this chapter we shall consider why and how partnerships are formed and some of the pitfalls to avoid. You may have thought of taking your wife or husband into partnership or you may want to set up a pop group with your friends. Whatever the situation, problems can arise if you're not careful. We shall also look at the changes which are necessary for a partnership accounting system and see how to prepare a set of accounts for a partnership.

Exercise 12.1

Complete the blanks in the following sentence to produce a definition of a partnership.

A partnership has ______________ or ______________ owners who each provide ______________ for the business and are usually ______________ liable for the debts of the business.

12.2 **WHY PARTNERSHIP?**

The reasons for going into a partnership, either when starting a business or at a later stage, are many and varied. Some of them have been illustrated in the case of John Jones and Kevin Crane (see above). It is important that you are aware of the practical business reasons for entering into a partnership as these will usually affect the formation of the partnership and the resulting accounts, so it will be worth spending five minutes on the following activity.

Activity

Put yourself in the position of John Jones and think of as many reasons as you can for bringing a partner into your business. (Include the reasons illustrated in the Kevin Crane example.) Make a list of those reasons, including any notes you feel you need to explain them.

Our list includes the following reasons:

- Additional skills – a new partner may bring new talents into the business which may help improve the range of products or services offered.
- More capital – a number of people in a business can obviously provide more finance for capital than any one person on their own.
- Expansion – with new skills, more labour and more capital the business will be able to grow if trading is reasonably successful.
- New ideas – these can be brought in with the stimulus of having a new partner.
- Shared strain – partners help share the worry and workload of the business, so that the excessive hours and overwork experienced by many sole traders are reduced.
- Specialisation – a sole trader has to be a 'Jack of all trades'. The introduction of a partner enables some specialisation to take place which should improve both job satisfaction and the efficiency of the business.

You may well have thought of many other reasons, but it is important to remember that a vital factor is that the partners are able to work well together, otherwise many of these benefits will not appear in practice. However, the advantages of partnership are such that they are a common feature of the business world, particularly in small to medium size businesses.

12.3 HOW IS A PARTNERSHIP FORMED?

The short answer is – very easily. No legal formalities are essential, so two or more people can just start trading as a partnership. However, there are certain regulations governing the operation of partnerships which you do need to know about. The first is the Companies Act 1985 which deals with the partnership' *name*. For example, if John Jones and Kevin Crane go into partnership and call their business 'Jones and Crane' or 'Crane and Jones' then there is no problem. However, if they decide to trade under a name which does not consist of the true names of all the partners – say 'Personal Plumbing Services', then they must put the name of each partner on all business letters and documents, together with the business address. Many partnerships have a large number of partners, so the business may often be described as, say, 'Pond and Co.' to give it a short name which customers or clients will remember. If there are more than twenty partners then their names need not be placed on all the paperwork of the business –

it would take up too much space! A list of the partners' names need only be shown at the premises of the partnership for anyone interested to inspect.

Exercise 12.2

Which of the following are partnerships? Tick the correct items.

(a) Albert Haddock, fishmonger
(b) Cook, Cook and Cook, solicitors
(c) McEnroe and Co, butchers
(d) Easthills Sports and Social Club
(e) United Consolidated PLC
(f) Smith and Jones

The second set of regulations governs the partnership's *size*. Under the Companies Act, an ordinary business partnership may not have more than twenty members. There are exceptions for certain types of professional partnerships such as solicitors, stockbrokers, accountants and estate agents, which have been given exemptions by the Department of Trade and Industry and can have as many partners as they wish.

The third set of regulations is by far the most important as it will determine the way in which the partnership operates. This third set of regulations may either be a *partnership agreement* or the provisions of the Partnership Act 1890.

12.4 **WHY HAVE A PARTNERSHIP AGREEMENT?**

Would you become a partner in a business and put your money into that business without agreeing the basis on which the partnership was going to operate? Obviously not, you may say. Many people do, however, which often leads to problems and disagreements at a later stage. Even if a partnership is between husband and wife it is advisable to see a solicitor and get a formal partnership agreement or deed drawn up.

If we take the case of John and Kevin and assume that Kevin has agreed in principle to become John's partner, they would then have to negotiate and agree on a number of issues. These might include:

- The fixed capital of the firm i.e. the amount to be contributed by each partner and left in the business as its permanent capital.
- The method of sharing profits and losses - are they to be shared equally or is John to get more as it was his business originally?
- The amounts that they may withdraw for their personal use and controls over this. For example, they might decide that both partners must sign the cheques. It has been known for a partner to empty the business bank account and disappear!
- Conditions under which the partnership may be brought to an end and procedures for dissolving it; also provision for the admission of new partners.

- Provisions restricting competition – for example, John would not want Kevin to be a partner for a few years, leave and then set up in competition only 200 yards away!

In other, more complex, situations further points may need to be dealt with, such as:

- The extent to which partners are to take part in the management of the business. You may be lucky enough to have a rich uncle who is prepared to put money into your business and receive a share of the profits but does not want to take an active part in running the business.
- Salaries to partners – because some partners are more active or experienced than others, it may be decided to give them a salary out of the profits in addition to their profit shares. In other cases, firms have 'junior' partners who receive only a salary and do not get a share of the profits as such.
- Interest on capital – this is sometimes given where the amount of capital contributed by the partners is very different. It is given as a recognition of these levels of investment by the partners.

A partnership agreement may include any matters the partners signing it wish and will vary depending on the nature of the partnership and the type of business concerned. Certainly anyone contemplating preparing a partnership agreement should ensure that the above factors are at least considered. They would also be wise to consult a solicitor as some of these points can prove very complex.

12.5 WHAT IF THERE IS NO PARTNERSHIP AGREEMENT?

In this situation which, as indicated earlier, is fairly common, the operation of the partnership is governed by the provisions of the Partnership Act 1890. The main rights given to a partner by the Act are:

1 To share equally in profits and losses.
2 To prevent the admission of new partners i.e. one partner can exercise a veto.
3 To receive interest of 5% per year on loans to the business above the agreed fixed capital.

Note: No salaries or interest on capital to partners are allowed.

Exercise 12.3

So far we have looked at the reasons for having partnerships and the way in which partnerships are formed. Before we go on to the accounting aspects in detail, try these questions:

3.1 What is a partnership? Give a brief definition.

3.2 Harry Clipper has worked for thirty years as a barber in Oldtown. Whilst he still has a regular number of older people as his customers, his business has declined steadily over the last few years. Some of his customers have died and a lot of other trade has been taken by a new and more modern 'unisex' salon which opened in the town centre. Jot down a list of brief points on the way in which the introduction of a partner might
   (a) be of benefit to him and his business, and
   (b) be a source of problems.

3.3 List the main points you would wish to see covered in a partnership agreement if you decided to go into a partnership with a friend in setting up and running a shop selling small computers.

3.4 If there is no partnership agreement then the Partnership Act 1890 states that:
   (a) Salaries and interest on capital are allowed — True/False
   (b) profits and losses are to be shared equally — True/False
   (c) loans to the partnership by a partner receive interest of 10% per year — True/False

Before moving on to the accounts, let's find out how important partnerships are in your area.

Activity

Look through your local paper or the Yellow Pages for your area, or just take a look at the names of businesses when you walk around. See how many partnerships you can identify.

You should be able to find quite a number - accountants, estate agents, solicitors and architects are obvious ones. But many local family businesses may be partnerships in such trades as butchers, coal merchants, greengrocers etc. I think you could be surprised at how many there are.

12.6 THE BOOKS OF ACCOUNT

12.6 1 Jones and Crane - 1

John Jones and Kevin Crane agree to begin their partnership on 1 January. Their partnership agreement specifies that John is to introduce fixed capital of £6,000 by transferring the assets of his sole trader business whilst Kevin is to provide capital of £2,000 in cash. John is to get a salary of £1,000 per year for the book-keeping and administrative work which he will do and interest on capital will be given at the rate of 5% per year. The remainder of profit or any losses will be shared in the ratio 3:2. Drawings from the business are to be restricted to a maximum of £600 per month per partner.

John has been used to keeping the accounts of his sole trader business in which all the capital and profit was his and was only reduced by the amount of money which he took out as drawings. However, the creation of the partnership will mean that a number of changes will be needed in his books of accounts:

1 John and Kevin will each need separate ledger accounts to record the fixed capitals they have contributed, the earnings they have made from the business and the money which they have drawn out. Obviously it would be very confusing and could lead to errors if this information was all in one account.
2 The fixed capital which they have each agreed to put in should be kept separate from the increase in capital which occurs when the profits earned by each partner are greater than their drawings. (This also helps to highlight when a partner's drawings are greater than the profits he has earned!) This enables the two elements in the partnership's capital structure to be easily identified. So each partner will have:

(a) a *capital* account - which records his fixed capital contribution and any changes which may, by agreement, be made to it; and
(b) a *current* account - which records his earnings from the partnership, e.g. from a salary, interest on capital and share of profits, and the drawings which he has made.

As far as the final accounts of the partnership are concerned, they will have to provide a statement which demonstrates that the partnership agreement has been complied with - this is an additional account which is added to the end of the profit and loss account and is called the *profit and loss appropriation account*.

What does this term 'appropriation' mean? Essentially it means 'to take possession of', which in this situation suggests that each partner 'takes possession of' his share of the business profits or losses according to the terms of the partnership agreement (see Figure 12.1). So the appropriation account shows the net profit earned by the business and the way in which this has been distributed between the partners as required by the partnership agreement.

The box represents the total net profit of the business to be shared between the partners. The partnership agreement will give the details of the way in which the 'box' is to be cut up.

Fig. 12.1 Appropriation of profit to partners

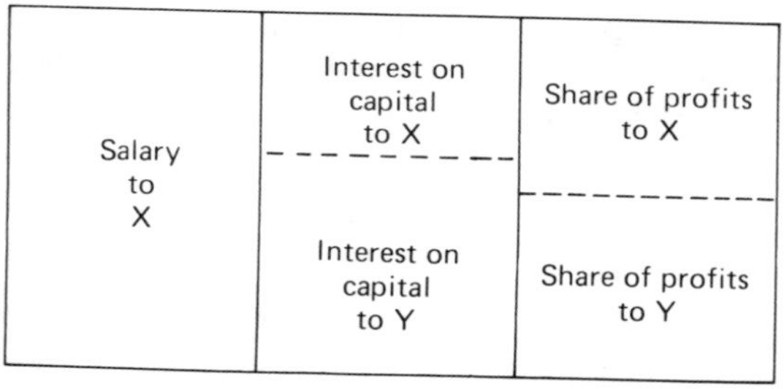

In this case X gets a salary, presumably for his additional work/responsibilities. Each partner gets interest on capital. Y has obviously invested more capital than X. The remainder of the profit ('the box') is then split equally between them.

Important. The salary and interest on capital are *not* actually paid in cash to the partners and are *not* running expenses of the business. They just provide a basis for calculating each partner's rights to the profits of a business. The cash which the partners receive from the business is from their drawings.

Exercise 12.4

John was trying to make some notes about the new accounts he needed now that his business was a partnership. See if you can help by completing the spaces in the sentences below.

4.1 We now need t___ ________________ accounts to record the fixed ________________ contributions which we've each agreed to put in.

4.2 We need t______ ______________ accounts to show what we've each earned from the partnership and what we have actually taken out in ________________.

4.3 When I prepare the final accounts, I will have to do a profit and loss ________________ account to show how the profits or losses have been shared.

12.6.2 **A note on ratios**

(You can miss out this section if you are happy about calculating ratios).

Before we go on to look at the keeping of these new accounts, we should quickly examine the way in which ratios are calculated and used. This is necessary because partnership agreements frequently say such things as profits and losses will be shared 'in the ratio of 3:2' or 'in the ratio of the partners' fixed capital account balances'. You will therefore need to be able to carry out the necessary calculations.

Let us take an example: Tom and Harry agree to put a bet on a horse called Be Lucky in the 4.30 pm race at Kempton Park. The odds are five to one against and they decided to bet £5. Tom provides £3 and Harry £2 and they agree to share any winnings in the ratio of their contribution.

Be Lucky is lucky and wins the race! Tom and Harry receive their winnings of £25 and get their stake back - a total of £30. How much will they each receive?

Calculation

The whole bet was £5. Tom gave £3 and Harry gave £2. The ratio of their contribution is therefore 3:2. Their total return was £30 of which Tom will get 3 parts and Harry 2 parts. The return is therefore divided by 5 parts to get the value of 1 part, i.e. £30 ÷ 5 = £6.

Tom therefore gets 3 × £6 = £18.
Harry therefore gets 2 × £6 = £12.

Note that their shares add up to £30, the amount to be shared. It is often a useful idea to check your calculations by doing this sum. Try the following calculations for some practice on ratios:

Exercise 12.5

5.1 Mary and Liz are partners in a boutique business. They agreed to share profits in the ratio 4:1 because Mary provided most of the capital. In their first year the business made a net profit of £4,500. How much does each partner receive?

5.2 In their second year they changed their ratios to 4:3 when Liz provided more capital. Their business made a net profit of £7,700. How much does each receive?

12.7 RECORDING ENTRIES IN THESE NEW ACCOUNTS

12.7.1 Jones and Crane – 2

At the beginning of the previous section we saw the main financial details of John and Kevin's partnership agreement. In the first year of trading as a partnership John and Kevin each put their capital contribution into the business on 2 January, the business made a net profit of £16,900 and John and Kevin's total drawings were £7,000 and £5,800 respectively.

See Figure 12.2 for the completed accounts. The entries in the accounts are made as follows:

1. Capital accounts: a separate account is opened for each partner and credited with the relevant capital contribution.
2. Current accounts:
   (a) throughout the year the drawings made by the partners are debited to their current account e.g. DR Current A/C, CR Bank when a partner takes money out of the business for his own personal use;
   (b) at the end of the financial year, the current account is credited with the partners' income earned, as shown in the profit and loss appropriation A/C;
   (c) the current accounts are then balanced off: if a balance is a credit balance when brought down, then this indicates that the partner has not drawn out as much as he has earned. Consequently the worth of the business has increased by the amount of his earnings which he has left in the business. If a balance is a debit balance then the partner has drawn out more than he has earned and reduced the value of the business.

3 Profit and loss appropriation account:
   (a) this account appears below the profit and loss account in the final accounts and begins with the net profit brought down from that account - this is the total amount which is available for distribution;
   (b) the debit side shows the split of the profit according to the partnership agreement: it is important to note that such features as salaries and interest on capital should be given before the share of profits is calculated, as they reduce the amount of net profit available for splitting according to the profit-sharing ratio.

Fig 12.2 Jones and Crane's new accounts for the partnership

Capital a/c–J. Jones

		2 Jan Assets	6,000

Capital a/c–K. Crane

		2 Jan Cash	2,000

Current a/c–J. Jones

31 Dec. Drawings	7,000	31 Dec.	Appropriation a/c: Salary	1,000
31 Dec. Balance c/d	3,600		Appropriation a/c: Interest	300
			Appropriation a/c: Share of profits	9,300
	£10,600			£10,600
		1 Jan	Balance b/d	3,600

Current a/c–K. Crane

31 Dec. Drawings	5,800	31 Dec.	Appropriation a/c: Interest	100
31 Dec. Balance c/d	500		Share of profits	6,200
	£6,300			£6,300
		1 Jan.	Balance b/d	500

Profit and loss appropriation account

Salary–J. Jones		1,000	Net profit b/d	16,900
Interest on capital:				
J. Jones (5% of £6,000)	300			
K. Crane (5% of £2,000)	100	400		
Share of profits:				
J. Jones ($^3/_5$ of £15,500)	9,300			
K. Crane ($^2/_5$ of £15,500)	6,200	15,500		16,900
				£ —

Having seen an example of these calculations and ledger accounts, try these questions in order to practise these techniques:

Exercise 12.6

6.1 Steve and Roger are in partnership with capital contributions of £10,000 and £7,200 respectively. The partnership agreement provides for:

- salaries of £2,400 per year to Steve and £1,800 to Roger.
- interest on capital of 10% per year
- a profit sharing ratio of 2:1

Select the correct answer:

(a) How much salary would Steve be entitled to for the period 1 March to 30 June?
i £600
ii £800
iii £750
iv £1,000

(b) How much interest on capital would Roger be entitled to for a period of five months?
i £330
ii £360
iii £240
iv £300

(c) How much profit share would Steve receive in a year when the net profit was £14,920?
i £6,000
ii £5,920
iii £3,000
iv £9,867

6.2 Pete Thomas and Frank Lock go into partnership whereby they provide capital of £6,000 and £5,000 respectively on 1 April. Their partnership agreement states that:

- Frank should receive a salary of £800 per year
- interest on capital should be given of 7% per year
- the profit-sharing ratio would be 1:1

In their first year of trading to 31 March they make a net profit of £12,000 and take out total drawings of £3,300 and £3,200 respectively.

Prepare the capital and current accounts of the partners and the business profit and loss appropriation account for the year ended 31 March.

Check your answers against ours – if there are any differences ensure, either by re-working your answer or re-reading the relevant part of the text, that you can see where you have made an error and why.

12.8 WHAT ABOUT THE BALANCE SHEET?

The only difference between the balance sheet of a sole trader and that of a partnership is the way in which the capital of the business is presented. We have already looked at the reasons for the creation of capital and current accounts in the books of a partnership. The balances on these accounts at the end of an accounting period represent the value of the partners interest in the business and must be included in the balance sheet. If we take the accounts for Jones and Crane shown in Figure 12.2 as an example, the balances on the capital and current accounts would appear as follows:

Balance sheet as at 31 December (extract)

Capital accounts		
J. Jones	6,000	
K. Crane	2,000	8,000
Current accounts		
J. Jones	3,600	
K. Crane	500	4,100
		12,100

So we have now covered all the new accounting points required when you are dealing with the accounts of a partnership. To make sure that you are completely happy with this new material try the following review questions.

Exercise 12.7

7.1 Dave, John and Jim have joined Fred in an electrical retail business. How many capital and current accounts will there be? Briefly note the information that you would expect to find in each type of account and explain why separate capital and current accounts are kept.

7.2 Jane and Jill began a partnership running a health food shop on 1 January when they contributed £3,000 and £2,000 respectively. Their partnership agreement stated that interest on capital of 10% per year should be given and that the profit-sharing ratio would be in the same ratio as their capital contributions. In their first year of trading to 31 December the business makes a net profit of £6,000 and the partners take out drawings of £1,400 (Jane) and £1,100 (Jill).

Complete the capital and current accounts of the partners, the profit and loss appropriation account for the year, and show the capital section of the final balance sheet.

12.9 A FULL SET OF ACCOUNTS

Congratulations! – you have now mastered the new material required to be able to prepare a set of accounts for a partnership. We would now like you to have a go at the following exercise which requires the preparation of a trading, profit and loss and appropriation account for a partnership business together with a balance sheet. Set aside about 45 minutes to tackle this exercise and to check your answer carefully against ours.

Exercise 12.8

Bill and Ben trade in partnership under the name 'The Master Potters'. Their partnership agreement allows for the payment of interest on capital at 12% per year and a salary to Ben of £2,000 per year. The remainder, whether profit or loss, is to be apportioned in the ratio of Bill 3:Ben 1. Using the trial balance and other information given below, prepare the trading, profit and loss and appropriation account for the year ended 30 April, and a balance sheet as at that date.

Trial balance as at 30 April

		dr	*cr*
Capital a/cs at 1 May, previous year	– Bill		6,000
	– Ben		4,000
Current a/cs at 1 May, previous year	– Bill		2,750
	– Ben		1,340
Fixtures and fittings at cost		1,000	
Provision for depreciation at 1 May, previous year			200
Delivery van at cost		4,400	
Provision for depreciation at 1 May, previous year			1,100
Stocks at 1 May, previous year		7,100	
Sales income			112,000
Purchases		71,200	
Salaries to employees		17,050	
Rent, rates, lighting and heating		6,580	
Advertising		1,020	
Motor expenses		2,200	
Telephone and postage		940	
General expenses		1,730	
Creditors			3,510
Bank and cash		17,680	
		£130,900	£130,900

The other information you need is as follows:

1 The closing stock at 30 April was £8,090.
2 Depreciation is to be provided as follows:
   (a) Fixtures and fittings at the rate of 10% per year on cost
   (b) Delivery van at the rate of 25% per year on cost.
3 Rent owing amounts to £1,000.
4 Rates prepaid are £800.
5 Telephone charges incurred and not yet paid amount to £70.
6 The partners' drawings have already been charged to the current accounts.

Finally, to round off the chapter tackle the following questions to give you plenty of practice:

Exercise 12.9

9.1 Gatting, Gower and Gooch are in partnership, sharing profits and losses in the ratio 3:2:1 respectively. On 1 January the balance of their capital accounts were: Gatting £25,000, Gower £30,000, Gooch £10,000. The following figures came out of the firm's accounts for the year ended 31 December.

1 Gatting took out £1,000 of his capital on 1 January; on 30 June Gooch increased his capital investment to £12,000.
2 During the year drawings amounted to – Gatting £8,000, Gower £7,000 and Gooch £5,000.
3 The net profit for the year was £36,000.

Prepare the partners' capital and current accounts for the year together with the profit and loss appropriation account.

9.2 Davies, Harris and Lord are in partnership with fixed capitals of £40,000, £30,000 and £10,000 respectively. Their partnership agreement allows for:

1 Lord receives a salary of £10,000 for acting as general manager.
2 Interest on capital is given at the rate of 5%.
3 The profit-sharing ratio is 3:3:1.

Drawings during the year to 30 September were Davies £9,000, Harris £7,000 and Lord £1,000. The net profit for the year amounted to £28,000.

Prepare the appropriation account and the partners' capital and current accounts for the year.

9.3 Nicholson and Marriott are in partnership, sharing profits and losses equally. On 31 March 19-9 the following balances were extracted from their books:

	dr	*cr*
Capital accounts:		
Nicholson		24,000
Marriot		36,000
Current accounts (1 April 19–8):		
Nicholson	2,000	
Marriott		4,000
Drawings:		
Nicholson	4,000	
Marriott	3,000	
General expenses	2,000	
Wages	15,000	
Rent, rates and insurance	9,000	
Purchases and sales	65,000	120,000
Cash and bank	2,000	

Stock at 1 April 19–8	10,000	
Fixed assets (net of depreciation)	73,000	
Debtors and creditors	10,000	5,000
	189,000	189,000

Additional information:

1 Stock on 31 March 19–9 was valued at 12,000.
2 Rent prepaid on 31 March 19–9 amounted to £1,000.
3 Fixed assets are to be depreciated by £9,000.
4 The partnership agreement provides that Nicholson is to receive a salary of £7,000 and that interest on capital of 10% is to be allowed.

Prepare the full final accounts and balance sheet for the partnership.

CHAPTER 13

LIMITED COMPANY ACCOUNTS

13.1 LUMLEY'S LAMPSHADES

'Of course I've heard of limited liability companies. I'm dealing with them all the time. Many of my suppliers are companies, my bank is and some of my customers are. But why should my business become one? What makes them so special?'

Joe Lumley, owner of Lumley's Lampshades, was talking to his accountant, Tim Weston. They had just reviewed Joe's latest accounts and were discussing the future development of the business.

Let's consider your business,' said Tim, 'it is growing fast and making large profits. However, you are paying huge amounts of income tax. You need additional finance for the three new shops you want to open. You can't provide all the capital yourself and bank loans are very expensive. You also want to let your son, Jamie, take over much of the day-to-day work as you aren't getting any younger. It would be easier to deal with these problems if you formed yourself into a limited company.

'What if I become a company?' said Joe. 'How can I still make all the decisions as I do now? Won't I get bogged down with red tape? Doesn't it cost a lot? Won't there be problems with . . .?'

'Hold it!' cried Tim. 'Let's go through this in detail. I'll explain to you the main features of limited liability companies, their advantages and disadvantages, the way in which one can be formed and some of the terms people use when discussing them. You can make up your mind then!'

In this chapter we shall look at the points which Tim would explain to Joe and then go on to see the way in which the accounts of limited companies are prepared. This is a very important topic as these companies are the most important form of business unit in the British commercial world. You may well be working for one; you will certainly have contact with companies every day if you buy a newspaper, go to a bank, shop in a supermarket, buy petrol for your car and in many other activities.

13.2 WHAT IS A LIMITED LIABILITY COMPANY?

It is a legal organisation created by registering a company with the Registrar of Companies under the provisions of the Companies Acts 1985 and 1989. So, for example, Lumley's Lampshades could be registered as Lumley's Lampshades *Ltd* and it would then continue in existence even if Joe Lumley died. It would be a separate being in law - you couldn't see it walking down the street but you could sue it in the courts!

So a company is a separate *legal being* created by registration under the *Companies* Acts 1985 and 1989.

This wonderful legal being has two features which distinguish it from the sole trader and partnership businesses which you have previously looked at:

1 There is no limit to the number of people who may become members of the company. The capital of a company is divided up into what are called *shares*, which may be of any amount decided by the members, e.g. 50p, £1, £5. Someone becomes a member or shareholder by purchasing one or more shares in the company. Therefore a company can find it easier to raise capital than a sole trader or partnership, as it need only issue more shares.
2 The members of the company have *limited liability*. This means that the maximum amount that a member can lose is the capital which he has actually invested in the company. So unlike a sole trader or a partner, the shareholder's private possessions cannot be used to pay for the debts of the business. This obviously helps in making people more willing to buy shares in a company.

Exercise 13.1

To test your understanding of these important points match each item in list A with the appropriate item in list B:

List A	*List B*
1 A company	(a) are members of a company.
2 Shareholders	(b) is limited to the amount of their investment.
3 Shares	(c) is a separate legal person.
4 The liability of shareholders	(d) are parts of the total capital of the company.

13.3 WHAT ARE PRIVATE AND PUBLIC COMPANIES?

They are the two types of limited liability company. A *public* company is defined by the Companies Act 1985 as one which:

- is registered as a public company with the Registrar of Companies.
- has at least two members or shareholders.

- has at the end of its name the words 'public limited company' or the letters 'plc' (or the Welsh equivalents of 'cwmni cyfyngedig cyhoeddus' or 'ccc').
- must have a minimum authorised share capital of £50,000 which must be issued before it can do business.

A *private* company is then a limited company which is not a public company. Its name is followed by the word 'limited' or letters 'Ltd' ('cyfyngedig' or 'cyf.' in Welsh).

What are the differences in practice between the two? There are more private than public companies in existence. The main advantage which public companies have is that it is possible for them to sell their shares to the general public. For example, a public company can apply to the Stock Exchange to have its shares dealt in on the Exchange; a private company cannot. The main disadvantages are that the public company has more regulations to comply with and has to provide more information about its affairs to such people as the Registrar of Companies. As a consequence, private companies tend to be smaller businesses which do not need to sell shares to the public e.g. family businesses. Public companies tend to be larger firms which operate on a large scale, require a lot of finance and are relatively well known.

Exercise 13.2

Can you define a public limited company? Underline the correct response to each part to test yourself:

A public company is one:

2.1 which has at least twenty shareholders True/False
2.2 which has a minimum authorised share capital of £50,000 True/False
2.3 whose name is followed by the letters 'ltd' True/False
2.4 which is registered as a public company with the Registrar of Companies True/False

Activity

How many do you know?

You will probably be aware of many public companies, more than you might realise. To test this, look at the business pages of a 'quality' newspaper. You will find a list of many public companies whose shares are quoted on the Stock Exchange. Look through the list and tick off those companies you recognise. If you manage more than 150 you have a good awareness of the commercial world. If you cannot tick off more than twenty, you need to read the business press more frequently!

13.4 HOW IS A COMPANY FORMED?

If Joe Lumley wished to create Lumley's Lampshades Ltd he would have to meet the requirements laid down in the Companies Acts so he would probably consult a solicitor! This would be a wise move as the law relating to companies is complex and there may be particular points which Joe would want to be sure of when setting up his company. The details of company law are beyond the scope of this book, so here I will just outline the procedure by which a private company can be formed:

1 Those wishing to form a company have to submit certain documents to the Registrar of Companies together with the relevant fee. The documents are:
   (a) The *Memorandum of Association* which gives the company's name, the address of its registered office, the objects of the company, the maximum amount of capital the company is allowed toi issue, and states that the liability of its members is limited. This document must be signed by at least two people who promise to pay for the shares they have agreed to take and state that they wish to be formed into a company.
   (b) The *Articles of Association* which give details of the intended internal constitution of the company. This can cover a wide range of issues such as the rights of shareholders, the conduct of meetings, the borrowing powers of directors and so on. The help of a solicitor can be very useful in dealing with these points. If you have no particular requirement you can use a model set of Articles produced in Companies Act 1985.
   (c) A statement regarding the company's share capital.
   (d) Details of the directors and secretary of the company.
   (e) A declaration that the Companies Acts have been complied with.
2 Once these documents have been checked and passed, the Registrar of Companies will issue a Certificate of Incorporation. This then means that the company has come into existence as a legal entity. As it is a private company it may then begin trading.

The procedure therefore is relatively straightforward. In addition to either 'doing-it-yourself' or with the help of a solicitor, it is also possible to buy a ready-made company from businesses who specialise in company formation, at a cost of approximately £120. Advertisements for these can usually be found in any financial paper.

Exercise 13.3

Complete the blanks in the following sentence:

A private limited company is ________________ and is able to trade when the ____________ of Companies issues a ____________ of ____________.

13.5 WHAT ARE THE ADVANTAGES OF LIMITED LIABILITY COMPANIES?

There are various features of limited liability companies which may have advantages for a particular business depending on its circumstances. The following are the most important:

- *Limited liability*: as mentioned earlier, the shareholders or owners of the business are liable to lose only the money they have invested in the company. Their personal assets cannot be touched.
- *Ability to raise capital*: there is no restriction on the amount of authorised share capital which a company can put in its Memorandum of Association. Also there is no maximum number of shareholders. Consequently, it is easier for companies to raise large amounts of finance through the issue of shares.
- *Transferability*: shares in a company can be sold without affecting the company's capital. So someone who is buying shares in a company is not necessarily making a decision which it is difficult to reverse.
- *Continuity*: the company continues in existence even if one of the major shareholders dies. If a partner dies then the partnership ceases.
- *Taxation*: companies are taxed under the corporation tax system whereas sole traders and partners pay income tax. There may well be tax advantages in turning a successful business into a limited company. However, the tax laws change regularly and advice should be sought from an accountant.
- *Loan capital*: as well as issuing shares a company can raise loan finance by issuing what are called debentures to those who wish to buy them. We shall look at these in more detail later. The important point here is that sole traders and partnerships cannot do this.
- *Image*: one intangible benefit which a limited company has is that it gives an air of respectability and permanence to a business. Consequently, people tend to be more willing to lend money to it, give credit to it and, in some cases such as mail-order selling, trade with it.

13.6 WHAT ARE THE DISADVANTAGES OF LIMITED LIABILITY COMPANIES?

The main disadvantages arise from the legal requirements imposed upon companies. If Joe Lumley set up Lumley's Lampshades Ltd, he could still make all the decisions by owning more than 50% of the shares, but more people would be aware of his affairs. Examples of the disadvantages would therefore be:

- *Accounts*: previously they may have been prepared by Joe's accountant for Joe, the Inland Revenue and the Customs and Excise to use. For a company the accounts must be audited and sent to every shareholder and the Registrar of Companies. Anyone who wishes to pay a search fee can examine the accounts at Companies House. Therefore, there is less privacy about the affairs of the business.

- *Annual return*: the company must also send the Registrar an annual return each year which gives various items of information about the company's affairs, e.g. current directors and shareholders; this also can be examined at Companies House.
- *Shareholders meetings*: there must be at least an annual general meeting of the shareholders of a company. There may also be special meetings if significant changes to the business are being proposed. This can result in slow decision-making and in embarrassing questions if you've got an awkward shareholder!

In general it can be said that a business which is formed as a limited liability company is able to raise finance more easily than a sole trader or partnership. However, it does have to meet with more stringent legal requirements and provide more information about its affairs. The decision to form a company is one which should be taken by a businessman together with his specialist advisers.

Exercise 13.4

Underline the correct response.

The main advantages of forming a limited liability company compared with a sole trader or partnership are:

1 There are more sources of finance available. True/False
2 There is limited liability for the owners. True/False
3 There are fewer formalities. True/False
4 Accounts do not have to be audited. True/False
5 The company continues in existence even if the major shareholder dies. True/False

So far then we have considered the very important legal and commercial points about limited liability companies. I hope you can see from this why they are such a common feature of the business world. Before we move on to the more technical accounting points, I would like you to review your understanding of the material covered by trying the following questions.

Exercise 13.5

5.1 What laws govern the operation of limited liability companies?
5.2 Which of the following are public companies? Tick the correct items:

(a) Dave Salmons, Motor Trader
(b) Cowley's Cars Ltd
(c) Vernon's Vehicles PLC
(d) Cardiff Vehicles CCC
(e) Cymru Cars Cyf.

5.3 The two main documents which have to be submitted to the Registrar of Companies in order to form a limited liability company are the ____________ of Association and the ____________ of Association. Complete the blanks.

5.4 Tom Downes, a friend of yours, had built up a thriving business selling computer systems. He is now in need of more finance and is thinking of forming his business into a company. He asks you for your advice. Briefly list the points you would bring to his attention.

Let's now look at some detailed points before we see the way in which a company's accounts are prepared.

13.7 WHO ACTUALLY RUNS A COMPANY?

As we have seen, the owners of a company are its shareholders. The day-to-day business of a company is, however, carried on by *directors*. Every company must have at least one director and usually has more. The directors are voted in or appointed by the shareholders at their annual general meeting. The directors are therefore entrusted with the management of the finance provided by the shareholders. At each annual general meeting they have to account for their use of the shareholders' funds. This is one of the main roles performed by the preparation of a company's accounts - to show the shareholders what the directors have done with their money. But in the case of many smaller firms the shareholders and directors will be the same people e.g. Joe Lumley, so the distinction is then of minor importance.

13.8 WHAT DO THE SHAREHOLDERS OBTAIN FOR THEIR INVESTMENT?

This will depend upon the type of share owned and upon the rights given to the share as detailed in the Memorandum and Articles of Association of a company. But generally a company's shares are of two types:

1 *Ordinary shares*. This is the most common type of share and entitles the holder to what is called a *dividend* out of the profits of the company. The rate of dividend is proposed by the directors and may vary from year to year. On occasions the directors may feel that no dividend at all should be paid. The directors will take into account in making their proposals such factors as the profits or losses of the company, the company's cash position, its tax position, any government regulations, the need to retain profits within the business and so on. It is important to note that the shareholders cannot propose a higher dividend for themselves at the annual general meeting where the directors' dividend proposals have to be voted on. They can, however, vote for a lower

dividend! Normally the ordinary shareholder will have voting rights. The other main feature is that he is the last person to be repaid out of the assets of the company if it should go into liquidation.

2 *Preference shares*. These entitle the holder to a *fixed* rate of dividend and so might be described, for example, as 10% £1 preference shares. The rate of dividend is decided upon when the shares are authorised in the Memorandum of Association. Therefore, if the profits of the company increase, the preference shareholder will not benefit from an increase in dividend. However, as their name implies, these shares have preference over ordinary shares both in dividends and normally in repayment on liquidation. They are therefore a safer form of investment than ordinary shares.

Many technical terms are used in relation to shares. For reference, here are some of the main ones which you may well meet, together with brief explanations:

- Authorised share capital - the total amount of share capital which a company is allowed to issue. It is specified in the Memorandum of Association and must be shown in the company's balance sheet.
- Issued share capital - the amount of share capital actually issued to shareholders and paid for by them. This forms the actual capital of the business in its balance sheet.
- Nominal or par value - this is the monetary amount of the share e.g. 50p, £1, 5p. The dividend which a shareholder receives is based upon this nominal value. If you held 100 £1 ordinary shares in a company which declared a dividend of 5%, you would receive 5% × £1 = 5p per share × 100 shares = £5.
- Redeemable shares - ordinary or preference shares may be bought back by a company if it is allowed in a company's Articles of Association. This may help in making people more willing to buy a company's shares as they know they can sell them back to the company, if necessary.
- Cumulative preference shares - with these shares the dividend must be paid. If the directors feel it cannot be paid in one year then the amount owing is carried forward to the next year. This is then payable before the ordinary shareholders receive anything.

We have covered a lot of detail here. Before we go any further try the following questions:

Exercise 13.6

6.1 Complete the blanks in the following:

There is a ______ rate of ______ payable on preference shares, but the amount payable on __________ shares may vary from year to year.

6.2 Tick the correct answer.
Coalmans Ltd has authorised share capital of 10,000 £1 ordinary shares of which 5,000 have been issued and fully paid for. The directors proposed a dividend of 20%. How much:
(a) will the company pay in total?
    (i) £1,000
    (ii) £2,000
    (iii) £3,000
(b) will the holder of one share receive?
    (i) 10p
    (ii) 20p
    (iii) 5p

13.9 WHAT ARE DEBENTURES?

I mentioned these earlier as a form of loan which a company could raise, which a sole trader or partnership could not. In addition to investing money in a company by buying shares, people can lend money in the form of a repayable loan, called a debenture. A debenture can be defined as the written acknowledgement of a debt – the debenture holder therefore receives a document in return for his loan to the company. In a company's balance sheet the debentures may be described as follows:

100,000	10%	£1	Debentures 1990–95
The number of units issued	The fixed interest rate paid annually on each £1 loaned to the company		The period during which the debentures will be repaid to the lenders

It is important to note that debenture holders are not shareholders or owners of a company. They are lenders to the company or creditors of it. Usually, a company when issuing debentures will make them more attractive by giving security for the amounts loaned to the company. This means that, if the company went into liquidation, the debenture holders are able to sell the assets which form their security in order to regain the money they have loaned.

Debentures are therefore quite an attractive form of investment. The company must pay the interest due on them and repayment is almost certain if sufficient security is provided.

Exercise 13.7

To summarise the main features of debentures complete the blanks in the following paragraph:

A ________________ is the written acknowledgement of a debt. Interest on debentures is charged at a ________ rate. Debenture holders are ________ to the company, not shareholders or owners of it. They will normally be provided with ________________ for the total of the loan.

13.10 WHAT ABOUT THE ACCOUNTS?

The accounts we shall consider are those which would normally be produced for internal use by any company. The accounts which are actually given to shareholders and sent to the Registrar of Companies are usually very different. The Companies Acts 1985 and 1989 describes the information which a company must give by law and directors will not normally go further than this for fear of giving away too many secrets to their competitors. The internal accounts will be much more detailed, especially regarding the costs of the business. How will these accounts differ from those of sole traders and partnerships? Let's look at them one by one:

1 *Trading and profit and loss account*. The only differences here will be the introduction of certain types of expenses peculiar to limited companies, e.g. directors' salaries and debenture interest.
2 *Profit and loss appropriation account*. As with a partnership, because there is more than one owner of the business, there must be a statement to show how the profits of the business are to be used. In the case of a company, the profits are either:
   (a) *distributed* - paid out in the form of dividends or taxation; or
   (b) *retained* - held within the business in what are called *revenue reserves*. These reserves may be of two types:
      - specific reserves which indicate that these retained profits are not to be used for dividends to shareholders but are to be held permanently within the business, e.g. fixed asset replacement reserve or general reserve.
      - undistributed profits - profits which have not been paid out to shareholders as dividends but are carried forward and may be distributed in future years. This is often called the profit and loss account balance or retained profits.
3 *Balance sheet*. In the assets part of the balance sheet there will be no difference. In the finance part the balance sheet must show:
   (a) the authorised share capital and the issued share capital separately, unless all of the authorised share capital has been issued, when the two can be combined.
   (b) the reserves of the company under their various headings.

A company balance sheet may also have to show any debentures as a long-term liability. As current liabilities it may well have amounts owing for proposed dividends and taxation. These will also be given in the appropriation account.

Exercise 13.8

8.1 Indicate where the following items would appear in the final accounts of a limited company, using 'P' for profit and loss account. 'A' for appropriation account and 'BS' for balance sheet. Some items may appear twice.

(a) Debenture interest paid (b) Proposed dividend
(c) Transfer to general reserve (d) Authorised share capital
(e) Retained profits (f) Directors' remuneration.

8.2 Indicate whether or not the following items are a true description of the reserves of a limited company. Reserves represent:

(a) the profits of the company which are held within it and not distributed to shareholders True/False
(b) the cash which the business has available to use. True/False
(c) increases in the assets - liabilities of the company. True/False

We have therefore seen the main differences in company accounts. You should, however, note that the Companies Acts 1985 and 1989 lay down strict formats for the formal presentation of company acccounts. They also introduce new terms for some of the categories in the accounts. These are beyond the scope of this book but you will encounter them at the next level of study.

Let's now see the way in which basic company accounts are prepared by looking at the overall figures for Joe's company after its first year's trading.

13.11 EXAMPLE - LUMLEY'S LAMPSHADES LTD

After a great deal of discussion with his accountant, Tim Weston and his solicitor, Joe, decided to form Lumley Lampshades Ltd. The company had an authorised share capital of £200,000 made up of 110,000 £1 ordinary shares and 90,000 10% £1 preference shares. In return for the net assets of his business at their balance sheet value, Joe received 100,000 ordinary shares and 20,000 preference shares from the company. Also 1,000 ordinary shares were issued to Joe's wife Edna and fully paid for.

At the end of the first year's trading the company's results could be summarised as follows:

1 The net profit for the year was £60,000. Out of this Joe proposed to transfer £10,000 to a general reserve, to pay the preference dividend and an ordinary share dividend of 10%.
2 The company had fixed assets of £141,000, current assets totalling £70,000 and its current liabilities for creditors and expenses were £30,000.

The final accounts at the end of the company's first year would appear as in Figure 13.1. Check them through carefully together with the notes which I've given.

Fig. 13.1 Lumley's Lampshades Ltd – final accounts

Profit and loss appropriation account for year ended 31 December

Net profit			60,000
Retained profits brought forward (*Note 1*)			—
Transfer to general reserve		10,000	
Proposed dividends: (*Note 2*)			
Ordinary	10,100		
Preference	2,000		
		12,100	22,100
Retained profits carried forward (*Note 3*)			£37,900

Balance sheet as at 31 December

Fixed assets			141,000
Current assets		70,000	
Current liabilities:			
Creditors and expenses	30,000		
Proposed dividends (*Note 2*)	12,100	42,100	
Working capital			27,900
Net assets employed			168,900
Authorised share capital (*Note 4*):			
110,000 ordinary shares			110,000
90,000 10% preference shares			90,000
			200,000
Issued share capital:			
101,000 ordinary shares			101,000
20,000 10% preference shares			20,000
			121,000
Reserves:			
General reserve		10,000	
Retained profits (*Note 3*)		37,900	47,900
Net capital employed			£168,900

Notes

1 Because this is the company's first year, there would not be any profits available for distribution which can be carried forward from previous years.

2 The proposed dividends are calculated on the issued share capital, i.e. 10% of £101,000 = £10,100, and 10% of £20,000 = £2,000. Note that because they have not been paid at the balance sheet date they will appear as a current liability in the balance sheet.
3 The retained profits held within the business, as shown in the appropriation account, will then appear under 'Reserves' in the balance sheet.
4 The authorised share capital is shown for information on the face of the balance sheet. It is double underlined to show that it does not form part of the capital of the company - that is the issued share capital.

We hope this has proved a clear illustration of the points we've discussed on limited company accounts. To practise the preparation of these, try the following exercises and then check them through carefully with our suggested answers.

Exercise 13.9

9.1 The Clarke Welding Company Ltd has an authorised capital of £200,000, split into 150,000 £1 ordinary shares and 50,000 6% £1 preference shares. On 1 January 19-8 the company had issued 100,000 ordinary shares and all the preference shares. At 1 January the company's fixed assets were valued at £100,000, current assets £75,000 and current liabilities £25,000. Prepare the company's balance sheet at 1 January 19-8.

9.2 During the year ended 31 December 19-8 the Clarke Welding Company Ltd made a net profit of £50,000. The directors propose to pay the preference share dividend and a 10% dividend on the ordinary shares. The fixed assets at 31 December were valued at £150,000, the current assets £90,000 and current liabilities £40,000.

Prepare the company's profit and loss appropriation account for the year ended 31 December 19-8 and the balance sheet at that date.

9.3 The Marston Co. Ltd has an authorised capital of £400,000 dividend into 300,000 £1 ordinary shares and 100,000 6% £1 preference shares. Of these, 60,000 preference shares and 250,000 ordinary shares have been issued and fully paid.

At the end of the year (31 December) the following information was available:

(a) The net profit for the year was £80,000. The directors recommended a transfer of £15,000 to a general reserve, and proposed the payment of the preference dividend and an ordinary share dividend of 15%.
(b) At the start of the year there were retained profits held in a profit and loss account of £36,000.
(c) The other closing balances in the books were:

Fixed assets	£350,000
Current assets	£126,000
Current liabilities	£50,000

Prepare the company's profit and loss appropriation account for the year ended 31 December and a balance sheet as at that date. Your answer should be fairly similar in format to Lumley's Lampshades Ltd in Figure 13.1.

9.4 The following trial balance was obtained from the books of Florists Ltd at 31 December:

	dr	*cr*
£1 ordinary shares, issued and fully paid		30,000
6% £1 debentures		15,000
Freehold buildings at cost	80,000	
Purchases	91,000	
Sales		165,000
Debtors and creditors	8,900	7,400
Rent receivable		450
General salaries	18,000	
Rates and insurance	500	
Motor expenses	1,000	
Directors' salaries	19,000	
General expenses	2,500	
Motor vans at cost	5,200	
Provision for depreciation on vans at 1 January		3,000
Stock at 1 January	1,200	
Bank and cash	5,400	
Debenture interest paid (to 30 June)	450	
Bad debts	600	
Profit and loss account balance at 1 January		12,900
	£233,750	£233,750

The following information was also available:

(a) Stock at 31 December was £1,400.
(b) General salaries unpaid at the end of the year were £200.
(c) Rent receivable due at 31 December was £150.
(d) Rates paid in advance at the year end were £50.
(e) Debenture interest for the six months to 31 December was due.
(f) Depreciation is to be charged on the motor vans at the rate of 25% per annum on cost.
(g) The directors proposed to pay a 10% dividend on the ordinary shares and transfer £5,000 to a general reserve.

Note: The authorised share capital of the business is 30,000 £1 ordinary shares.

Prepare the trading, profit and loss appropriation accounts for the year ended 31 December, and a balance sheet as at that date.

Notes: Remember to tackle these long accounting questions in small separate stages:

- Trading account – this is straightforward.

- Profit and loss account - identify all the expenses in the trial balance and don't forget the adjustments needed because of notes (b), (d), (e) and (f). The rent is income and must be adjusted for note (c).
- Appropriation account - don't forget the opening balance on the profit and loss account.
- Balance sheet - note that the authorised and issued share capital are the same. Remember to include the items in the notes in your balance sheet.

9.5 The following trial balance was extracted from the books of Shorts Ltd as at 30 June 19-9:

	dr	*cr*
Share capital - ordinary shares		50,000
10% debentures		20,000
Building at cost	36,000	
Purchases and sales	180,000	240,000
Debtors and creditors	18,000	14,000
Rent receivable		1,000
Salaries	24,000	
Rates and insurance	2,000	
Motor vehicle expenses	3,000	
Directors' salaries	6,000	
General expenses	5,000	
Motor vans at cost	12,000	
Provision for depreciation on vans at 1 July 19-8		3,000
Stock at 1 July 19-8	30,000	
Bank balance	30,000	
Debenture interest to 31 December 19-8	1,000	
Bad debts	2,000	
Profit and loss account at 1 July 19-8		21,000
	£349,000	£349,000

The following matters are also to be taken into account:

1 Stock at 30 June 19-9 was £32,000.
2 Salaries outstanding at 30 June 19-9 amounted to £1,000.
3 Rent receivable due at 30 June 19-9 was £1,000.
4 Debenture interest for the 6 months to 30 June 1989 is payable.
5 Depreciation on motor vans is calculated at 25% per annum on cost.
6 The directors propose to pay a dividend of £5,000.

Prepare the final accounts for the year and a balance sheet at 30 June 19-9.

13.12 CONCLUSION

As with the previous chapter, the last exercise has covered material which you will have studied at an earlier stage, such as depreciation and adjustments. If you had problems on those points, then go over them again as they are very important to the study of accounting.

If you have tackled the chapter successfully you will now have a good grasp of the basic elements of limited companies and their accounts. There are a great many aspects of the operations of companies which could be studied in greater depth. To obtain a taste of the world of limited companies, try the following final activity.

Activity

Information about public companies is more readily available than that on private companies. For example, the *Stock Exchange Year Book* (available in most public libraries) gives details of the addresses, shares, activities and so on of all companies whose shares are bought and sold on the Exchange. Many newspapers include information on the share prices of public companies, announcements of companies' results and comments on their performances. A public company will usually be very willing to send you a copy of their annual report and accounts.

So think of a public company you are interested in. Find their address in the *Stock Exchange Year Book*. Write to the company secretary asking for a copy of their latest annual report and accounts. Read through this - it can be very interesting and will give you some idea of the accounts produced by a real company. Keep an eye on your company's share price and cut out any articles on its performance. All of this will help to improve your knowledge of the business world and of a particular company. This can be a very valuable exercise, especially if you buy a few shares yourself!

CHAPTER 14

MANUFACTURING ACCOUNTS

14.1 INTRODUCTION

So far you have studied various aspects of the accounts of sole traders, partnerships and limited companies - different types of ownership of businesses. All of these have been involved in *trading*, i.e. the buying and selling of finished goods, as their method of operation. This type of business activity is very common and familiar to us all when shopping, whether it be at the local newsagent's, supermarket or large store. However, other firms have to supply the goods which these traders sell. Many of Britain's largest and best known companies, such as GEC, ICI, Rover Group, Plessey, BP and Unilever, are mainly involved in this different business activity of *manufacturing* goods and then selling them. Overall, manufacturing firms account for approximately 20% of people employed and so constitute an important sector of the economy. The main characteristic of such manufacturing firms is that they obtain raw materials and components and convert them into finished products ready for sale. This work will obviously be reflected in the accounts which will, therefore, be slightly different to those which you have previously seen and prepared.

Exercise 14.1

Briefly define the work of a manufacturing firm.

In this chapter we shall examine the way in which the accounts of a manufacturing firm differ from those of a trading concern. To do this we shall look at the different types of costs which a manufacturing firm incurs and the way in which the costs are recorded and then summarised in the final accounts. You will then be able to prepare the accounts of a manufacturing business and understand the content of them. The chapter also introduces the idea of adapting the accounts to the type of business and to the needs of the owners or managers of that business - an important theme throughout the rest of the book.

14.2 TRUEMAN'S TABLES LTD

To begin our study of manufacturing accounts let's look at Trueman's Tables Ltd. This private limited company was set up a few years ago by Dennis Trueman and his wife Bella to manufacture a range of pine tables. Since its incorporation the company has expanded rapidly and now occupies three separate buildings on their local trading estate. One building is the factory, the second is the finished goods warehouse and the third is the administrative offices and showroom.

14.2.1 The factory and the manufacturing account

Activity

Think about the factory - this is where all of the production of the tables is carried out. Briefly note the main costs which the company is going to incur in making the tables and running the factory.
Our answer includes the following:

1 The pine which is used in making the tables. In accounting language this is called the *direct materials cost* - the materials used in making the finished product.
2 The wages paid to the workers who make the tables, i.e. those involved in cutting the wood, making the joints, assembling the parts and sanding and finishing the final product. This is called the *direct labour cost* - the wages paid to those who actually make the finished product.
3 There may be a royalty to pay if the table follows a design which is patented by someone outside the company. This is an example of a *direct expense* - an expense incurred specifically for a particular unit of a product.
4 There will then a host of expenses such as factory rent, rates and insurance, depreciation of machinery, factory light, heat and power, salaries paid to the production director and factory foremen, costs of the factory canteen.
   These are just examples, you may have thought of many more. These are all instances of what are called *factory indirect expenses* or *factory overheads* - all those costs which are incurred in the production function of a business but are not directly traceable to a particular finished product.

To summarise then, the costs of a factory and its work are as shown on the diagram overleaf.

Direct materials
+
Direct labour
+
Direct expenses

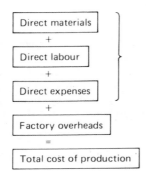

The direct costs when added together are called the *prime cost* - the basic costs incurred in making the products.

+
Factory overheads

The costs of running production and providing the premises and machinery.

=
Total cost of production

All of these would be shown in the company's *manufacturing account* when the final accounts are prepared. The purpose of that statement is to calculate the cost of production of goods completed and transferred to the stock of finished goods. Clearly it would also give the management of the business an analysis of the costs which are involved in the manufacturing process.

Exercise 14.2

These definitions are important in understanding manufacturing accounts and occur again when we discuss product costing. So try the following two questions about them:

2.1 Complete the blanks in the following sentences:

Direct materials are those materials ________ in the ________ product.
Direct labour costs are the wages paid to those who actually ________ the finished product.
Direct expenses are those incurred ________ for a particular ________ of product.
Factory overheads are all those costs incurred in the ________ function of the business but are not ________ traceable to a particular finished product.

2.2 For each of the following items, tick the correct column to show its place in a manufacturing account.

Type of business/cost	*Direct materials*	*Direct labour*	*Direct expenses*	*Factory overheads*
Tomato grower:				
(a) Seeds and plants				
(b) Repairs to glasshouses				
(c) Weeders' wages				
Newspaper:				
(a) Printer's wages				
(b) Rolls of paper				
(c) Lump sum paid to Mr and Mrs Brown for their story				

14.2.2 **The warehouse and the trading account**

When the tables are completed they are transferred from the factory to the finished goods warehouse where they are stored until delivered to customers. In running the warehouse the company again suffers costs such as the wages of the storemen, the depreciation and expenses of fork-lift trucks, and premises costs such as rent, rates and insurance. These warehousing costs are shown in the *trading account* when the final accounts are prepared. They are regarded as part of the cost of the finished goods and are therefore charged before calculating the gross profit on the sales of the tables.

14.2.3 **The offices, showrooms and profit and loss account**

The third premises of the company contain the administrative offices and showrooms. The costs incurred here will be the same as for the trading businesses you have dealt with so far in your studies and will be charged in the *profit and loss account*. However, the various expenses are often grouped under headings in order to bring together the costs involved in a particular aspect of the business. The main headings used tend to be administrative expenses, selling and distribution expenses and finance expenses (e.g. bank charges, interest on overdrafts and loans, discount allowed).

14.2.4 **Conclusion**

The different types of costs which Trueman's Tables Ltd incurs are therefore displayed in the final accounts of the business according to the activity on which they are spent. This enables Dennis and Bella to ascertain the costs of the company's different activities and premises and to control such costs if they need to.

Exercise 14.3

3.1 Briefly describe the work carried out by two manufacturing firms that you are aware of. Trueman's Tables Ltd convert pinewood into tables, what do your companies do?

3.2 Identify where the following cost groups are shown in the final accounts by matching the two lists:

(a) Warehouse costs	(i) Profit and loss account
(b) Selling costs	(ii) Manufacturing account
(c) Factory overheads	(iii) Trading account

3.3 State which part of the final accounts the following individual costs would be shown in by putting the appropriate letter(s) beside the cost – M for manufacturing account, T for trading account, P(A) for profit and loss account (administration), P(S) for profit and loss account (selling and distribution) and P(F) for profit and loss account (finance):

(i) Factory foreman's wages
(ii) Interest on bank overdraft
(iii) Salesman's commission
(iv) Depreciation of plant and machinery
(v) Rent of factory buildings
(vi) Advertising
(vii) Discounts allowed
(viii) Warehouse storekeeper's salary
(ix) Costs of factory cleaning
(x) Plastic casings for ballpoint pens
(xi) Depreciation of accounting machinery
(xii) Bad debt

If there were problems with these questions then you should read through the section on Trueman's Tables Ltd again, paying particular attention to the way in which the definitions relate to the actual workings of the business and the costs it incurs.

14.3 A FULL SET OF ACCOUNTS

Having mastered the basic definitions involved in manufacturing accounts, we shall now see the way in which a full set of final accounts is prepared for a manufacturing company by looking at the figures for Trueman's Tables Ltd.

On 31 December the company's trial balance was as shown below.

	dr	*cr*
Issued share capital, 50p ordinary shares		23,000
Profit and loss account balance at 1 January		125,000
Stocks of timber at 1 January	8,520	
Purchases of timber	164,590	
Direct factory wages	52,110	
Factory rent and rates	2,435	
Factory salaries	6,808	
Factory light and power	1,177	
Factory general expenses	5,946	
Sales		325,175
Warehouse salaries	4,205	
Warehouse rent and rates	1,272	
Warehouse expenses	897	
Administration rent and rates	650	
Showroom rent and rates	400	
Administration salaries	12,975	
Selling and distribution salaries	18,017	
General administration expenses	4,983	

General selling expenses	3,500	
Directors' remuneration	22,092	
Leasehold premises at 1 Jan.		
Factory	24,350	
Warehouse	12,720	
Offices	10,100	
Plant and machinery (net)	75,700	
Motor vehicles (net)	15,855	
Office equipment (net)	10,200	
Showroom fixtures (net)	3,480	
Stocks of finished goods at 1 January	16,095	
Debtors	55,908	
Creditors		35,313
Bank balance		27,797
Bank interest	1,200	
Cash	100	
	£536,285	£536,285

At the year-end the following information was ascertained:

1 Stocks held were: timber £10,083
finished goods £22,178

2 The company depreciates its fixed assets as follows:

Leasehold –	Factory	£1,350 per annum
	Warehouse	£628 per annum
	Offices and showroom	£550 per annum – split equally between the two functions
Plant and machinery		10%
Motor vehicles		20% – these are distribution and salesmen's vehicles
Office equipment		10%
Showroom fixtures		20%

All percentages are to be calculated on the net value of the assets.

3 The directors, Dennis and Bella, decide to propose a dividend of 10% or the ordinary share capital.

This would be a long example as the first part of the final accounts would be the manufacturing trading, profit and loss and appropriation account!

To make this easier to follow, we shall look at each section separately. Try and work out for yourself how the figures are arrived at. I hope the notes below will deal with any problems you may have:

The manufacturing account (see Figure 14.1). This collects the various types of production costs to arrive at the total cost of production. Most of the figures are picked up from the trial balance, apart from the adjustments for closing stock and depreciation.

Note 1 The calculation of the direct materials cost is similar to that used in ascertaining the cost of goods sold in the trading account. Here, however, you are calculating the raw materials used in production.
Note 2 The detailed factory overheads are indented so that a total for this category of costs can be shown separately.

Fig. 14.1 The manufacturing account

Opening stock of timber		8,520
Add Purchases of timber		164,590
		173,110
Less Closing stock of timber		10,083
Direct materials (*Note 1*)		163,027
Direct labour		52,110
Prime cost		215,137
Factory overheads:		
Rent and rates	2,435	
Salaries	6,808	
Light and power	1,177	
General expenses	5,946	
Depreciation on leasehold	1,350	
Depreciation on plant	7,570	25,286 (*Note 2*)
Cost of production		240,423

The trading account (see Figure 14.2). This is much as you will have previously seen except for the items in the notes:
Note 1 The cost of production replaces purchases as the company is making the goods rather than buying them in.
Note 2 The warehouse costs are identified in the trial balance and notes. Again, they are indented and a sub-total shown to enable the costs to be easily seen. These are added to the cost of goods sold to arrive at the cost of sales.

Fig. 14.2 The trading account

Sales			325,175
Cost of production (*Note 1*)		240,423	
Add Opening stock of finished goods		16,095	
		256,518	
Less Closing stock of finished goods		22,178	
Cost of goods sold		234,340	
Add Warehouse expenses: (*Note 2*)			
Salaries	4,205		
Rent and rates	1,272		
General expenses	897		
Depreciation of leasehold	628	7,002	

Cost of sales	241,342
Gross profit	83,833

The profit and loss and appropriation account (see Figure 14.3). The content is standard but note the way in which the expenses are classified under separate headings and sub-totals shown.

Figure 14.3 Profit and loss and appropriation account

Gross profit			83,833
Administration expenses:			
Rent and rates	650		
Salaries	12,975		
General expenses	4,983		
Directors' remuneration	22,092		
Depreciation of office equipment	1,020		
Depreciation of leasehold	275	41,995	
Selling and distribution expenses:			
Showroom rent and rates	400		
Salaries	18,017		
General expenses	3,500		
Depreciation of leasehold	275		
Depreciation of showroom fixtures	696		
Depreciation of motor vehicles	3,171	26,059	
Finance expenses:			
Bank interest		1,200	69,254
Net profit			14,579
Profit and loss account balance at 1 January			125,000
			139,579
Proposed ordinary dividend			2,300
Profit and loss account balance at 31 December			137,279

The balance sheet (see Figure 14.4). The only addition is the fact that this manufacturing business has two types of stock – its raw materials (the timber) and the finished goods. The fixed assets are shown net of depreciation.

Fig. 14.4 Balance sheet as at 31 December

Fixed assets:			
Leasehold premises:			
Factory		23,000	
Warehouse		12,092	
Offices and showroom		9,550	44,642
Plant and machinery			68,130
Office equipment			9,180
Motor vehicles			12,684
Showroom fixtures			2,784
			137,420
Current assets:			
Stocks:			
Timber		10,083	
Finished goods		22,178	
		32,261	
Debtors		55,908	
Cash		100	
		88,269	
Current liabilities:			
Creditors	35,313		
Bank overdraft	27,797		
Proposed dividend	2,300	65,410	
Working capital			22,859
Net assets employed			160,279
Share capital:			
46,000 50p ordinary shares			23,000
Reserves:			
Profit and loss account			137,279
Net capital employed			160,279

This comprehensive example will be useful for reference. I hope it also illustrates clearly the way in which the accounts can be structured to show the costs of the different functions of the business. Now try the following questions to test your understanding of this material.

Exercise 14.4

4.1 How is the direct materials cost calculated in the manufacturing account?

4.2 From the following list of balances, prepare a manufacturing and trading account for the year ended 30 June (this should be a useful exercise in practising the preparation of these accounts):

	£	
Stock of raw materials at 1 July	4,200	Closing stocks at 30 June were:
Direct factory wages	38,300	raw materials £6,200
Purchases of raw materials	82,000	finished goods £15,700
Sales	200,000	
Stock of finished goods at 1 July	13,200	
Royalties	1,000	
Factory power, light and heat	1,650	
Warehouse power, light and heat	800	
Factory rates	3,000	
Warehouse rates	1,500	
Depreciation of machinery	1,850	
Indirect factory wages	15,700	
Warehouse wages	4,700	

4.3 From question 4.2, what would the total stock figure be in the closing balance sheet?

14.4 WORK-IN-PROGRESS

So far we have considered the treatment of two types of stocks - raw materials and finished goods. However, most manufacturing firms are likely to have a third type - partly manufactured goods, which are called *work-in-progress*.

These items will have to be valued at the year-end as they represent costs which have been incurred but must be carried forward to the next accounting period when the goods will normally be completed and then sold. The valuation will usually be done by the factory staff in conjunction with the accountant. Also the opening work-in-progress must be included in the accounts as costs carried forward to the current year when the goods were completed.

Work-in-progress therefore represents an adjustment in preparing the manufacturing account and is treated as in this simplified example:

Manufacturing account

Direct materials	50,000
Direct labour	100,000
Prime cost	150,000
Factory overheads	100,000
	250,000
Add Opening work-in-progress	10,000
	260,000
Less Closing work-in-progress	12,000
Cost of production	£248,000

Note also that the balance sheet figure for stocks could include three different stock figures - raw materials, work-in-progress and finished goods.

14.5 WHERE DOES THE INFORMATION COME FROM?

As we have seen, one of the main features of these accounts is the way in which costs are analysed between the main activities of the business in order to assist the management of the business in controlling costs. We have also seen some examples of the types of expense accounts used and their treatment in the final accounts. But where does the information for the entries in the ledger accounts come from?

Essentially the information is arrived at from two processes:

- Allocation - the charging of whole items of cost to a specific function, e.g. Sid Smooth is a sales representative, therefore his salary will be charged to the selling and distribution salaries account.
- Apportionment - the sharing out of a cost between functions which benefit from it. Here common sense has to be used and it must be recognised that some estimation does take place. For example, the rates bill for a company may be split between functions on the basis of floor space occupied by each function; the lighting and heating bills may be split on the basis of cubic feet for each function or it may, more accurately, be measured by meters and split accordingly. Various approaches are used but the key point to remember is the aim - to try and show a fair view of the costs incurred by each of the firm's main activities. We shall look at this process in more detail in the next chapter.

14.6 CONCLUSION

This chapter is important for a number of reasons:

- It introduces you to the important world of manufacturing.
- It provides you with some key definitions which will be referred to and used later when we look at the costing of products.
- It also provided an introduction to the way in which accounting systems can be modified to produce useful information for the management of a business through the analysis of costs - an approach we shall take up again in the next chapter.

Therefore to consolidate on the work of this chapter we would like you to tackle the exercises and activities which follow:

Exercise 14.5

5.1 The following information relates to the Ashton Products Company Ltd:

Stock of raw materials:	
1 January 19–9	6,000
31 December 19–9	5,000
Depreciation of plant and machinery	8,000
Factory wages and salaries:	
Direct	55,000
Factory supervisors and manager	24,000
Rates and insurance	3,000
Sales	150,000
Purchases of raw materials	35,000
Fuel and power	6,000
Stocks of manufactured goods:	
1 January	4,000
31 December	8,000

Prepare the company's manufacturing and trading accounts for the year ended 31 December 19–9.

5.2 Prepare a manufacturing, trading and profit and loss account for the year ended 30 September 19–9 for Brazier Ltd from the figures given below:

Stocks on 1 October 19–8:	
Raw materials at cost	6,000
Work-in-progress at factory cost	4,000
Finished goods at factory cost	8,000
Purchase of raw materials	43,000
Manufacturing wages	65,000
Factory expenses	18,000
Office and administration expenses	9,000
Depreciation of plant and machinery	7,000
Factory power	5,000
Salespersons' salaries and commissions	14,000
Salespersons' expenses	4,000
Advertising	3,000
Rates and insurance	4,000
Light and heat	8,000
Sales	190,000
Stocks at 30 September 19–9:	
Raw materials at cost	9,000
Work-in-progress at factory cost	5,000
Finished goods at factory cost	10,000

Note: Three-quarters of rates and insurance and light and heat are to be allocated to the factory and one-quarter to the office.

5.3 Bradley's Bats Ltd is a manufacturing company which produces cricket bats and associated products. From the trial balance and other information given, prepare the manufacturing, trading and profit and loss account for the year ended 31 October, and a balance sheet as at that date.

Other information:

1 The stocktaking at 31 October valued the closing stocks as follows:

Raw materials	£6,250
Work-in-progress	£11,150
Finished goods	£17,380

2 Depreciation on the assets of the business is to be provided as follows using the straight-line method:

Plant and machinery	15% per annum
Fixtures and equipment	10% per annum

3 The provision for bad debts is to be 5% of total debtors.
4 Amounts are outstanding as follows – factory light, heat and power £750; bank interest £450; selling and distribution expenses £300.
5 The directors propose an ordinary share dividend of 15% and to pay the preference share dividend.

Trial balance as at 31 October

	dr	*cr*
Issued share capital:		
40,000 £1 ordinary shares		40,000
20,000 6% £1 preference shares		20,000
Profit and loss account at 1 November, previous year		61,200
Stocks at 1 November, previous year:		
Raw materials	5,300	
Work-in-progress	10,200	
Finished goods	16,120	
Factory rent	2,400	
Factory light, heat and power	4,250	
Factory wages (direct)	52,180	
Factory salaries (indirect)	14,630	
Factory general expenses	4,730	
Warehouse costs	5,970	
Sales		245,010
Purchases of raw materials	89,160	
Purchases of finished goods	3,240	
Administration expenses	9,840	
Selling and distribution expenses	14,620	
Office premises (at cost)	76,500	
Plant and machinery at cost	80,000	
Plant and machinery depreciation provision at 1 Nov. previous year		45,000
Fixtures and equipment at cost	15,000	
Fixtures and equipment depreciation provision at 1 Nov. previous year		5,000

Debtors	51,000	
Creditors		16,450
Provision for bad debts at 1 Nov. previous year		3,200
Bank balance		20,480
Bank interest	1,200	
	£456,340	£456,340

Activities

Here are two suggestions which should help strengthen your understanding of manufacturing businesses and their costs and accounts:

1 See if you can arrange a visit to a manufacturing firm. This may be your own place of work or part of an organised visit (trips to breweries are very popular!), or through a friend. The idea of this is to enable you to see the various activities which a manufacturing business undertakes and to easily identify the types of costs that business will incur. They may be willing to let you look at their accounts if you express a particular interest!

2 Find the address of a manufacturing company in which you are interested using the sources mentioned in Chapter 13. Write to them asking for a copy of their latest annual report and accounts and any other information which they will send you concerning the work which they do. Many companies are very willing to do this and the material they send out is often very interesting, informative and well presented and should help you gain a good understanding of manufacturing business.

CHAPTER 15

DEPARTMENTAL ACCOUNTS

15.1 GOLDCROFT SPORTS LTD

'Well, how is *my* department doing? That's what I need to know. It's all very well you telling us that the business is not very profitable. We're only department heads. What can we do about it if you can't tell us how well or badly each of our sections is performing?'

As you can see tempers were wearing thin! The occasion was the management meeting of Goldcroft Sports Ltd held to discuss the year's results which had just been produced by the company's accountant, Brian Jameson. The managing director, Marian Golding, had just been complaining at length about the company's performance as shown in the trading and profit and loss account. This had produced the angry response above from Joan Taylor, head of the winter sports department.

'She's got a good point you know, Brian. Our accounting systems only give us the results for the business as a whole which doesn't help me or the heads, such as Joan, in managing the business. Is there anything we can do about it?' asked Marian.

'Of course,' said Brian, 'with some modification to your systems and a little more work in entering transactions, you could have all the information you need.'

Activity

Briefly state the company's main problem in the above situation.

Essentially it can be described as lack of information. More particularly the problem is lack of information in a useful, relevant and detailed form which will help the management of the business in making decisions about it.

To look at this problem in more detail, try the following activity.

Activity

Look around a department store or large shop in your area (or think about one you are familiar with). List the main departments which you can identify and briefly note the questions which you think the management of the business might want to ask about each department.

Let's have a look at a possible approach in relation to Goldcroft Sports Ltd. The company has just one store in a market town with a large population in its area and no specialised competitor in sports goods. The store has three main departments:

1 Winter sports – specialising in clothing, footwear and equipment for skiing, mountaineering and hillwalking.
2 Main sports – selling the necessary goods for football, rugby, cricket, tennis, squash, athletics and fishing.
3 Other sports – dealing with such sports as snooker, darts, chess, cards, some children's games and any other product lines Marian Golding wants to sell.

These departments are backed up by an administrative section which handles all the accounting, advertising, buying and other matters of running the business.

What sort of questions would be asked about each department?

- How much gross profit is made by each department?
- How much stock is held by each department? How frequently is that stock sold?
- What running costs are there for each department, e.g. salaries?
- What profit does each department make?
- What are the costs of the administrative section? Are these costs covered by the profits of the departments?
- What percentage does each department make in relation to its sales?
- What sales and profit per square foot does each department make?

These are some examples. You may well have thought of others for the firm you choose.

Answering these questions would provide useful information to the management of the company and enable them to make rational decisions on a range of important issues such as:

- deciding where costs might be cut
- deciding where stock levels might be reduced
- increasing the size of one department's sales area at the expense of another
- wage increases and their effect on departmental profitability
- deciding what products to promote and what prices to charge.

In this chapter we shall look at the way in which accounting systems can be organised and final accounts produced so as to provide the vital information which we have seen is needed to effectively manage a business. Whilst we shall use the retail store as an example, the principles illustrated can equally be applied to: different factories in a manufacturing company; different products in a manufacturing or trading business; or different types of work in a service industry, e.g. conveyancing, criminal work, divorce etc. for a solicitor. The key to providing useful information is the accounting system.

15.2 HOW SHOULD WE DESIGN AN ACCOUNTING SYSTEM?

The design of the accounting system should follow two basic principles:

1 It should produce the information the management requires.
2 It should reflect the structure of the business and its activities.

In the case of Goldcroft Sports Ltd, the information required could be provided by a trading and profit and loss account for each department, and a summary account for the firm as a whole which deducted the costs of the administrative section and other costs from the profits of the departments. The structure of the accounts would then follow the simple example in Figure 15.1.

Fig. 15.1 Goldcroft Sports Ltd – the structure of the accounts

	Winter sports	Main sports	Other sports	Total
Sales	100	100	100	300
Less Cost of goods sold	50	40	60	150
Gross profit	50	60	40	150
Less Departmental costs	40	30	20	90
Departmental profit	10	30	20	60
Less Administrative section costs			10	
Other costs			20	30
Company net profit				30

15.3 HOW WOULD THE INFORMATION BE OBTAINED?

Let us look at the *trading account* first of all:

1 *Sales*. A separate sales account would be needed for each department. A business such as Goldcroft Sports might have a cash till in each department so that the cash sales made by each department can easily be

counted at the end of each day and then recorded. Alternatively, if only one cash till is used, the transactions can be coded by the use of an appropriate machine and a daily summary produced. Sales on credit can be recorded by putting the details of the invoice into an analysed sales daybook (this may also be used for the summary of cash sales). A daybook lists the details of the sale but also analyses it into a predefined column according to the type of item sold. There are many companies who produce standard stationery for accounting staff to use for this purpose. Computerised accounting systems of course produce all of the information required automatically.

2 *Purchases.* Again a separate purchases account would be kept for each department. Most purchases would be on credit so the information on the invoices could be recorded, as for sales, in an analysed purchase daybook.

3 *Stock figures.* These can easily be obtained for each department by counting and valuing their stock separately.

As you can see, the necessary information for the trading account can be readily obtained for each department at the cost of a little more work in recording and analysing transactions.

As far as the *profit and loss account* is concerned, the expenses of the business will be recorded as normal from expense invoices, contracts and so on. Their treatment in the final accounts will depend on the type of expense they are. For this purpose there are two basic types, as mentioned in Chapter 14:

1 Those which can be *allocated* in full to a particular department and can therefore be regarded as a cost of running that department. In the case or Goldcroft Sports these would probably be just the wages and salaries paid to the staff working in each department. This would only require the wages and salaries paid to be analysed and separate ledger accounts to be kept for each department. If a firm had two separate factories it wished to keep departmental accounts for, then a whole range of expenses could be allocated separately to each factory. This would then require two ledger accounts for each expense and correct entering of invoices to these accounts.

2 Those *common costs* which are incurred for the benefit of a number of departments. Examples of such costs would be those relating to premises, accounting work, purchasing etc. With these costs there are two possible approaches:

   (a) to leave these costs as amounts which need to be covered by the profits of the departments before the company as a whole makes a profit -- the *contribution method*; or
   (b) to apportion these costs between the departments using reasonable methods of calculating the share to be borne by each department - the *apportionment method*.

In the next section we shall see both approaches used, but before going on, try the following questions to summarise the main points on obtaining departmental information:

Exercise 15.1

1.1 Tick the correct answer.
Entries for the purchases and sales figures for different departments are usually obtained from:
(a) Credit notes (b) Analysed daybooks (c) Cash payments

1.2 Complete the gaps in the following sentences:

Departmental costs are those which can be __________ in full to a particular department. Other expenses are those common costs ______ for the benefit of a number of ________ ; they may be deducted from the total of departmental profits or ________ between departments.

15.4 A FULL SET OF ACCOUNTS WITH THE CONTRIBUTION METHOD

In this first example we shall see how the final accounts of Goldcroft Sports Ltd are prepared using the first approach i.e. where non-departmental expenses are left as totals and not apportioned to departments.

At 31 January the trial balance of the company was as shown opposite. The following additional information is also given:

1 The closing stocks at 31 January were:

Winter sports	£3,000
Main sports	£7,000
Other sports	£2,000

2 Depreciation on fixtures and equipment is charged at the rate of 10% per annum on cost.

3 The directors propose an ordinary share dividend of 10%.

From this information the accounts would be prepared as in Figure 15.2. Look at this answer and the notes below in relation to the information given and make sure you can see where the figures come from.

	dr	cr
Opening stocks at 1 Feb. (previous year)		
Winter sports	2,000	
Main sports	6,000	
Other sports	1,000	
Sales:		
Winter sports		25,000
Main sports		60,000
Other sports		15,000
Purchases:		
Winter sports	16,000	
Main sports	31,000	
Other sports	9,000	
Wages and salaries:		
Winter sports	6,000	
Main sports	15,000	
Other sports	4,000	
Administrative section	6,000	
Directors' remuneration	6,000	
Rent, rates and insurance of premises	2,000	
Insurance of stock	900	
General administrative expenses	3,000	
Light and heating expenses	100	
Fixtures and equipment at cost	10,000	
Provision for depreciation of fixtures and equipment at 1 Feb (previous year)		4,000
Debtors	400	
Bank	28,300	
Cash	300	
Creditors		8,000
£1 ordinary shares, issued and fully paid		10,000
Profit and loss account at 1 Feb. (previous year)		25,000
	£147,000	£147,000

Fig. 15.2 *Departmental trading and profit and loss accounts and appropriation account for the year ended 31 January*

(*Note 1*)		*Winter sports*	*Main sports*	*Other sports*	*Total*
Sales	(A)	25,000	60,000	15,000	100,000
Opening stock		2,000	6,000	1,000	9,000
Add Purchases		16,000	31,000	9,000	56,000
		18,000	37,000	10,000	65,000
Less Closing stock		3,000	7,000	2,000	12,000
Cost of goods sold	(B)	15,000	30,000	8,000	53,000
Gross profit	(A–B)	10,000	30,000	7,000	47,000
Less Departmental costs:					
Wages and salaries		6,000	15,000	4,000	25,000
Departmental profits (*Note 2*)		£4,000	£15,000	£3,000	22,000
Administrative costs					
Wages and salaries			6,000		
Depreciation of fixtures and equipment			1,000		
General expenses			3,000	10,000	
Other costs					
Rent, rates and insurance of premises			2,000		
Insurance of stock			900		
Directors' remuneration			6,000		
Light and heating expenses			100	9,000	19,000
					3,000
Add Profit and loss account balance b/fwd					25,000
					28,000
Less Proposed ordinary dividend					1,000
Profit and loss account balance at 31 January					£27,000

Note 1 Note the layout of the trading and profit and loss accounts in what is called a *vertical* form. This makes it easier to present the accounts where a number of columns are required.

Note 2 When the profit of each department has been calculated, the column is ruled off. From the figure for total departmental profits the other costs of the business are deducted.

As you can see, these accounts do highlight the direct profitability of each of the departments of the business. The figures for each department can then be used to answer some of the questions we discussed earlier.

Balance sheet as at 31 January

Fixed assets:			
Fixtures and equipment at cost		10,000	
Less depreciation		5,000	5,000
		41,000	
Current assets:			
Stocks		12,000	
Debtors		400	
Bank		28,300	
Cash		300	
Current liabilities:			
Creditors	8,000		
Proposed dividend	1,000	9,000	
Working capital			32,000
Net assets employed			37,000
Share capital:			
£1 ordinary shares			10,000
Reserves:			
Profit and loss account			27,000
Net capital employed			37,000

15.5 THE APPORTIONMENT METHOD

The second approach goes a step further by charging each department with a fair share of the general costs of the business. To do this an appropriate basis of apportionment should be used for each type of cost. Usually it is not fair just to share the costs out equally between each department as, for example, one department may be much larger than another. In the case of Goldcroft Sports Ltd the following methods may be used:

Basis of apportionment	*Costs*
Sales of each department	Administrative wages and salaries; depreciation of fixtures and equipment; general expenses; directors' remuneration
Square feet occupied by each department	Rent, rates and insurance of premises; light and heating expenses.
Opening stock held by each department	Insurance of stock.

The basis of apportionment will be used to calculate the ratio by which the costs will be charged to each department. We looked at ratios in detail in Chapter 12 of the book but let's take administrative wages and salaries as an example.

	Winter sports	*Main sports*	*Other sports*
The sales of each department were:	£25,000	£60,000	£15,000
We can divide through by 5,000 to make the figures simpler and give the ratio:	5 :	12 : (a total of 20 parts)	3
The administrative wages and salaries cost is £6,000 which is split as follows	($^5/_{20}$ × £6,000) =£1,500	($^{12}/_{20}$ × £6,000) =£3,600	($^3/_{20}$ × £6,000) =£9,000

Exercise 15.2

Calculate the amount which should be charged to each department for insurance of stock.

Let us now see what the profit and loss account of Goldcroft Sports Ltd would look like using this apportionment method; we shall start from the gross profit figures as in the previous answer. The additional piece of information required is that the area occupied by each department is:

Winter sports	300 square feet
Main sports	500 square feet
Other sports	200 square feet

See Figure 15.3 for the departmental accounts using the apportionment method.

15.6 **INTERPRETING THE RESULTS**

As can be seen from Figure 15.3, the winter sports department makes a final net loss after other costs have been charged to it. Whilst this approach may give some useful information to management, it could be dangerous to base drastic action upon it because:

- different net profit/loss figures would be produced if different apportionment bases were used
- many of these costs would still be incurred by the business even if the winter sports department were closed down. For example, directors' remuneration, lighting and heating, rent, rates and insurance would still have to be covered by departmental profits.

Fig. 15.3 Departmental profit and loss account for the year ended 31 January

	Winter sports	*Main sports*	*Other sports*	*Total*
Gross profit (as in Fig. 15.2)	10,000	30,000	7,000	47,000
Less Departmental costs:				
Wages and salaries	6,000	15,000	4,000	25,000
Departmental profits	4,000	15,000	3,000	22,000
Administrative costs				
Wages and salaries	1,500	3,600	900	6,000
Depreciation of fixtures and equipment	250	600	150	1,000
General expenses	750	1,800	450	3,000
Other costs				
Rent, rates and insurance of premises	600	1,000	400	2,000
Insurance of stock	200	600	100	900
Directors' remuneration	1,500	3,600	900	6,000
Light and heating expenses	30	50	20	100
	4,830	11,250	2,920	19,000
Net profit/(loss)	£(830)	£3,750	£80	£3,000

So for practical purposes we would recommend using the first approach where the departmental profits represent the 'contribution' which each department makes to the overall profitability of the business. These contributions obviously reflect the efforts of the departmental managers. The other costs of the business are not affected by the work of these managers and are therefore listed as totals which must be covered by the departmental profits if the business is to make an overall profit. The apportionment approach has been covered because it is used in practice and its limitations should be appreciated. It is also relevant to our studies of costing in Chapter 19. Also it does appear in exam papers in accounting - examiners like to make you calculate ratios!

To complete this chapter try the following exercises. These are designed to help you make sure you have understood the material in the chapter and give you some practice in preparing departmental accounts.

Exercise 15.3

3.1 What is the purpose of preparing departmental trading and profit and loss accounts?
3.2 Explain the term 'allocated cost' in relation to departmental accounts.
3.3 Explain the term 'departmental profit or contribution'.

3.4 If all of the expenses of the business are to be apportioned to the departments, then appropriate bases of apportionment should be used. Decide which is the most appropriate basis for each cost below by matching the items in the two lists:

Cost	*Basis of apportionment*
(a) Rent	(i) Equally
(b) Advertising	(ii) Number of employees in each department
(c) Canteen costs	
(d) Managing director's salary	(iii) Sales of each department
	(iv) Floor area of each department

3.5 A furniture retailer keeps accounts for his three sales departments – bedroom, kitchen, and other furniture. The following information relates to the six months ended 28 February:

	Bedroom	*Kitchen*	*Other*
Sales	20,000	40,000	60,000
Purchases	13,000	25,000	34,000
Opening stock	4,000	8,000	15,000
Closing stock	3,000	9,000	14,000

The other expenses of the business have not been analysed and are to be apportioned between the departments. These are: Advertising £6,000; rates and insurance £4,000; salaries £25,000; other expenses £9,000.

Advertising and other expenses are to be apportioned in relation to sales.

Rates and insurance are to be split in proportion to floor areas, which are: bedroom department 400 square feet, kitchen department 600 square feet, and other furniture 1,000 square feet.

Salaries are to be charged according to the number of staff employed in each department; these are bedroom 1, kitchen 2, other 2.

Prepare departmental trading and profit and loss accounts for the six months ended 28 February using the apportionment method.

3.6 The Yeovale Hardware Company Ltd is a trading company with two departments – hardware and timber. The trial balance of the company at 31 July is as follows:

	dr	*cr*
Stock at 1 August, previous year:		
Hardware	40,000	
Timber	10,000	
Purchases: Hardware	240,000	
Timber	70,000	
Sales: Hardware		400,000
Timber		180,000
Wages and salaries: Hardware	40,000	
Timber	18,000	
Freehold property at cost	220,000	
Fixtures and equipment at cost	60,000	
Depreciation of fixtures etc. at 1 August, previous year		18,000
Administration expenses	30,000	
Selling and distribution expenses	40,000	
Premises expenses	20,000	
Debtors and creditors	60,000	70,000
Bank balance	40,000	
50p ordinary shares		80,000
Profit and loss account at 1 August previous year		140,000
	£888,000	£888,000

The stocks of 31 July were: hardware £45,000; timber £20,000.
The directors proposed an ordinary share dividend of 20%.
Depreciation on fixtures and equipment is to be charged at the rate of 10% per annum on cost.

Prepare the departmental trading, profit and loss and appropriation accounts for the year ended 31 July, and a balance sheet as at that date. Use the contribution method for your trading and profit and loss accounts.

We hope you managed to tackle these successfully and enjoyed the chapter. It is an important one as it illustrates the way in which accounting can be adapted to meet the needs of the management of a business. It also deals with the uses of accounting in rather more complex firms where a range of activities is carried out.

CHAPTER 16

INCOMPLETE RECORDS AND CLUB ACCOUNTS

16.1 TWO CASES

Edith Purchase runs a profitable business selling ladies clothing on a party-plan basis. She, or her friends and contacts, will hold a tea or sherry party to which women are invited; Edith will then display and sell her stock to those who attend. As far as book-keeping and accounting are concerned, she says, 'I just pay the bills as they come in and bank the cash I earn at my parties. So long as my bank balance is OK then I'm happy - so far it always has been. Every year I send my box of bills and bank statements to my accountant and he prepares my accounts for the tax man. Mind you, he charges me an exorbitant fee for them!'

Tom Friar has set up a small business selling secondhand books. He rents a small shop and uses that and his garage at home to store the books. He has only been trading for about a year and is still building the business up. Tom is very conscious of the need to control costs and see how his business is doing. But, as he asked a friend recently, 'I only keep a cash book. How do I find my profit?'

Activity

What is the major difference between the book-keeping systems employed by Edith and Tom and those which you have studied so far? Give a brief comment.

The main difference is the lack of a double-entry book-keeping system. Transactions made by Edith and Tom will only be shown by documents and, in the case of cash and bank transactions, may be recorded in a cash book. This situation is very common, especially in small businesses where the owners tend to spend as little time as possible on paperwork. The transactions are not recorded using a double-entry system and so the system used is called *incomplete records* or single-entry.

In this section we shall answer Tom Friar's question and see how a set of accounts can be prepared from a cash book and documents. So if Tom or Edith asked you to prepare their accounts for them, then you could do so! A knowledge of these techniques therefore is very useful to anyone who may be involved with small business book-keeping. To start with, however, we shall look at the worst possible situation where there are no records kept by the business at all.

16.2 **THE WORST CASE**

This may arise where records and documents have been lost or destroyed through fire, flood or a similar disaster, or where the owner of the business just does not keep records of any kind. How then can you possibly assess the profit of the business?

The technique which is used here is the *accounting equation* which you will have met at the beginning of your studies of accounting. Just to remind yourself try this question:

Exercise 16.1

Complete the blanks in the following:

The accounting equation states that ________ equal ________ plus ________.

Profit can therefore be calculated if it is remembered that profit is an increase in capital. The basic technique is to calculate the capital at the start and end of the accounting period; the difference is then adjusted for any capital introduced or drawings made in order to find the profit or loss of the business for the relevant period.

How do you find the assets and liabilities figures needed if there are no records kept by the business? The general approach is to use physical checks and information from parties who deal with the business. See if you can work out how this could be done by tackling the following activity:

Activity

Think of an ordinary business which has lost all its records. How would you value the following items: freehold premises; plant and machinery; stock; debtors; bank; cash; creditors? Make brief notes for each one.

A range of approaches are possible but here are our suggestions:
Freehold premises – the solicitor who dealt with the purchase should have a copy of the contract giving its cost; an estate agent could give a current valuation of the property.

Plant and machinery - physically check and list the items the business owns; they could then be valued using current price lists, adjusted for the approximate age of the items.
Stock - physically count and list the items held and value them using suppliers' price lists.
Debtors - write to the customers of the business; or estimate the debtors from the amounts received after the accounting year end.
Bank - obtain a copy of the bank statement.
Cash - count it.
Creditors - write to the usual creditors of the business; or wait until they send reminders - they certainly will!

As you can see, it is possible to make reasonable estimates even when the business has no records. The calculation of the capital figures is done by preparing what are called *statement of affairs* - these are the same as balance sheets but the different title is used to indicate that the figures are not based on ledger accounts.

16.3 **PROFIT CALCULATION**

Let us now see the way in which profit can be calculated using the methods we've outlined:

Example

David Perkins wanted to assess his profit for the year ended 31 March. He started a part-time business on 1 April of the previous year when he put £1,000 into a business bank account. At 31 March his assets and liabilities were estimated as follows: fixed assets £600, stock £700, debtors £100, bank and cash £50, creditors £250. He estimated that he had put a further £500 into the business from his own resources and that his drawings for the year were £1,250.

Step 1 Calculate the opening capital

Statement of affairs at 1 April

Bank	1,000
Capital	1,000

Step 2 Calculate the closing capital

Statement of affairs at 31 March

Fixed assets		600
Current assets:		
Stock	700	
Debtors	100	
Bank and cash	50	
	850	
Current liabilities	250	
		600
		1,200
Capital (see Note below)		1,200

Note: The capital figure is the difference between the assets and liabilities, i.e. 1,450 – 250. It is the last figure entered on the statement of affairs.

Step 3 Calculate the difference; closing capital £1,200 - opening capital £1,000 = £200.

Step 4 Adjust the difference for any capital introduced and/or drawings:

	Difference	200
Add	Drawings	1,250
		1,450
Less	Capital introduced	500
	Net profit	£950

The calculation enables us to identify how much of the increase in capital is due to profit rather than the other factors.

So far then we have seen that many businesses keep few accounting records and have looked at the method for calculating profit from a mimimum of information. To assess your understanding of this material try the following questions.

Exercise 16.2

2.1 What do you understand by the term 'incomplete records'?
2.2 Briefly state why some businesses operate using only incomplete records.
2.3 What does the accounting equation state?
2.4 Ivor Record wants to know how much profit he has made during the year. He has not kept proper records but, with his help, you are able to ascertain the following:

	1 January	*31 December*
Furniture and fittings	£850	£1,250
Stock	£810	£1,020
Debtors	£350	£460
Bank and cash	£175	£300
Creditors	£340	£420

In addition Ivor discloses that during the year he withdrew a total of £1,200 for his own use.

16.4 **THE USUAL SITUATION**

The majority of businesses will have basic records. Like Tom Friar in our earlier example, a cash book will be kept and documents recording transactions will be filed. Consequently, it is possible to prepare a trading and profit and loss account in detail to arrive at the final net profit. Also it will be much easier to ascertain figures for assets and liabilities.

What then are the stages in preparing final accounts from incomplete records?

1 The opening capital is required for the closing balance sheet. This may be available from the cash book if it is a new business, from the previous year's accounts for an existing business or it may have to be calculated using the statement of affairs approach.
2 The cash book entries should be analysed and summarised with the help of cheque stubs, bank statements and invoices. This summary will then give details of all the receipts and payments which have taken place in the accounting period.
3 The sales and purchases are then calculated using the cash book entries and the details of outstanding invoices. Let us take the calculation of sales as an example using some imaginary figures. The principle used is that income is the amount earned in the accounting period; this is not necessarily the same as the cash received. The process is as follows:

Total receipts from customers, say	10,000
Less Amounts received in settling debts from sales in the previous period i.e. opening debtors, say	2,000
	8,000
Add Amounts due for sales made during the period but not yet settled i.e. closing debtors	3,000
Sales	£11,000

Exercise 16.3

Following the same approach as for sales, how would you calculate purchases? Use your own figures. The basic principle here is that the expense to be charged in the accounts is that incurred in the accounting period. This is not necessarily the same as the money paid.

With the addition of the stock figures it should therefore be possible to prepare a trading account.

4 Expense and income items are calculated for the profit and loss account. This is done using the cash book entries and details of any prepayment or amounts outstanding.
5 The closing balance sheet will be prepared from the information available on assets and liabilities. As noted earlier, this will usually be more extensive than in the worst case.

Before we look at a full example of this accounting process, try the following questions.

Exercise 16.4

Tick the correct answers.

4.1 At the start of the year Dave Harris was owed £1,000 by his customers. During the year he received £22,000 from them and was owed £1,500 at the end. His sales for the year were:
(a) £22,000; (b) £22,500; (c) £23,500; (d) £21,000.
4.2 At the start of the year Dave owed his suppliers £750. During the year he paid them £10,250 and owed £1,000 at the end. His purchases for the year were:
(a) £12,000; (b) £11,250; (c) £10,250; (d) £10,500.
4.3 At the start of the year Dave owed £40 rent. He paid £1,300 during the year but still owed £60 at the end. How much should be charged in his profit and loss account for rent for the year?
(a) £1,380; (b) £1,320; (c) £1,420; (d) £1,400.

If you had difficulties with these questions then re-read point 3 above or, if necessary, look at your earlier studies on prepayments and expenses outstanding.

16.5 **TOM FRIAR'S ACCOUNTS**

Let us now answer Tom's question in full. We have seen the steps involved in preparing his accounts from a cash book and other documents, we shall now do it for him.

Tom began his business on 1 July with £2,000 from his personal savings which he put into the business bank account and a stock of books which he had bought worth £500. His cash book, when summarised, gave the following information for his bank transactions:

		£
Receipts:	capital	2,000
	amounts banked from sales	6,000
Payments:	to suppliers of books	5,000
	rent	400
	rates	600
	heating and lighting	200
	purchase of shelving and equipment	800
	general expenses	1,300

In addition to the sales banked, Tom had also made sales for cash out of which he had paid cash purchases £1,000; assistants' wages £500; general expenses £300 and taken drawings for himself of £1,300.

At the end of the year Tom's stock of books was valued at £700, he had debtors of £200 and owed book suppliers £100. He also owed £20 for rent and had prepaid rates of £150. He felt the shelving and equipment should be depreciated at the rate of 10% on cost.

Step 1 Opening capital

Statement of affairs at 1 July

Stock	500
Bank	2,000
	2,500
Capital	2,500

Step 2 This information is given above.
Step 3 Sales: Receipts from customers

–banked	6,000
–cash (1,000+500+300+1,300)	3,100
	9,100
Add Closing debtors	200
	£9,300

Purchases: Payments to suppliers

bank	5,000
cash	1,000
	6,000
Add Closing creditors	100
	£6,100

Steps 4 and *5* will be shown in the final accounts themselves which are now as follows:

Trading and profit and loss account for year ended 30 June

Sales			9,300
Opening stock		500	
Add Purchases		6,100	
		6,600	
Less Closing stock		700	
Cost of goods sold			5,900
Gross profit			3,400
Expenses:			
Rent (400+20)		420	
Rates (600–150)		450	
Heating and lighting		200	
General expenses		1,600	
Depreciation of shelving and equipment		80	
Assistant's wages		500	3,250
Net profit			£ 150

Balance sheet as at 30 June

Fixed assets:			
Shelving and equipment at cost			800
Less Depreciation			80
			720
Current assets:			
Stock		700	
Debtors		200	
Prepayment		150	
		1,050	
Current liabilities:			
Creditors	100		
Rent owing	20		
Bank	300	420	
			630
			£1,350
Capital:			
Opening balance			2,500
Add Net profit			150
			2,650
Less Drawings			1,300
			£1,350

Now try the following exercises:

Exercise 16.5

5.1 J. Connors did not keep proper accounting records for his new business but you are able to ascertain the following:

1 He started on 1 January with equipment of £12,000 and a bank balance of £5,000.
2 Receipts and payments as shown by a simple cash book were:

Receipts:	
Initial deposit	5,000
Receipts from debtors	29,000
Payments:	
Sundry expenses	5,000
Payments to creditors	15,000
Equipment	3,000
Furniture	1,000
Drawings	9,000

3 On 31 December debtors totalled £3,000 and creditors £4,000; stock was valued at £2,000; it was decided to depreciate the equipment by 10%; expenses outstanding totalled £100.

You are required to:
1 Calculate Connors' capital on 1 January.
2 Calculate Connors' credit sales and credit purchases for the year.
3 Calculate the bank balance on 31 December.
4 Prepare a trading and profit and loss account for the year and a balance sheet as at 31 December.

5.2 Ian Lindley, a general dealer, had the following assets and liabilities at 1 October 19-8: equipment £5,100; vehicle £3,500; stock £4,000; trade debtors £1,000; cash £50; bank overdraft £500; creditors £1,500.

The only book of account he uses is a cash book. The following is a summary of the entries he made in the year ended 30 September 19-9:

Paid:	
for stock purchased for resale	9,000
for equipment	1,000
assistant's wages	3,000
light and heat	300
vehicle running costs	2,200
drawings	4,500
Received:	
for goods sold	21,100

Prepare the trading and profit and loss accounts for the year ended 30 September and a balance sheet at that date, taking the following into account:

1 The fixed assets are valued as - equipment £5,500, vehicle £2,500.

2 At 30 September stocks were £5,000, debtors £2,000 and creditors £2,000, cash in hand amounted to £50.
3 At 30 September £50 is owing for light and heat.

5.3 The following information was obtained relating to Stan Walker's business.

On 1 January his assets and liabilities were as follows:

	£
Furniture and fittings	1,000
Stock	910
Bank balance	3,550
Debtors	390
Creditors	140

A summary of his cash book for the year ended 31 December showed:

		£
Receipts:	from debtors	6,640
Payments:	to creditors	2,420
	wages	1,020
	drawings	1,500
	general expenses	680
	rent and rates	1,650

At 31 December the following assets and liabilities were identified:

1 Debtors totalled £650, but of this £20 was thought to be a bad debt and was to be written off.
2 Creditors were listed as £320.
3 Stock was valued at £1,200
4 Wages to his assistant of £40 were owing and the rates prepaid amounted to £140.
5 The furniture and fittings were to be depreciated by 10%.

Prepare Stan's trading and profit and loss account for the year and a balance sheet as at 31 December.

We hope you managed to complete the exercises successfully as the methods used in preparing these accounts are very common. We shall be using them again in the next section when we look at the accounts of clubs and societies. To round off your study of the preparation of accounts from incomplete records try this activity.

Activity

It would be useful if you could see the records kept in practice by the owner of a small business. This would help to relate your studies to real life. Try and find someone who would be prepared to show you his book-keeping systems and accounts and explain to you the way in which he keeps his records. Discuss with him the way in which his accounts are prepared using the knowledge you've acquired in this chapter. Owners of businesses tend to be reluctant to disclose information about them so you could emphasise that you are interested in the systems used and records kept rather than any detailed figures. Good luck!

16.6 SHERBORNE CRICKET CLUB

One of George's main interests is cricket, which he used to play for the Dorset team, Sherborne Cricket Club. As a member of such a club he paid an annual subscription. He also paid for each match he played; he bought drinks from the bar after games; he attended club social evenings and so on. The money raised for the club by these means is then used to pay its running expenses, improve its facilities and so ensure that members can play cricket.

You too may be a member of a club or association - many people are, although they may not realise it! A knowledge of the accounts of such organisations should therefore be of interest to you. Once people realise that you know a lot about keeping accounts you could well find yourself elected as treasurer! You will then have to account to your fellow members for the activities of the organisation and the work which you have carried out. By the end of this section you should able to undertake that work quite happily.

First of all we shall define exactly what a club is, consider how it is likely to be organised and the reasons why accounts need to be prepared. We shall then look in detail at the preparation of club accounts. This will use some of the techniques covered in the previous section but our main concern will be with presentation - ensuring that any club member could appreciate his club's financial position from the accounts prepared by you!

16.7 WHAT IS A CLUB?

It is an example of what is legally called an *unincorporated association*. This may be defined as two or more people who have joined together to pursue a matter of common interest with no profit-making motive.

Such organisations are very common and are usually identified by the use of 'club', 'society' or 'association' as part of their name. Examples range from specialist bodies such as building societies, the Football Association and the National Union of Students to the smaller ones like a village small business association, a school parent-teacher association and the local chess club. It is probable that the majority of adults are members of at least one unincorporated association.

The key element in the definition is the lack of a profit-making motive. These organisations exist not to make money for their members but to enable them to pursue or promote particular activities or interests. Raising money will be necessary but it is not the main aim.

Exercise 16.6

Tick the organisations in the following list which can be classed as unincorporated associations:

1 The Keep Fit Gym Club Ltd
2 Fenton Tennis Club
3 Bridge & Bridge Partners
4 The Social Democratic Party
5 John Booth & Associates
6 The Save our Fish Society

16.8 **WHY PREPARE CLUB ACCOUNTS?**

Let us consider Sherborne Cricket Club in more detail. As we have seen, all the members will provide money for the running of the club. Not all of these members will want to, or be able to, say how that money will be spent. They may be too busy with other activities; they may not be interested and so on. It would slow up decision-making if all the members had to be consulted on such day-to-day matters. This question of the financial and administrative part of the club's affairs is dealt with in the club's *constitution*.

A constitution is a set of rules which governs the operation of an association. It is usually designed by the founder members when an association is first formed and may be altered if an appropriate majority of the members agree.

In the case of Sherborne Cricket Club the constitutuion allows for the affairs of the club to be managed by a *committee* which is elected by the members of the club. The committee consists of officers, such as the chairman, secretary and treasurer (i.e. those who hold specific posts), and other ordinary committee members. At the end of each year the committee is required to hold an *annual general meeting* of all of the members of the club.

Activity

From your own experience or from the description of Sherborne Cricket Club, jot down a few brief ideas on the reasons for having an annual general meeting.

The main reasons we think are:

- Accountability – the committee members are required to account for their conduct of the club's affairs during the previous year.
- Involvement – it gives the other members an opportunity to review the operation of the club and make a contribution to its development.
- Future progress – it enables the members to elect the committee for the next year and to put forward ideas on the future of the club for that new committee to look into.

At the annual general meeting the treasurer will have to present to the members the accounts of the club for the previous financial year. This is required by the constitution of my cricket club and is normal for any association. There are two main reasons for this:

1 It is only right that the committee should show what funds have been raised for the club and the use it has made of those funds for the benefit of the members.
2 All the members of a club can be legally liable for any debts incurred by the committee on behalf of the club. So accounts are necessary to show the liabilities of the club and the assets available to meet them.

Exercise 16.7

Complete the blanks in the following sentences:

A ____________ is a set of ____________ which governs the operation of an association. It will usually allow a ____________ to be elected by all of the members of the club in order to ____________ its affairs. The treasurer will have to produce the ________________ of the club at an ________ ________ ____________.

16.9 **HOW WOULD YOU PREPARE THE ACCOUNTS?**

Say you are appointed the treasurer of a club. What do you have to do? It would be a good idea to check with your club's constitution and the previous treasurer, but normally the job will require two main tasks:

1 Recording all of the transactions of the club - the book-keeping.
2 Accounting to the club's members - preparing the accounts.

Let's look at each of these in detail.

1 *The book-keeping.* The key element here is to keep a cash book which records all of the club's cash and bank transactions. Ideally, the cash book will have analysis columns which will enable you to allocate income and expenses to appropriate headings such as subscriptions, bar takings, dance ticket sales etc. The procedures you should then follow would be:

   (a) At the end of each month balance the cash book and reconcile your figures with the bank statement and physical cash count.
   (b) Total your analysis columns for each month. Add those to the previous months figures so that you then have figures for the year so far. This will provide useful information for the committee at its regular meetings and will save you work at the end of the year when you come to prepare the accounts. This summary of the cash book is sometimes called a *receipts and payments account*.

2 *The final accounts.* As we have seen earlier, it is possible to produce a full set of accounts for an organisation from a cash book by making appropriate adjustments for such items as accruals, prepayments, fixed asset depreciation and so on.

How then will a set of accounts for a club differ from those for a business? Study the accounts for Sherborne Cricket Club given in Figure 16.1. I have tried to highlight the main differences by making notes which are explained below.

Note 1 As we have seen, a club is not primarily aiming to make a profit. The main revenue account is therefore called an income and expenditure account rather than a profit and loss account.

Note 2 A club will usually run various activities in order to raise finance for it. These activities are intended to be profit-making! It is usual to show either the profit or loss on these activities as one figure, rather than show the income on one side and the expenditure on the other and leave the members to work out the result.

Note 3 Many clubs will run a bar as a major source of income. Often a separate bar trading account will be prepared to take into account opening and closing stocks and allow for such costs as wages to stewards for running the bar.

Note 4 In the case of clubs, net profit is described as a surplus and a net loss as a deficit. This again reflects the fact the profit-making is not the main aim.

Note 5 The capital of a club is called a fund. The term accumulated fund recognises that this fund will be built up over the years as surpluses are made.

As we can see, the main differences are in terminology and in the presentation of information about the activities of the club. Before going into the mechanics of account preparation, try the following question:

Exercise 16.8

Match the items in the two lists given below:

Business terms	*Club terms*
(a) Profit and loss account	(i) Deficit
(b) Net loss	(ii) Accumulated fund
(c) Net profit	(iii) Income and expenditure account
(d) Capital	(iv) Surplus

Fig. 16.1 Sherborne Cricket Club

(Note 1) Income and expenditure account for the year ended 31 January

Expenditure		*Income*		
Payments to umpires	20	Subscriptions		228
Pavilion rent	75	Sale of sausages etc.		20
Pavilion expenses	201	Profit on discos (*Note 2*)		320
Ground and tea expenses	425	Profit on fork supper (*Note 2*)		24
Playing equipment	161	100 Club profit (*Note 2*)		234
Insurance, entry fees and subscriptions	107	Profit on race evening (*Note 2*)		750
Printing, postage, stationery and telephone	61	Match fees and teas		351
Sundry expenses	22	Building society interest		20
Stock of ties written off	15	Bank deposit interest		99
Depreciation of pavilion improvements	326	Profit on bar: (*Note 3*)		
Loss on dance (*Note 2*)	85	Sales	1,675	
Surplus for the year (*Note 4*)	903	Purchases	1,320	355
	£2,401			£2,401

Balance sheet as at 31 January

Fixed assets:		
Pavilion improvements at cost		1,631
Less Depreciation		326
		1,305
Current assets:		
Stock of cricket balls	77	
Debtors	407	
Premium bonds at cost	85	
Cash on bank deposit	659	
Cash at bank	50	
	1,278	
Current liabilities:		
Creditors	58	
		1,220
		£2,525
Accumulated fund (*Note 5*):		
Opening balance		1,622
Add Surplus for the year		903
		£2,525

16.10 SUBSCRIPTIONS

The amount of subscriptions which should be credited to the income and expenditure account in an accounting year can be a complex calculation, especially as practice and accounting theory tend to differ.

What is a subscription? It is an annual payment made by a member towards the running expenses of a club. The amount is usually fixed at the annual general meeting and will be payable by members early in the club's financial year.

To follow correct accounting principles then the income and expenditure account should be credited with the subscriptions due from the members for the accounting year. This may be analysed as:

Subscriptions paid in previous year for this year
+
Subscriptions paid this year for this year
+
Subscriptions for this year, not paid by year end

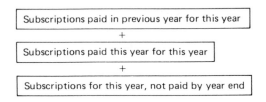

In practice, this last section would not normally be included. If a member has not paid a subscription by the year end then he would normally be excluded from the club and no money would be expected to be received. However, if you are answering exam questions you will be expected to include this as income and regard the amount involved as 'income due' - a current asset.

Exercise 16.9

The Trenthall Sports Club has fifty members. The annual subscription is £10 for 1989. During 1988, ten members pay their 1989 subscriptions and during 1989 £380 is received for subscriptions. Following normal accounting principles, how much should be credited to the 1989 income and expenditure account?

Tick the correct answer:

1 £380 3 £500
2 £480 4 £400

To complete this chapter we would now like you to tackle the following exercises. These will help you to assess your understanding and give you an opportunity to practise the preparation of accounts for clubs and societies.

Exercise 16.10

10.1 Define the term 'unincorporated association'.
10.2 Why should a club have a constitution? Briefly note the reasons.
10.3 The Coalite Rugby Club operates a bar. For the year ended 31 December, the treasurer was able to ascertain the following:

	£
Bar takings	15,000
Payments to suppliers for purchases	10,000
Opening creditors	1,000
Closing creditors	2,000
Opening stock	1,500
Closing stock	2,500
Payments to barman	3,000

Prepare the bar trading account for the year.
(Remember to use the techniques studied earlier in the chapter to arrive at your purchases figure.)

10.4 Subscriptions received in 1989 for 1990 should be treated as what in 1989's balance sheet?
10.5 The following information relates to the income and expenditure of a club:

1 Rent owing at the beginning of the year £18; paid during the year £80; owing at the end of the year £28.
2 Members' subscriptions overdue at the beginning of the year £120; received during the year £4,580; payments in advance included in receipts £40.
3 Rates prepaid at the beginning of the year £400; paid during the year £1,900 which includes £300 in respect of the following year.

Calculate the amounts which would be shown in the income and expenditure account for the year for rent, subscriptions income and rates.

10.6 The following information was extracted from the cash book and records of the Haven of Rest Social Club for the year ended 31 December:

Receipts and payments account

Balances at 1 January	765	Creditors for bar supplies	16,980
Subscriptions for the year	1,980	Costs of socials	720
Bar takings	22,970	Wages to steward	2,500
Receipts from socials	980	General expenses	1,760
		Repairs to premises	1,400
		Purchase of new furniture	1,900
		Balances at 31 December	1,435
	£26,695		£26,695

Balance sheet as at 1 January

Fixed assets:			
Buildings at valuation			15,000
Furniture at net book value			1,600
			16,600
Current assets:			
Bar stocks		920	
Bank		765	
		1,685	
Current liabilities:			
Creditors for bar supplies	1,300		
Subscriptions in advance	20	1,320	
			365
			£16,965
Accumulated fund:			£16,965

Depreciation of 10% is to be provided on the net book value of the old furniture and on the cost of the new purchases of furniture.

The bar stocks at 31 December are £960, when the creditors were owed £1,380 for bar supplies. Prepare the club's bar trading account and income and expenditure account for the year and a balance sheet as at 31 December.

We hope you managed all this without too much trouble, if so you should feel confident about taking on the role of a treasurer. To add the final touches to your appreciation of this topic it would be a help to you if you could try the following.

Activity

As with other topics, see if you can look at a real life example. If you belong to a club or know someone who would be prepared to help you, contact the treasurer. Ask him to show you the records he keeps and systems he uses to record the club's transactions. Look at a copy of the club's constitution and accounts to see the framework within which the club operates and the information presented to the members. Try and attend an annual general meeting - you never know, you might be elected as treasurer!

PART III

ACCOUNTING AND MANAGEMENT

CHAPTER 17

RATIO ANALYSIS

17.1 INTRODUCTION

It is time now to broaden our view of accounting. So far we have concentrated on the mechanics of accounting - the way in which accounts are prepared and presented. But consider the view taken by John Slater, managing director of Slater's Stores Ltd:

> I have to pay my accountant/auditor a large fee to prepare and approve my company's accounts. What a waste of money! I don't understand them, so the business doesn't benefit. The only people that do are the taxman and the VAT man! OK by law I have to prepare them for the shareholders, but they are me and my wife. The only other person who gets a copy is the Registrar of Companies, but I don't suppose he's interested.

It is vital that the information contained in accounts is *understood* and *used*. There is little point in preparing them otherwise. In this chapter we will consider the various groups of people who may want to use a company's accounts and the tools of analysis used to help them make sense of the figures in those accounts. This is a very important chapter in your studies as it begins to show how accounts are used in the business world and how it is possible to understand what they mean.

17.2 WHO USES ACCOUNTS?

Let's begin by using the quote from John Slater as a starting point. He has indicated some groups of people who could use accounts. Using these, and any others you can think of, try the following activity.

Activity – users and uses

Draw up a table listing the main groups of people who may be interested in the accounts of a limited company. For each group identify the main areas of the company's performance it would be interested in. Here is an example as a starting point:

Group	*Areas of interest*
Employees	Profitability – as a basis for wage bargaining; it also may be of interest for job security. Efficiency and productivity – the figures reflect employees' efforts. Liquidity – can the company meet its debts and therefore are our jobs secure?

Hopefully you have managed to list a good number of groups. Below I have indicated the main parties you could have mentioned. I have expanded on the areas of interest in order to help indicate some of the ways in which accounts are used in business:

Group	*Areas of interest*
Shareholders	Level of profits and dividend – has the company made sufficient profits to maintain or increase the dividend? Is the dividend a sufficient return for the shareholders' investment? Liquidity – has the company sufficient cash to pay the proposed dividend?
Management	Everything, because the accounts reflect the performance of the management during the year. Specifically, the accounts may highlight areas of weakness in the company which the management will need to tackle.
Inland Revenue and Customs and Excise	The accounts are used as the basis of tax assessment. Profitability is looked at carefully – are the profits reasonable given the nature of the business? Are all sales transactions being recorded?
Registrar of Companies	Do the accounts comply with the Companies Acts? They are then filed and are available for anyone to see them, e.g. journalists, credit agency, the police, an accountancy student etc.
Long-term lenders, e.g. banks, debenture holders	Accounts are often used to assess whether or not a loan should be given in the first place. They are then used to se see if the loan should be continued. Areas looked at are: Profitability – does the profit performance mean that the company will continue trading? Liquidity – does it have the cash to pay interest and make loan repayments? Assets – what assets are available as security for loans, debentures, overdrafts?

Trade and expense creditors	Liquidity - what current assets are available to meet current liabilities? What do the current assets consist of? Will they realise their balance sheet values?
Potential investors and their advisers	As for shareholders but with the question - is this company worth investing in?

You may well have thought of other groups and points - well done! But we can see from this that John Slater's main complaint is not really justified. Lots of people can benefit from the preparation of a company's accounts if they can understand them - including John as a manager and shareholder! We shall now move on to look at the problem of understanding.

17.3 HOW CAN YOU UNDERSTAND A COMPANY'S ACCOUNTS?

What is meant by the term 'understand' here? We feel that you should aim to be capable of analysing a set of accounts so that their significant features are apparent to you. In order to achieve this you need:

1 A knowledge of the terms used in the accounts - this you have already obtained from your studies so far.
2 An awareness of the key figures in the accounts. Again you will already have appreciated that figures such as sales, gross profit, net profit and capital are important.
3 An appreciation of the relationship between two figures in the accounts. For example a net profit of £1 million would be amazing for a small fish and chip shop but not very good for British Telecom! This analysis of the key relationships in a set of accounts is carried out through the calculation of *accounting ratios*.
4 The ability to assess whether a given ratio is good or bad. An aid to this is the use of comparisons. These may be of two types:
   (a) Internal - comparisons with previous results of the business or with expected results.
   (b) External - comparisons with other businesses, particularly those in similar types of business.
5 The ability to make reasonable deductions from the analysis carried out. This is achieved with practice and through a full understanding of the material involved in steps 1-4.

In the remainder of this chapter we shall look in detail at the way in which accounting ratios are calculated, the use of comparisons and the way in which deductions may be made. This would enable someone like John Slater to assess how well his company has done from the accounts he pays for!

17.4 WHAT ARE THESE ACCOUNTING RATIOS?

They are figures which express the key relationships in a set of accounts by comparing one figure with another. We shall now see the way in which the main ratios are calculated, what they are attempting to demonstrate and how they can be assessed. This should provide you with the basic tools to interpret a set of accounts.

For ease of reference the ratios are often split into categories covering the main features of interest. They are given in Figure 17.1 together with the method of calculation. Below, we comment on these ratios and their purpose and assessment.

Fig. 17.1 Table of ratios

Ratio	*Method of calculation*
Overall performance	
1. Return on capital employed (%)	$\frac{\text{Net profit before tax and interest}}{\text{Capital employed}} \times 100$
2. Return on owners' equity (%)	$\frac{\text{Net profit after tax}}{\text{Owners' equity}} \times 100$
Profitability	
3. (a) Gross profit margin (%)	$\frac{\text{Gross profit}}{\text{Sales}} \times 100$
(b) Mark-up on cost (%)	$\frac{\text{Gross profit}}{\text{Cost of goods sold}} \times 100$
4. Net profit margin (%)	$\frac{\text{Net profit}}{\text{sales}} \times 100$
Productivity	
5. Sales per employee (£)	$\frac{\text{Sales}}{\text{Number of employees}}$
6. Asset turnover (times)	$\frac{\text{Sales}}{\text{Total assets} - \text{Current liabilities}}$
7. Stock turnover (times)	$\frac{\text{Cost of goods sold}}{\text{Average stock}}$
8. (a) Debtor turnover (times)	$\frac{\text{Sales}}{\text{Debtors}}$
(b) Debtor collection period (days)	$\frac{\text{Debtors}}{\text{Average sales per day}}$
Liquidity	
9. Current ratio	Current assets: Current liabilities
10. Acid test or liquid ratio	Current assets–Stock: Current liabilities

Investment

11. Dividend yield (%) $\dfrac{\text{Gross dividend per share}}{\text{Market price per share}} \times 100$

Capital structure

12. Gearing ratio (%) $\dfrac{\text{Long-term loans}}{\text{Capital employed}} \times 100$

13. Interest cover (times) $\dfrac{\text{Profit before interest charge}}{\text{Interest charged}}$

17.5 OVERALL PERFORMANCE RATIO

1 *Return on capital employed (ROCE).* This is the key ratio as it relates the profit earned to the amount of long-term capital invested in the business. Capital employed in this calculation means owners' capital plus any long-term liabilities. This is the finance for total assets - current liabilities.
2 *Return on owners' equity.* This gives the actual return to the shareholders only, as the payment of interest to long-term lenders has been deducted.

What should these ratios be? It is difficult to give a set figure but they could be related to the possible returns from investment with a bank or building society. Given that business is riskier then desirable ratios should be a little higher.

Here are some example ROCE figures for well known companies in different types of business:

			YEAR		
Company	*1*	*2*	*3*	*4*	*5*
British Petroleum	13.8	15.3	33.3	28.7	19.4
Tesco Stores	34.7	21.3	20.9	20.2	21.6
Scottish & Newcastle Breweries	15.6	13.9	13.2	15.0	13.0

Exercise 17.1

Which of these three companies has had the most consistently high performance?

A relatively low ROCE will indicate that there are weaknesses in either the profitability or productivity of the business. These can be assessed by using further ratios.

17.6 **PROFITABILITY RATIOS**

Here you are assessing the amount of profit that has been or can be made on sales. The other factor in determining overall profit will be the volume of sales - the productivity of the business.

3 *Gross profit margin/mark-up*. These ratios are used to analyse the trading profitability of the business. They are very similar ratios which express the cost + gross profit = sales relationship in different ways.

Acceptable gross profit percentages vary from one type of business to another as can be seen from the survey examples given in Figure 17.2.

As the ratios are based on the cost of goods, labour intensive businesses such as plumbers and driving instructors will have much higher gross profit margins.

A fall below expectations may be the result of a number of factors such as:

- reduction in selling prices
- poor buying
- poor stock control

All these are areas which the management could look into in order to improve the performance of the business.

Fig. 17.2 Profit margin survey

Cash trade classification	*Mark-up on cost (%)*	*Gross profit on sales (%)*
Antique dealer	51	34
Bakers	54	35
Builders' merchants	27	21
Builders and decorators	43	30
Butchers	27	21
Coal merchants	33	25
Confectioners and tobacconists	19	16
Chemists	39	27
Cycle and motorcycle dealers	37	27
Dentists	59	37
Driving instructors	100	50
Fish and chip shops	72	42
Florists	64	39
Footwear retailers	41	32
Grocers	16	14
Greengrocers	27	21
Jobbing plumbers	203	67
Milk retailers	31	24
Off licences	33	25
Opticians	35	26
Public houses	45	31
Restaurants	100	50
Radio and electrical retailers	49	33

Exercise 17.2

A business finds that its gross profit percentage has fallen from 25% to 22% in the current year. Tick which of the following factors might have accounted for the decrease:

(a) fewer items had been purchased during the year
(b) selling prices were reduced during the year
(c) pilferage of stock was high
(d) fewer items were sold during the year
(e) increased costs of purchases which were not passed on in selling prices.

4 *Net profit margin*. This measures the final profit made on sales after all of the running expenses have been deducted from the gross profit. If this percentage has fallen whilst the gross profit margin has remained constant then increases in running costs should be investigated and efforts made to reduce them.

17.7 **PRODUCTIVITY RATIOS**

This is the other factor which determines overall profit. It can be regarded as the level of sales obtained from the assets employed by the business - obviously the higher this is the better from the viewpoint of the business.

5 *Sales per employee*. This is used to measure the productivity of the employee of the business. The effective use of labour is one of the key tasks of the management of a business so this is an important ratio. It is also relevant to employees as it does reflect their efforts during the accounting period. The Business Section of the *Observer* newspaper reports periodically on productivity in Britain's major companies using this ratio amongst others.

6 *Asset turnover*. This expresses the number of times the value of assets utilised by the business have been covered by sales.

7 *Stock turnover*. This is an important measure of the effective use of stock by the business. The adequacy of the ratio will depend upon the type of industry. For example, a supermarket is likely to turn over or sell its stock much more quickly than an engineering company carrying

a wide range of components. If the turnover is declining then the reasons should be investigated. Possible factors would include:

- a large amount of slow-moving or obsolete stock
- higher levels of stocks being held
- lack of control over purchasing
- a wider range of products being stocked

Note that the average stock is usually calculated as the total of the opening stock plus the closing stock divided by two.

8 *Debtor turnover/debtor collection period.* These ratios assess the speed with which a business collects amounts owing from customers. The higher the turnover rate or the lower the collection period the more effective is this control of credit. The average day's sales is usually calculated by dividing sales by 365, the number of days in the year. Most firms operate on a normal credit period to customers of thirty days. An acceptable debtor collection period might therefore be something like fifty days. Very high collection periods would indicate that the credit control system needs to be improved and that either incentives should be given to customers or effective sanctions applied against slow payers.

Exercise 17.3

Which of the following ratios represents an improvement in the productivity of a business in the second year?

Tick the ratios which do.

	1st year	*2nd year*
(a) Sales per employee	£3,500	£5,000
(b) Asset turnover	4 times	3.9 times
(c) Stock turnover	12 times	13.2 times
(d) Debtor collection period	64 days	62 days

17.8 **LIQUIDITY RATIOS**

A business must be able to pay its debts. The two ratios given measure its ability to do so from its current resources.

9 *Current ratio.* This compares all current assets with current liabilities and indicates the ease with which, given time, a business will be able to meet its debts. As a guide, most businesses will require a ratio of 1.8:1. Too high a ratio would suggest too much money tied up in current assets; whilst too low a ratio could be dangerous if the creditors press for a quick payment.

10 *Acid test ratio.* This takes a tougher view as it excludes stock from current assets. This is done because in some businesses it can take a long time to turn stock into cash. As it is rare for creditors to all ask

for payment at once, time is allowed for money to be obtained from debtors. A reasonable level of cover would be about 0.8:1.

17.9 **INVESTMENT RATIO**

The shareholder or prospective investor will be very interested in the return he is obtaining from his purchase of shares in a business. This is calculated by:

11 *Dividend yield.* This relates the income from shares, the dividend, to the value of the investment in the business. Consequently, the result can be compared with interest rates from other types of investment. Another factor which would also be considered would be any increase in share price as this represents a capital gain to the shareholder. You will find dividend yield figures quoted along with share prices in the business section of any quality daily paper.

17.10 **CAPITAL STRUCTURE RATIOS**

The long-term finance of a business will be provided by its shareholders and long-term lenders:

12 *Gearing ratio.* This is an assessment of the extent to which a firm is financed by long-term loans. It is a very important ratio for prospective lenders as many like to see the owners/shareholders providing at least half the overall capital of a business. They may not be prepared to lend if further lending would push the gearing ratio too high.

13 *Interest cover.* An important factor affecting lending decisions is the ability of a business to satisfactorily meet its interest payments. If the gearing ratio is very high, a business will have large interest costs to meet out of its profits. Interest cover ratio indicates the level of cover which the business has achieved.

If the gearing ratio becomes too high or if interest rates rise and the interest cover reduces, the business must look at ways to improve the situation. Two of the methods used are:

- to raise more shareholders' funds by issuing shares and perhaps using some of this cash to repay loans.
- selling fixed assets and using the proceeds to repay loans.

That completes our review of accounting ratios. Remember that not all of these ratios would be used by everyone examining a set of accounts. A particular interest group will be most concerned with specific aspects of the accounts and will therefore use the ratios relevant to those aspects.

Try the following:

Exercise 17.4

A bank manager has been asked to lend money to a small company. Which of the following ratios would he use *first* in examining the company's accounts?

1 Return on capital employed
2 Sales per employee
3 Gearing ratio
4 Net profit margin

Exercise 17.5 – Slater's Stores Ltd

We must now have a look at the actual calculation of the ratios and start to see the way in which they can be interpreted. To do this we shall analyse the accounts of Slater's Stores Ltd, given in Figure 17.3, from the viewpoint of John Slater as managing director.

Fig. 17.3 Slater's Stores Ltd

Trading and profit and loss accounts for the year ended 31 December

			(000's)	
		1988		*1989*
Sales		600		800
Opening stock	50		60	
Add Purchases	430		600	
	480		660	
Less Closing stock	60		80	
Cost of goods sold		420		580
Gross profit		180		220
Less Running expenses		100		140
Net profit before interest and tax		80		80
Less Interest		8		16
Profit before tax		72		64
Less Tax		30		41
		42		23
Less Dividends (10p per share)		2	(15p per share)	3
Retained profit for the year		£40		£20

Balance sheets as at 31 December

	1988		*1989*	
Fixed assets		140		250
Current assets:				
Stocks	60		80	
Debtors	2		4	
Bank and cash	38		36	
	100		120	
Current liabilities	40		70	
Working capital		60		50
Net assets employed		£200		£300
Share capital:				
Ordinary shares		20		20
Reserves:				
Profit and loss account		100		120
		120		140
10% Debentures		80		160
Net capital employed		£200		£300

Number of employees: 1988 20; 1989 25. There is no market price for the shares – use the nominal value of £1.

5.1 The first step in the analysis of these accounts is the number-crunching! Try calculating the ratios for yourself first and then check your results with ours.

A calculator is a great help in this type of exercise!

5.2 What can we now deduce from these ratios, the accounts and the knowledge that this business is a chain of general stores? Study the figures yourself and jot down brief notes explaining the points you would make to John Slater.

You can see from the answers how very useful accounting ratios are in helping anyone to understand the accounts of a business. Even they, however, are of little use in isolation. Comparisons are needed.

17.11 WHY HAVE INTERNAL COMPARISONS?

Desirable ratios will differ depending on the nature of the business being assessed. For example, newsagents will have a much higher rate of stock turnover than an aeroplane manufacturer. Consequently an internal comparison which monitors ratios in the same business on a regular basis is one of the best ways of understanding the performance of that business. Any changes in the trend of results can be spotted and corrective action taken if required.

Some firms may also use ratios as *targets*. For example, a business may want to increase its stock turnover rate and might therefore introduce controls over buying in order to reduce stock levels. The actual ratio will then be compared with the target to see if it has been achieved through that course of action.

17.12 WHAT ABOUT EXTERNAL COMPARISONS?

A weakness of internal comparisons is that they do not show what it is possible for a particular type of business to achieve. A comparison with similar firms or competitors can show that, as well as highlighting where specific improvements might be made.

A number of industry-based schemes provide this type of information. The most significant schemes are run by the Centre for Interfirm Comparison which provides data for over 100 sectors of activity - ranging from book publishers to mechanical engineering to residential homes for the elderly. It is possible through this system to provide confidential information about the detailed operation of your business and to be able to compare it with very detailed ratios from similar firms. The data is all collected in a standard manner and the analysis can contain 60–100 ratios for each business. All this work is computerised needless to say!

17.13 WHAT ARE THE LIMITATIONS OF THESE RATIOS?

Whilst they are valuable in assessing a company's performance, they do have limitations which should be recognised:

- They will help to identify strengths and weaknesses in a business but will not necessarily provide answers. For example, a low rate of stock turnover may be identified but the reasons for it will not.
- They must be related to the particular activities and circumstances of the business. This is why internal analysis of accounts using 'inside' knowledge is very valuable.
- Comparisons must be used as much as possible to help in the correct interpretation of them.
- The source from which the ratios were calculated must be considered. If you have used an old balance sheet then the results will obviously be outdated.

17.14 CONCLUSION

Whilst these limitations should be borne in mind, I hope this chapter has shown you the way in which ratios can be used to help you understand a company's accounts. As we have seen, lots of different people will want to use accounting information. The ratios provide the tools which help them to do this. In the next chapter we shall see the benefits which can be obtained from comparing the ratios of your business with those of a similar one. But before that, ensure that you have a good grasp of all the material in this chapter by tackling the following:

Exercise 17.6

6.1 Briefly explain why a trade creditor might be interested in examining a company's accounts. What ratios would he use to assess the information relevant to him?

6.2 Why are ratios needed to help understand a company's accounts?

6.3 The chairman of Rising Stores Ltd claimed in his report on the company's latest accounts 'a greatly improved current ratio'. The balance sheets at 31 March 1988 and 1989 showed the following:

Current assets	*1988*	*1989*
Stocks	32,000	75,000
Debtors	41,000	106,000
Bank	—	54,000
Current liabilities		
Creditors	29,000	45,000
Bank overdraft	4,000	—

Calculate the relevant ratio(s) and comment briefly on the chairman's claim.

6.4 Computer Services Ltd was formed in 1985 to manufacture and sell a small business computer. Until 1988 the company expanded very rapidly and was very successful. However in 1989 the combined impact of technical change and very heavy competition from the market leaders resulted in a slow down in the company's rate of growth and severe financial problems. The company's main ratios from 1985 to 1989 were as follows:

	1985	*1986*	*1987*	*1988*	*1989*
ROCE (%)	55.5	50	53	58	5
Gross profit margin (%)	50	50	50	40	30
Net profit margin (%)	10	9	8	7	0.3
Stock turnover (times)	20	20	20	20	18
Debtor collection period (days)	37	36	36	36	40
Current ratio (:1)	5.1	4.8	2.6	2.7	1.4
Acid test ratio (:1)	3.9	3.5	1.7	1.9	0.9

From the above information identify the main features of the company's performance over this period with particular reference to 1989.

CHAPTER 18

CASH FLOW

18.1 MATHER MACHINES LTD

'These should keep you happy. You've made a good profit over the past year.' Chris Tompkins, auditor of Mather Machines Ltd had just given a set of the company's finalised accounts to Mike Mather, managing director.

'That's true,' said Mike, 'but tell me, why then is my bank manager always on the phone going on about my bank balance and cash flow and things like that? Surely, if the company makes a good profit then there won't be any problems with the bank.'

'Not necessarily,' said Chris, 'there are many businesses which have been profitable, have expanded rapidly and then suddenly gone into liquidation because of the lack of cash.'

Chris has highlighted a problem which anyone involved with business must appreciate - the difference between being profitable and having cash. In this chapter we shall look at the whole question of cash flow. We shall see how a company's balance sheets can be used to prepare cash flow statements and consider some of the techniques which businesses can use to improve their cash flow. This is a very important chapter because of the emphasis on cash flow and cash control in modern business. A firm can continue for a time when it is making losses but if it has not got the cash to pay its suppliers or its employees' wages it won't last for long! A major factor leading to the downfall of many businesses, especially smaller businesses, has been poor control of cash because people have relied on the belief that profit always equals cash.

18.2 HOW TO MAKE A PROFIT BUT HAVE NO CASH!

Let's consider a simple case where Tony Parrott decides to set himself up in business as a hardware supplies wholesaler. He buys a range of stock from various manufacturers and has to pay cash for it as he is new to the trade. His sales will have to be on one month's credit if he is to compete successfully with other wholesalers. When he begins selling he has £10,000 worth of stock and nothing in the bank, having spent all the capital he is able to invest.

On the first day of selling, he makes the following two transactions:

1 He sells a bathroom suite (cost £1,000) for £1,800.
2 He sells some guttering (cost £100) for £200.

Exercise 18.1

1.1 What is Tony's profit at the end of the day?
1.2 What is his bank balance at the end of the day?

On the second day, Tony wants to replace the items he has sold and pays £1,000 for a bathroom suite and £100 for more guttering. He also sells some kitchen units (cost £500) for £800.

Exercise 18.2

2.1 What is his profit for transactions in day two?
2.2 What is his bank balance at the end of the day?

If we summarise the effects of Tony's trading we can see that he has been very profitable - £1,200 in two days' can't be bad! However, he hasn't any cash - his bank balance has gone from £0 to £1,100 overdrawn. His business is only able to survive because his bank manager is willing to allow him to have an overdraft. He has made a profit but he doesn't have any cash! Of course, Tony should ultimately receive the money from the sales made and his bank balance will then improve. But this distinction between profit and cash is important as a short-term influence on the cash flow of a business.

18.3 **WHAT DOES THE TERM 'CASH FLOW' MEAN?**

The term tries to summarise the effects of all of the inflows and outflows of cash which a business has. A business will have various sources of cash and will use that money in various ways, e.g. on running expenses, buying machinery and vehicles and purchasing stock. If more cash is used in a given period than comes in, then the business might be said to have a poor cash flow. This will be reflected in the business's cash balance, i.e. the money it actually holds in cash and has in its bank account - a poor cash flow will result in a fall in the cash balance.

What then are these sources of cash and uses of cash within a business?

Activity

Let's first of all put this into a personal context and consider your personal finances (or if you are too young to have much money, those of your parents). Make a brief list of where you obtain money from and what you use it for (use major headings for expenses - not too much detail is needed).

Considering our own circumstances, we were able to make the following list:

Sources of cash - Salary from job.
- Mortgage from building society for the purchase of a house.
- Income from writing this book (!)

Uses of cash - Living expenses of house and family, e.g. food, gas, electricity, clothes, holidays, entertainment etc.
- Mortgage repayments to building society.
- Purchase of a car.
- Savings in a building society.

Your affairs may be simpler or more complex but doubtless you will have included some of these items. Now let us transfer these ideas to the affairs of a limited company.

Activity

First, let us take sources of cash - in what ways could a limited company get more cash? Think about the various transactions which a business makes and list as many sources as you can.

Our list is as follows:

1 *Share capital*. The original cash for the company will come from the issue of shares; more shares could be issued to raise more money.
2 *Borrowing money*. Cash could be obtained in the form of loans, debentures, mortgages etc.
3 *Trading profit*. Cash will be generated from trading as the excess of cash received from sales over cash paid out on the expenses of operating the business. This is a very important source. The healthy company should be able to generate sufficient cash from trading to cover the majority of its uses - it would then be regarded as a company with a good cash flow.
4 *Proceeds from the sale of fixed assets*. Whilst not frequent transactions these can be major cash inflows. For example, in one year Tesco Stores raised cash of £46.4 million through the sale of properties, in the same period generating £67.2 million from trading.
5 *Decreases in current assets*. A company's cash balance can be improved by reducing the amount of money which is tied up in other current assets. So by reducing stock levels i.e. not replacing stock when it is sold, or by reducing the level of debtors (e.g. chasing them more vigorously for payment), the cash balance will increase whilst these other current assets will fall.

6 *Increases in current liabilities*. Here, for example, you might delay the payment of creditors and so retain cash in the business for a longer period. For example, if you owed trade creditors £10,000 at the start of the year, bought goods to the value of £60,000 during the year, and owed £15,000 at the end of the year, your cash balance would have benefited by £5,000. You have only paid £55,000 for goods purchased of £60,000.

We hope you managed to get a good number of these items. If we now consider the uses or applications of cash, then the list is fairly straightforward as most of them will be the opposite to the sources.

Activity

Make a brief list of the uses of cash by a typical company.

Here we would include:

1 The repayment of borrowings - that is, the loan itself; the payment of interest is a running expense of the business.
2 Trading losses - where cash paid for expenses is greater than the income from sales.
3 The purchase of fixed assets.
4 Increases in current assets e.g. investing more in stock.
5 Decreases in current liabilities.

Before we go on to summarise the cash flow of a business, try the following exercise on the component parts which we've looked at here.

Exercise 18.3

Mark each of the following items with an S if you think it is a source of cash or an A if you think it is an application.

1 The purchase of a milling machine by a manufacturer.
2 The receipt of a loan from a bank.
3 An increase in debtors.
4 An increase in creditors.
5 An issue of shares.

Just to summarise this examination of cash flow we shall look at it in diagrammatic form (refer to Figure 18.1). The top part of the diagram contains the more constant sources and applications of cash. The lower section describes the flow of cash around the trading cycle of a business, whereby money will be paid to creditors for stock or stock may be bought and sold for cash. Expenses will be incurred in the course of trading which must be covered by sales income. Therefore the money which is received from debtors must be greater than that spent in buying stock and paying

Fig. 18.1 The cash flow of a business

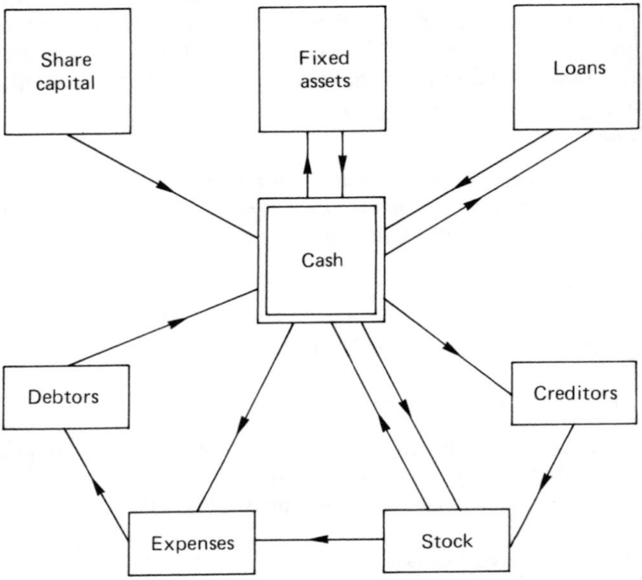

for expenses. All of this is what is covered by the term cash flow - the overall effect of the various sources and applications of cash on the cash balance of a business.

18.4 HOW CAN YOU MEASURE THE CASH FLOW OF A BUSINESS?

The cash flow of a business can be measured over any period by comparing the balance sheet at the start of a period with that at the end.

From that comparison can be seen:

1 The sources of cash of the business during the period.
2 The application of cash.
3 The overall effect on the cash balance.

This is usually shown in the form of a cash flow statement which gives a picture of the liquidity of a business and often highlights areas of strength and weakness in the management of its funds.

18.5 HOW IS A CASH FLOW STATEMENT PREPARED?

Let us look at a simple example using the last two balance sheets of Mather Machines Ltd, given in Figure 18.2. We might be able to see why his bank manager was worried! The approach to use is as follows:

Step 1 List the two balance sheets side-by-side in vertical form.
Step 2 Calculate the difference for each item in the balance sheet. These two steps have been illustrated in Figure 18.2.

Fig. 18.2 Mather Machines Ltd

Balance sheets as at 31 December

	Year 1	*Year 2*	*Movement*
Fixed assets	43,000	80,000	37,000 (A)
Current assets			
Stock	11,000	17,000	6,000 (A)
Debtors	9,000	15,000	6,000 (A)
Cash at bank	4,000	—	4,000*
	£67,000	£112,000	
Share capital	30,000	30,000	—
Reserves	30,000	40,000	10,000 (S)
Loan	—	25,000	25,000 (S)
Current liabilities			
Creditors	7,000	11,000	4,000 (S)
Bank overdraft		6,000	6,000*
	£67,000	£112,000	

Step 3 Calculate the overall movement in the bank and cash balances. In this case there was an opening bank balance of £4,000 and a closing overdraft of £6,000. Therefore the cash flow of the business has been £10,000 negative in the course of the period.
Step 4 Identify the movement on each balance sheet item as either a source (S) or an application (A) of funds. Again this is illustrated in Figure 18.2. Note that the bank/cash figures are not included as they are what you are reconciling to.
Step 5 Prepare the cash flow statement as in Figure 18.3. This will merely contain a list of the sources and applications identified in *Step 4*. It is usual to begin the sources with the cash generated through trading because, as mentioned earlier, it should be the most important source of funds to the business. In this case the total sources are £39,000 and the total applications £49,000 so that there is a decrease in cash of £10,000 which agrees, as it should with our answer in *Step 3*.

Fig. 18.3 Mather Machines Ltd

Cash flow statement for year ended 31 December

Sources of cash		
Cash from trading		10,000
Loan		25,000
Increase in creditors		4,000
		39,000
Applications of cash		
Purchase of fixed assets	37,000	
Increase in stock	6,000	
Increase in debtors	6,000	49,000
Decrease in cash		£10,000

Try the following exercise before we go on to discuss the significance of these cash flow statements.

Exercise 18.4

From the following two balance sheets, prepare a cash flow statement using the method outlined above:

Balance sheets as at 31 December

	Year 1	*Year 2*
Fixed assets	55,000	70,000
Current assets		
Stock	30,000	40,000
Debtors	15,000	30,000
Bank	1,000	6,000
	£101,000	£146,000
Share capital	40,000	60,000
Reserves	45,000	52,000
Loan	—	20,000
Creditors	16,000	14,000
	£101,000	£146,000

18.6 WHAT DOES THE CASH FLOW STATEMENT SHOW MIKE MATHER?

It should at least give him some idea why his bank manager is worried! The statement in Figure 18.3 shows that his business has been profitable but its liquidity has worsened over the year by £10,000. The major reason for this has been the money he has spent on fixed assets. Whilst this has been partly financed by the loan he has raised, it has also taken up all of the cash from trading. He has also allowed more money to be invested in stock and permitted debtors to take more credit.

This is the main purpose of the cash flow statement - to concentrate on the liquidity of the business and show how its funds are being managed. This is now considered so important that all companies with sales of over £25,000 per annum are required to produce a similar statement, called a Sources and Applications of Funds Statement, with their annual accounts.

18.7 HOW COULD MIKE MATHER IMPROVE HIS COMPANY'S CASH FLOW?

The basic principle must be to increase the sources and reduce the applications of cash as far as possible. Try the following to see if you are thinking along the right lines.

Exercise 18.5

Indicate whether each of the following items would improve the immediate cash flow of Mather Machines Ltd. Tick *Yes* or *No:*

	Yes	*No*
1 Issue more shares or debentures		
2 Decrease the level of debtors		
3 Hold more stocks of finished machines		
4 Pay key suppliers more quickly		
5 Increase the selling prices of finished machines		
6 Buy fewer assets		
7 Sell and lease back the factory		

In this chapter we have looked at the very important topic of cash flow. It is a term frequently used in the press when discussing the performance of companies. I hope you now feel that you have a good understanding of it. To consolidate your learning try these:

Exercise 18.6

6.1 Explain why a business trading on credit may make a profit on a sale without receiving any cash.

6.2 Draw a diagram to illustrate cash flow in a business.

6.3 Prepare a cash flow statement from the balance sheets in Figure 18.6 and comment briefly on what the statement shows you.

Fig. 18.6 Balance sheets as at 31 March

	Year 1	*Year 2*
Fixed assets	20,000	38,000
Current assets		
Stock	16,000	28,000
Debtors	12,000	20,000
Bank	6,000	—
	£54,000	£86,000
Share capital	10,000	30,000
Reserves	4,000	14,000
10% Debentures	22,000	13,000
Current liabilities		
Creditors	18,000	27,000
Bank overdraft	—	2,000
	£54,000	£86,000

6.4 Tom Race runs a small hardware shop in which he sells a massive range of small items. He is well known in the market town where his business is situated for stocking items which cannot be found in the main 'do-it-yourself' stores. He has however experienced a drop in sales because of a general fall in people's spending and is nearing his overdraft limit. The vast majority of the capital of the business is invested in his stocks. What would you advise him to do to ease his cash flow difficulties?

Finally, to investigate this area in more detail and more practically, you might like to try the following:

Activities

1 Have a look at the Sources and Applications of Funds Statements in the published accounts of various businesses (you should have the accounts available from the activities in Chapters 13 and 14). Reading these in conjunction with the rest of the accounts should give you a picture of the major sources and uses of cash of different types of business.
2 Try and discuss the question of cash flow with someone involved in it, either in your own business or one you know of. You could learn a lot about the techniques used to control cash in the day-to-day running of a business.
3 Why not try and apply some of these ideas to your own personal finances?

CHAPTER 19

ABSORPTION AND MARGINAL COSTING

19.1 THE PRESENTATION

The research and development and marketing departments of Sportstuffs Ltd had made their presentation of a new product idea to the managing director, Chris Disley.

The company specialised in sports shoes and had captured a sizeable share of the British market in squash and tennis shoes. The marketing people said that they now wanted to get into the rapidly expanding, but competitive, market in running shoes. This idea had been investigated by the research and development staff who had come up with a production model which has the required qualities of shock absorption, flexibility, lightness and wear. It was also attractively designed to appeal to the jogger or even to the non-runner who wanted a striking pair of casual shoes. The suggested name for the shoe was the 'Marafun' shoe – an attempt to cover both the serious runner and the jogger or casual wearer. The target price was in the region of £18 to £25.

Chris Disley was impressed by the basic idea. He was aware of the interest in jogging and running and agreed that there was a market in which Sportstuffs Ltd should have an interest. However, nothing had been said in the presentation about finance, apart from the projected selling price. It was time for some questions . . .

Activity

If you were Chris Disley, what questions would you ask about the financial aspects of this idea? Jot down your main questions.

The main questions you might ask could include:

- How many pairs are expected to be produced and sold?
- Could production be met using existing capacity or would other lines have to be reduced or would more capacity have to be bought, i.e. money spent on new machinery, more employees, more factory space etc?

- How much would each pair cost to produce and what would the profit per unit be? Is this profit adequate and how does it compare with the profit on other lines?
- How much would need to be spent on advertising and promotions? Launching a new product into a new market is always expensive.

These are typical of the questions that would be asked; you may have thought of many others. Certainly before Chris Disley could make an informed decision about this product idea he would need to have those questions answered. The answers could only come from a detailed study of expected costs of various kinds and from estimates of future sales.

There are many special situations in which managers in business have to make decisions. For example:

- setting wage and salary levels
- opening or closing departments, factories, retail stores etc.
- deciding where costs can be cut
- introducing computers into the accounting system

All of these decisions have financial implications which should be assessed before the decision is made.

On a more routine basis managers need information on what has happened in the area they are responsible for, so that they can control the work of their area and plan to improve performance. At the very least they need information on the costs of:

- The different goods they produce and sell.
- Each department or activity in the business for which they are responsible.

So Chris Disley could rightly ask 'How much will this product cost?' and expect an answer before giving the go-ahead to produce and market the shoe.

Activity

Could the financial accounts that we have looked at so far give him the answer? Think about the different types of accounting we have considered so far and briefly jot down your answer and reasons for it.

Your answer should be no. We saw in the chapter on departmental accounts that it is possible to analyse costs to ascertain the costs of running a particular department. We also saw in looking at manufacturing accounts that details can be obtained on the different types of cost incurred by a business. But the financial accounts will not tell you the likely cost of producing one pair of shoes. This is because the financial accounts:

- record what has happened not what may happen
- record transactions for the business as a whole or a department not for an individual product.

- are not usually prepared more frequently than monthly. Information for control and decision-making may be needed much more frequently, even daily.

In this chapter we shall move into the field of cost and management accounting. This is that part of accounting work which tries to provide the detailed information managers need, in the form in which they want it. In particular we shall concentrate on the way in which the cost of producing and selling a product is arrived at. By the end of the chapter you should be able to produce a cost statement for a given product and will know how firms operate product costing systems. We shall be using definitions and terms which we first used when preparing manufacturing accounts - there we were assembling the costs of all of the firm's production, now we will be working out the cost of one pair of shoes. We shall also be looking at the use of costings in management decision-making.

Let's first of all revise some of the definitions we used in manufacturing accounts. Figure 19.1 is a diagram showing the main categories of cost incurred by a manufacturing company.

Fig. 19.1

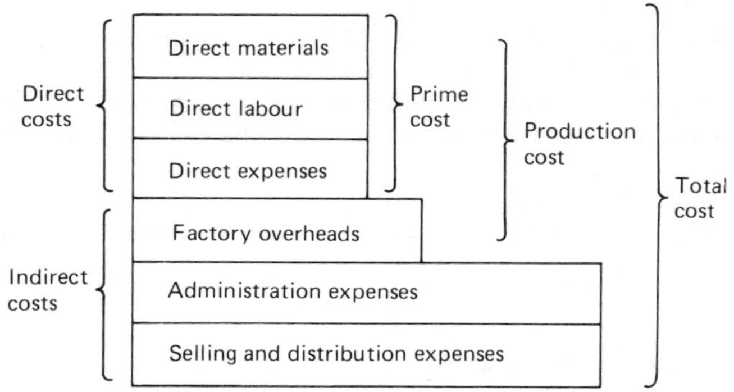

Exercise 19.1

Define the following terms by completing the blanks in the sentences below:

Direct materials are those materials __________ in the __________ product.
Direct labour costs are the wages paid to those who actually __________ the finished product.
Direct expenses are those incurrred __________________ for a particular unit of product.
Factory overheads are all those costs incurred in the __________ function of the business but are not directly traceable to a particular finished product.

If you had trouble with these definitions refer to Chapter 14 on manufacturing accounts.

19.2 HOW CAN YOU FIND THE DIRECT COSTS OF A PAIR OF SHOES?

The methods used to obtain costs depend on whether a product is new or is already being produced. If items are in production then you can calculate costs from actual transactions which are taking place. If a product is new, then estimates will need to be made. Let's look at possible approaches for material, labour and expenses in turn.

19.2.1 Direct materials

Here you want to get the amount of materials which have been or will be used in making the finished product. If the shoes were in production, materials would have to be purchased, e.g. nylon for the shoe uppers, foam for the cushioning, rubber for the sole etc. These materials would then be held in stock until they were needed for production when they would be issued from the stores. This process and the documents usually involved are shown in Figure 19.2.

So in a well-organised firm with good systems the quantity of materials used to produce a certain number of units would be obtained from the *materials requisition notes*. By consulting the *stock records* and the *purchase invoices* it is then possible to calculate the cost of those materials used.

If the items are not in production or if you are preparing estimates, then other methods will have to be used. If we take the shoes as an example,

Fig. 19.2

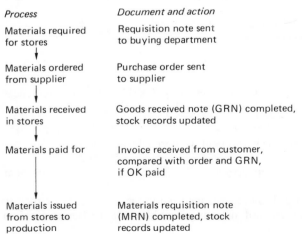

Process	*Document and action*
Materials required for stores ↓	Requisition note sent to buying department
Materials ordered from supplier ↓	Purchase order sent to supplier
Materials received in stores ↓	Goods received note (GRN) completed, stock records updated
Materials paid for ↓	Invoice received from customer, compared with order and GRN, if OK paid
Materials issued from stores to production	Materials requisition note (MRN) completed, stock records updated

the research and development department will have prepared some drawings of the shoes and a detailed technical specification of the quality and quantity of the materials to be used. By contacting suppliers for quotations of prices and allowing for wastage in production, it would be possible to make a sound assessment of the materials cost. Common sense is the key in carrying out such calculations!

19.2.2 **Direct labour**

This cost is obviously the time spent by the production staff actually making the shoes multiplied by their wage rates. If the shoes are in production it is possible to ascertain the time taken in two ways:

1 By allocating a job number to each pair of shoes produced and requiring the production staff to write on a job card the time which they spend on that particular job. This is a commonly used system but it does rely on the accuracy of the staff when booking their time.
2 By observation (known as time study). Here a person would be asked to time the production of a pair of shoes using a stopwatch. By carrying out this exercise a number of times, a sound assessment of the time to be taken can be obtained (though you must be aware that people tend to work a little more slowly when they know they are being observed for time study purposes!).

If the shoes are not in production then estimates would have to be used. Here it would be sensible to consult those with considerable production experience and ask them to estimate the time to be allocated for each operation and so arrive at a total time for the job.

19.2.3 **Direct expenses**

These are items such as royalties, payable at a specific cost per unit. Consequently, it is usually easy to obtain this cost from invoices or contracts.

As we can see from these sections, it is relatively straightforward to obtain the direct costs of manufacturing a pair of shoes and therefore in total, the prime cost. The problems come with overheads!

19.3 **HOW MUCH OVERHEAD IS IN A PAIR OF SHOES?**

This is the main difficulty when trying to work out the cost of one unit, one pair of shoes. The overheads of the business are incurred because of the needs of the business as a whole, because of all of its production. Sportstuffs Ltd does not pay rent for its premises just to produce one pair of shoes but to produce a large number of different types of sports shoes and other sports equipment. However, if the total cost of the pair of shoes is to be arrived at, a part of the rent expense must be included as part of its cost.

Activity

Think about the problem of how much overhead should be charged for one pair of shoes. How would you tackle it? Jot down a few brief ideas.

You might say - add up all the units produced by the business, add up all the overheads and divide one into the other to give you an amount of overhead per unit. For example: units produced 100,000, total overheads £500,000. Overhead cost per unit = £500,000/100,000 = £5.

This system would work well when all the finished products of the firm are identical. However, when products are different and take different amounts of time to produce, fair costings would not be arrived at as all products would be charged the same overhead despite requiring different production time.

Another idea then would be to say - if overhead is incurred mainly on a time basis, then divide the total overheads by the number of man-hours worked and get a rate per labour hour. If a pair of tennis shoes takes one hour to produce whilst a pair of running shoes takes four hours, then overheads could be fairly charged.

Again this system would work well if all the finished products took fairly similar amounts of time in the different production departments of the business. However, it must be remembered that in a lot of firms it costs much more to run some departments than others, e.g. departments with a lot of machinery. If different products took differing amounts of time at various stages of production, again overheads would not be fairly charged.

Nonetheless, if you were thinking along these lines you were correct. The process by which overheads are charged to cost units is called *overhead absorption.* What we have been considering above are some of the different types of overhead absorption rates which may be used. As we have seen, in practice this will depend upon the type of product and methods of production which a particular firm uses.

Exercise 19.2

Match the following systems of overhead rates with the relevant type of production:

A Single overhead rate per unit.
B Single overhead rate per hour.
C Departmental overhead rates.

1 The firm produces items which take similar amounts of time in each production department.
2 The firm's production is varied, different units take different amounts of time in each department.
3 All units produced are identical.

We have already considered systems A and B, which are fairly simple to operate as there is just one rate for the firm as a whole, however system C is a little more complex.

19.4 HOW ARE DEPARTMENTAL OVERHEAD RATES CALCULATED?

The process can be taken in stages as in Figure 19.3.

Fig. 19.3

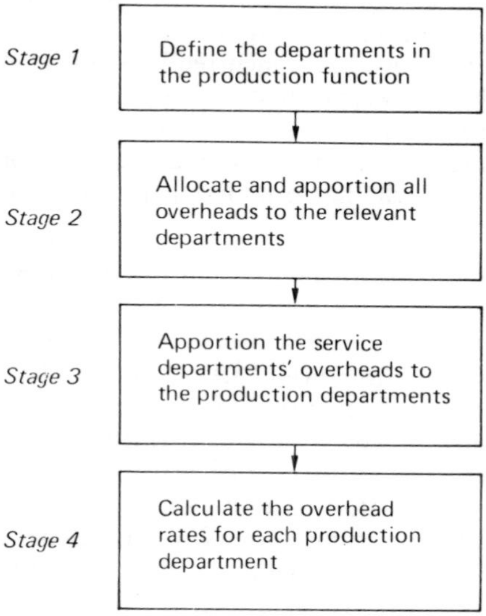

Stage 1
Define the departments in the production function
Stage 2
Allocate and apportion all overheads to the relevant departments
Stage 3
Apportion the service departments' overheads to the production departments
Stage 4
Calculate the overhead rates for each production department

Notes

Stage 1 Another term commonly used for departments here is cost centres. The idea is to identify parts of the production function for which costs can be collected. The cost centres can be either production centres, i.e. where products are actually made, or service centres i.e. activities in the production area which are not directly involved in the production function. In the case of Sportstuffs Ltd it has three production centres - cutting, assembling and finishing - and two service centres - stores and inspection. Remember that we are only considering production costs here. Administration, selling, distribution and other costs will be dealt with separately.

Stage 2 We looked at allocation and apportionment when considering departmental accounts - exactly the same principles are used here.

Items of cost which are for the benefit of one department only are *allocated* in full to that department. For example, an inspector's wages would be charged to the inspection department; the costs of a computerised stores system would be regarded as a cost of the stores department.

Other costs are known as common costs, i.e. the costs are incurred for the benefit of a number of departments. These costs are *apportioned* between departments using a reasonable basis to estimate each department's share. For example, rent might be apportioned on the basis of the floor area which each department occupied; the production director's salary might be split on the basis of the number of man hours worked in each department.

The aim of this stage is to charge each cost centre with its fair share of the production overheads incurred by the business.

Stage 3 The idea of this is that all of the overheads incurred in production should end up in the production departments. They will then be taken into account when the overhead rates are calculated.

Stage 4 The most common rates used are on the basis of labour hours or machine hours, depending on whether production is labour or machine intensive.

All this may be difficult to appreciate at this point but let's now look at an illustration of how this might work for Sportstuffs Ltd by referring to Figure 19.4. We shall assume that the company wishes to calculate what it has cost to produce its products over the previous month. It therefore has the details of the production overheads incurred in the month – the total of £16,000. The cost centres/departments have been defined. *Stage 2* shows the way in which costs are charged to the cost centres – obviously there is a significant amount of approximation but the aim is to gain a reasonably accurate approximation of the running costs of each department. In *Stage 3* the costs of the service departments are charged to the production departments and in *Stage 4* the overhead rates are calculated. The overhead rates to be used for the work of each department vary quite considerably.

19.5 HOW IS THE PRODUCTION COST OF A PRODUCT CALCULATED?

Let's take an example for Sportstuffs Ltd: Job 491, a pair of tennis shoes which was produced last month:

1 Direct materials booked to the job on materials requisition notes were priced at £4.

2 Direct labour booked consists of:

Cutting	½ hour at £3 per hour;
Assembling	½ hour at £4 per hour;
Finishing	¼ hour at £2 per hour.

Fig. 19.4 Calculation of production overhead rates

Production overhead	£	Basis of apportionment	Production departments			Service departments		
			Cutting	Assembling	Finishing	Stores	Inspection	Stage 1
Indirect wages	6,000	Actual allocation	1,500	2,000	800	1,000	700	
Maintenance	1,200	Estimated	400	700	—	100	—	
Rent and rates	2,200	Floor area	550	550	500	500	100	
Consumables	800	Estimated	200	300	200	100	—	
Depreciation	1,000	Value of machines	300	300	200	200	—	
Light and heat	1,100	Floor area	275	275	250	250	50	
Insurance	200	Insured values	50	50	30	70	—	Stage 2
Production director's salary and benefits	2,000	Equally	400	400	400	400	400	
General expenses	1,500	Estimated	400	600	300	100	100	
Total	16,000		4,075	5,175	2,680	2,720	1,350	
Apportionments of:								
Stores (equally between cutting and finishing)			1,360	—	1,360	(2,720)		
Inspection (equally)			450	450	450		(1,350)	Stage 3
			£5,885	£5,625	£4,490	—	—	
Labour hours worked			1,177	1,250	449			
Overhead rate per labour hour			$=\frac{£5,885}{1,177}$	$=\frac{£5,625}{1,250}$	$=\frac{£4,490}{449}$			Stage 4
			= £5	= £4.50	= £10			

The production costing would be as follows, using the production overhead rates calculated in Figure 19.4:

Direct materials			4.00
Direct labour:			
Cutting	(½ hour @ £3 per hour)	1.50	
Assembling	(½ hour @ £4 per hour)	2.00	
Finishing	(¼ hour @ £2 per hour)	0.50	4.00
Prime cost			8.00
Production overhead:			
Cutting	(½ hour @ £5 per hour)	2.50	
Assembling	(½ hour @ £4.50 per hour)	2.25	
Finishing	(¼ hour @ £10 per hour)	2.50	7.25
Production cost			£15.25

As you can see, once the overhead rates have been calculated, it is easy to use them to get the production cost.

19.6 **WHAT ABOUT THE TOTAL COST?**

A charge will need to be added to production cost for selling, distribution and administration expenses. Most firms use a blanket rate per unit for this because the time it takes to produce a unit has little effect on these costs. So, for example, Sportstuffs Ltd may have incurred total selling, distribution and administration costs of £30,000 in the last month, during which they produced 10,000 units. They would therefore use a rate of £3 per unit.

Therefore the total cost of Job 491 would be:

Production cost (as above)	15.25
Selling, distribution and administration overheads	3.00
Total cost	£18.25

19.7 **SUMMARY OF ABSORPTION COSTING**

As can be seen, the process by which the total cost of a product is arrived at is relatively simple for direct costs. However, indirect costs cause more of a problem and require many estimations and approximations to be made. But remember, as we saw at the beginning of the chapter, managers need information which is relevant and useful even if it is not absolutely accurate. To consolidate your understanding of this topic try the following:

Exercise 19.3

3.1 Match the costs which make up the total cost of a product with their relevant sources:

A	Direct materials	1	Departmental labour hour rates
B	Direct labour	2	Invoices and contracts
C	Direct expenses	3	Job card and wage rates
D	Production overheads	4	Materials and requisition notes and invoices
E	Selling, distribution and administration overheads	5	Overhead rate per unit

3.2 In the chapter we concentrated on calculating the cost of a product after it had been produed. The 'Marafun' shoes have not yet been produced – briefly describe how you would set about obtaining a costing for that new product.

3.3 Tubular Products Ltd has four departments in its production function – the machine shop, assembly shop and paint shop, which are the production departments, and the maintenance department, a service department.

The actual production overheads incurred in a month are given on the worksheet below. You are also given the following information:

	Machine Shop	*Assembly Shop*	*Paint Shop*	*Maintenance Department*
Area (sq metres)	1,000	750	500	250
No of employees	20	25	10	5
Value of plant	£20,000	£30,000	£5,000	£5,000
Machine capacity in horsepower	1,000	1,200	200	200

Worksheet

Production overhead	£	*Basis of apportionment*	*Machine shop*	*Assembly shop*	*Paint shop*	*Maint. dept*
Canteen exp	2,400					
Maint. wages	1,510					
Rent	2,500					
Depreciation	1,200					
Power	5,200					
	£12,810		___	___	___	___
Appointment of maintenance to prod depts (equally)						
			£ ___	£ ___	£ ___	£ Nil

Apportion the costs to the departments, using the most logical methods. Then apportion the maintenance department's costs to the production departments. Check your answer before going on.

3.4 Tubular Products Ltd use labour hour rates. In the month in question the following hours were worked in production:

Machine shop	– 3,100
Assembly shop	– 3,900
Paint shop	– 1,500

Calculate the overhead absorption rate for each department (to the nearest p).

3.5 During that month Tubular Products Ltd carried out job No. 86201 for a selling price of £90. The details are as follows:

Direct materials – £22.67
Direct labour

Machine shop	– 3 hours @ £4 per hour
Assembly shop	– 2 hours @ £3.75 per hour
Paint shop	– 3 hours @ £3.50 per hour

Production overheads are charged using the rates from question 3.4. Other overheads are charged at the rate of £8 per unit.

What was the total cost of Job No. 86201 and what profit did the company make on it?

Now let's move on to another situation with . . . .

19.8 SUPERBENCH LTD

'Times are hard. Our benches are not selling',' said Tom Wood, managing director of Superbench Ltd. The company manufactures a special type of workbench which is specifically aimed at the up-market, do-it-yourself fanatic. Its major advantages over cheaper models are the storage space it offers and its built-in fixtures for using drills. But the recession was biting deep and people preferred to buy the cheaper, less sophisticated benches offered by the company's competitors.

The board of directors were looking at the company's results from January to the end of September which showed a loss of £150,000 on sales of 30,000 benches.

'The problem is that we planned production and sales of 80,000 benches this year. At our present level of sales we will only manage another 10,000 in the last quarter, giving us 40,000 for the year and a loss of £200,000.'

'Perhaps I can help,' said David Bucknall, the sales director. 'I've just been on the phone to the retailers, Merryhomes Ltd and they would be prepared to take 10,000 benches if we can price them at around £55.'

'You're joking,' exploded Tom Wood. 'I know we need the contract but at what price? Our normal selling price is £80 and it costs us £60 to produce the benches. We can't sell our products at below cost!'

Activity

Think about the situation of this company. What is its key problem?

Its main difficulty is lack of sales. It has the capacity to produce 80,000 units but is only likely to produce 40,000 units in the year. The company's losses are due to the fact that it will still have to pay the costs of its capacity e.g. rent and rates, depreciation of machinery, insurance of buildings and machinery etc, although it lacks the sales income. It needs more sales, but not at any price.

Back at the board meeting:

'Let's look at David's idea more closely,' suggested Andrew Weir, the finance director. 'The cost of that bench is made up as follows:

	£
Direct materials	10
Direct labour	20
Production overheads	20
Selling, distribution and administrative overheads	10
	60

Now if we produce these 10,000 benches for Merryhomes Ltd what costs will we actually incur? The materials and labour certainly and some production overheads for light, heat, power and consumables. But the major part of our production and other overheads are costs we are going to pay anyway whether or not we take on this order, e.g. rent, rates, depreciation, our salaries, the foreman's salary and so on. So for a one-off contract like this, as we've got the spare capacity and need the work, we could price the benches much lower and still make some money.'

Andrew has pointed out that costs behave in different ways when the volume of production of a business improves. Some costs will increase and some will remain static. In this section we shall look at cost behaviour in detail and see how an appreciation of this is useful to managers when making decisions about one-off contracts or when trying to identify the level of sales at which their business breaks even. This is a part of costing known as *marginal costing*.

19.9 WHAT IS THE AIM OF MARGINAL COSTING?

We've seen in the case of Superbench Ltd that, whilst it is useful to know the total cost of making a product, other information may be more relevant. The board would here like to know exactly what additional costs they would incur by taking on a contract when they are already operating at a production level of 10,000 units per quarter. The board needs to know the *marginal cost* of the workbench. The formal definition is:

Marginal cost is the total cost of increasing the volume of output of a component, product or service by one unit at a given level of output.

19.10 HOW IS THE MARGINAL COST CALCULATED?

We need to know what costs will increase when production is increased and what costs will be unaffected. Consequently, the costs of a business are analysed and classified as one of the following:

1 *Fixed costs* - those which are unaffected by changes in the volume of output. Examples might include rent, rates and salaries.
2 *Variable costs* - those which vary *directly* with changes in the volume of output. Examples here would be all the direct costs - materials, labour and expenses.
3 *Semi-variable costs* - those which vary with changes in the volume of output, but not in direct relationship. Examples might be telephone costs, supervisory wages and power costs.

Exercise 19.4

A good way to remember these definitions is to think about the various costs of running a car. Jot down examples of fixed, variable and semi-variable costs in doing that.

For marginal costing purposes the semi-variable costs are separated into their fixed and variable elements. For example, telephone costs have a fixed element - the standing charge - and a variable element - the cost per unit used. Other costs may be split using statistical methods or more simply by using the high-low method.

19.10.1 Example of the high-low method

In order to split a cost into its fixed and variable elements, a number of steps have to be gone through. Let's take production supervisors' wages as an example.

Step 1 Ascertain the cost incurred at the highest and lowest level of activity of the business:

Units produced	*Cost*
60,000 (lowest level)	£16,800
100,000 (highest level)	£24,800

Step 2 As the fixed element of the cost must, by definition, stay the same at the two levels of production, the increase in cost must be the variable cost:

An increase in production of 40,000 units has increased the total cost by £8,000 which is the variable cost. The variable cost per unit must therefore be £8,000 ÷ 40,000 units = 20p per unit.

Step 3 The total variable overhead in the two levels above is then calculated:

At 60,000 units it will be 60,000 × 20p = £12,000
At 100,000 units it will be 100,000 × 20p = £20,000

Step 4 The fixed element will be the difference between the total cost and the total variable overhead. It should be the same figure at the two levels.

At 60,000 units it will be £16,800 – £12,000 = £4,800
At 100,000 units it will be £24,800 – £20,000 = £4,800

To practise this, try the following:

Exercise 19.5

A firm's records for its power costs give the following information:

Units produced	*Cost*
8,000	£5,000
12,000	£7,000

1 Calculate the variable power cost per unit.
2 Calculate the total fixed power cost.

Having split all of the costs of the business into fixed and variable, the marginal cost of a product will be the total of its variable costs.

If we take the workbench as an example, its marginal cost might be as follows:

	£
Direct materials	10
Direct labour	20
Prime cost	30
Variable production overheads	5
Marginal cost	35

Exercise 19.6

Briefly explain what this marginal cost of £35 means.

19.11 WHAT EFFECT WOULD THE MERRYHOMES CONTRACT HAVE?

The board of directors would have to look at these figures:

Income (10,000 benches @ £55)	= 550,000
Less Marginal costs (10,000 benches @ £35)	= 350,000
Contract contribution	£200,000

The contract would give a contribution of £200,000 to the business and mean that the company would break even for the year rather than make a £200,000 loss.

Note that the term *contribution* has been used rather than profit. This is because no account has been taken of the fixed costs of the business. Contribution is defined as the difference between the selling price and the marginal cost of a product, i.e. £20 per bench in this case. This contribution per unit multiplied by the units sold represents the total contribution which a product makes towards covering the fixed costs of the business and then generating a profit.

The main features of marginal costing are, therefore, that:

1 The profitability of a product or contract is shown by its contribution and this is the key element to look for in making decisions. If there is a contribution, it's worth considering.
2 Fixed overheads should not be treated as part of the costs of a product. As we saw in the last chapter, the process of apportionment and absorption can require a lot of estimating and therefore produce inaccurate total costs. As we've seen in this chapter, the total cost can be misleading when making some decisions.
3 Fixed costs should therefore be pooled and will represent a cost commitment which a business has to cover from the sales of its products before it starts making a profit.

Before going on, try the following questions to check your understanding of the material covered so far.

Exercise 19.7

7.1 Below are three diagrams which outline fixed, variable and semi-variable costs. Identify each diagram.

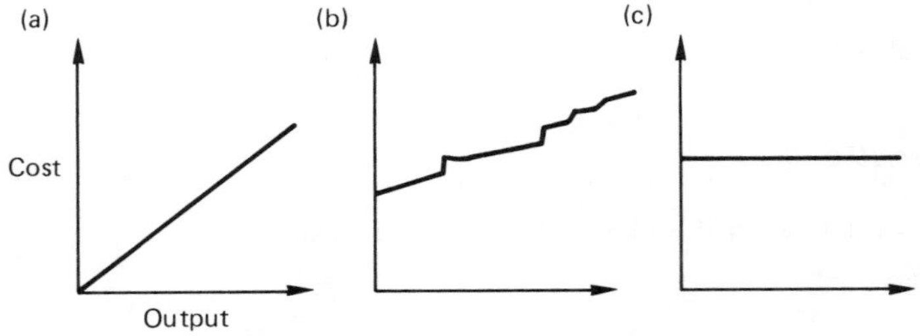

7.2 A company's factory has the capacity to produce 13,000 units a year. Its normal production is 10,000 units, the costs of which are:

Direct material	30,000
Direct labour	20,000
Production overheads	40,000
	90,000
Administration and other overheads	10,000
	£100,000

The normal selling price is £12 per unit. A salesman says that a foreign buyer will take 2,000 units a year if the price can be cut to £8.50 per unit.

Additional distribution costs would be 50p per unit for these export items. Of the production overheads, a quarter is variable and three-quarters is fixed. All of the administration and other overheads should be taken as fixed.

(a) Should the company accept the order?
(b) What effect would it have on the normal profit of the business?

19.12 WHAT DO I HAVE TO DO TO BREAK EVEN?

Information on the break-even level of sales can be very useful to a businessman. It gives a goal to aim at and can act as a warning that a business is not doing well. Marginal costing enables the break-even point of a business to be easily calculated. It also allows the financial shape of a firm to be presented in the form of a graph which is relatively easy to understand.

What has to be done to break even? Enough sales have to be made so that the contribution from those sales exactly covers the fixed costs of the business, i.e.

Break-even point (in units) = *Total fixed costs ÷ contribution per unit*

For example, a company has total costs of £200,000. Its product has a selling price of £200 and a marginal cost of £100. Its break-even point is therefore:

$$\frac{£200,00}{£100} = 2,000 \text{ units}$$

Exercise 19.8

A company has total fixed costs of £80,000. Its one product sells for £8 and has a marginal cost of £6. What is the company's break-even point?

The technique can be adapted to calculate the number of sales units required to achieve a target profit. The profit is added to the total fixed costs to give the total contribution required. Following the example above, if we say the company has a target profit of £150,000, then the level of sales required would be:

$$\frac{£200{,}000 + £150{,}000}{£100} = 3{,}500 \text{ units}$$

But even more useful is the ability to present this information in the form of a break-even chart.

19.3 HOW IS A BREAK-EVEN CHART PREPARED?

Figure 19.5 is an example of a chart. It shows the financial shape of a business which has the following vital statistics:

Expected sales: – 10,000 units @ £8 per unit
Marginal cost: – £5 per unit
Total fixed costs: – £21,000

Fig. 19.5

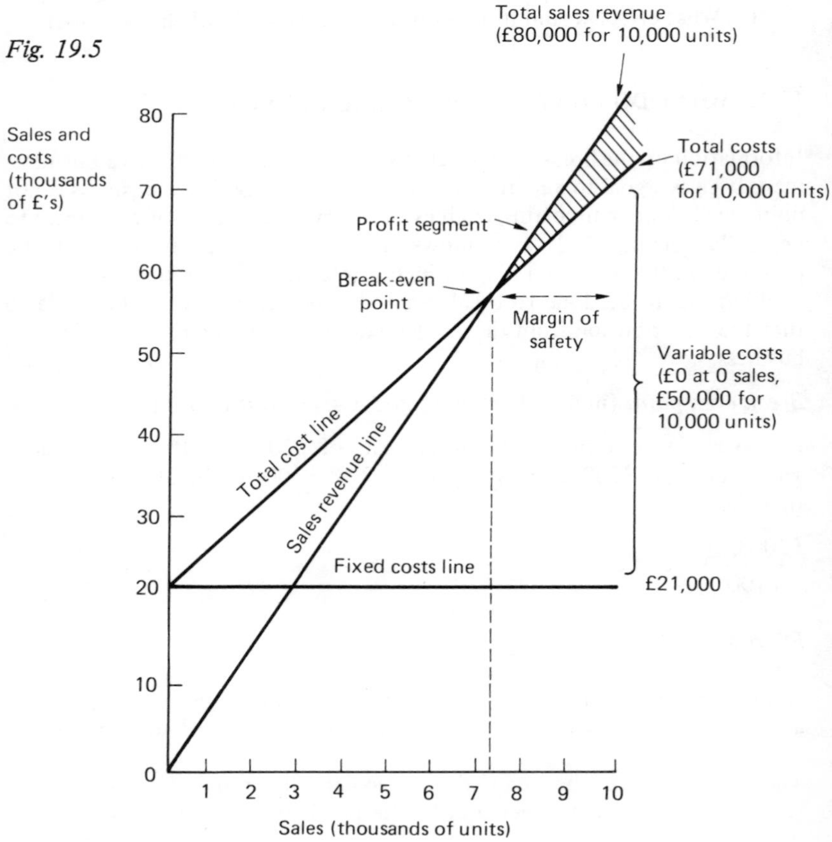

The chart is prepared as follows:

1 The horizontal axis (going across!) is used to show the number of units sold. The vertical axis shows sales and costs in money values.
2 The total sales will increase with the number of units sold, and will be a straight line from £0 to £80,000 (10,000 units @ £8).
3 The fixed costs will remain static, beginning at £21,000 at 0 units sold and going across in a horizontal line.
4 The variable costs will increase as production and sales take place. They will be added to the total fixed cost to give the total costs of the business. In this case, at 0 sales there will be £0 variable costs, at 10,000 sales the total variable cost will be £50,000. The total costs are therefore £21,000 and £71,000 respectively.

When preparing these yourself, try and use graph paper, a sharp pencil and a ruler. These help make the charts more accurate.

19.14 WHAT DOES THE BREAK-EVEN CHART SHOW?

1 *Break-even point.* This is where the sales revenue line crosses the total cost line. The further to the right of the graph the break-even point is then the riskier the business. This can be checked by calculation, e.g.

$$\frac{£21,000}{£3} = 7,000 \text{ units.}$$

This is quite a high break-even point, as we can see, when expected sales are only 10,000 units.

2 *Margin of safety.* This reinforces the risk idea. It is the difference between the total expected sales and the break-even point, i.e. 10,000 units minus 7,000 units equals 3,000 units. Obviously, the greater this is, the less chance a business has of making a loss.
3 *Profits and losses.* These can be seen on the chart, losses diminishing and profits increasing as sales take place.
4 *Make-up of total costs.* It is possible to easily see from the chart which is the most important part of total costs, in this case variable costs. Consequently, if the management of this business wanted to cut costs they could see that variable cost was the area they needed to concentrate on.

These charts are therefore very useful in that they present a lot of useful information about a business in an easily understood way. They are also very flexible in that you can use them to show the effects of changes in selling prices and costs or volume of sales on the performance of the business.

To practice this very useful technique try the following:

Exercise 19.9

9.1 Prepare a firm's break-even chart from the following summarised results:

Sales (6,000 units)			60,000
Costs:	Variable	24,000	
	Fixed	14,000	38,000
	Profit		£22,000

Check your break-even point by calculation.

9.2 Figure 19.6 shows two break-even charts. Both companies earn the same profit from the same level of sales. Explain:
(a) what the charts indicate to you.
(b) the type of industry you think each company is in.

As we have seen, marginal costing can be very useful in management decision-making. If you are in a position to do so, you might like to try the following:

Activities

1 List areas where application of marginal rather than absorption costing might be useful in *your* firm, e.g. pricing for contracts, considering whether to buy out or make components, decisions on pricing for bargains, loss leaders, obsolete stock, etc. You may well find that some products or services can be priced lower and still be profitable.

2 See if you can prepare a roughly estimated break-even chart for your business. You could try applying the high-low method to total costs at different levels of sales to get some general idea of the fixed and variable cost split.

Fig. 19.6

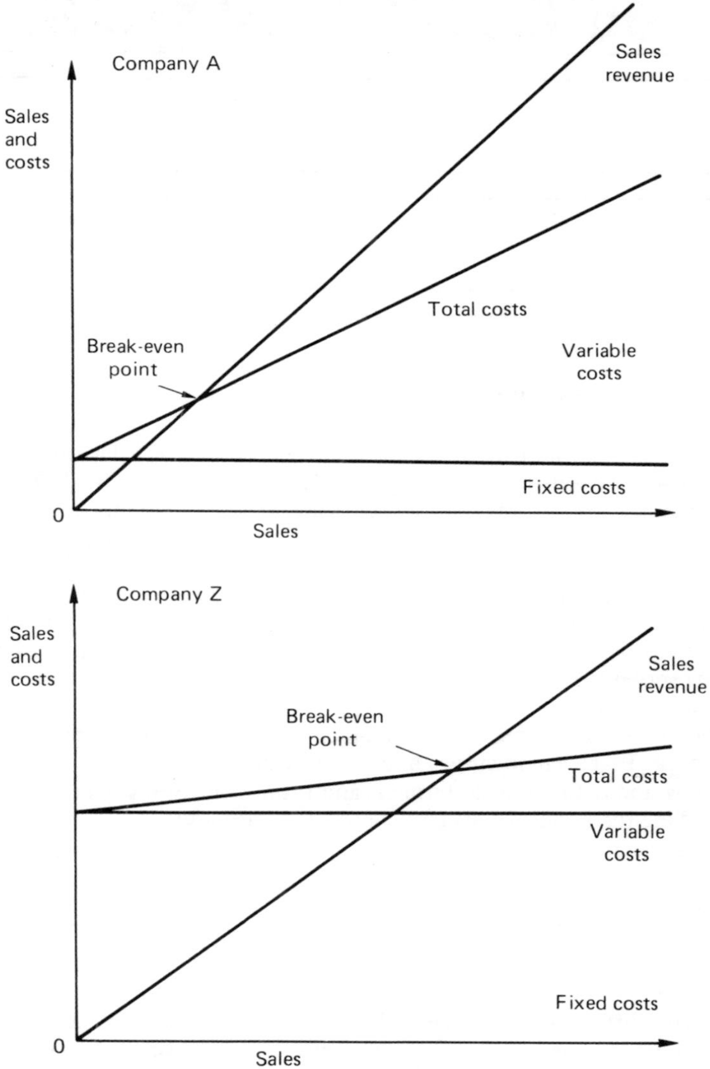
Company A
Sales
and
costs
Sales
revenue
Total costs
Break-even
point
Variable
costs
Fixed costs
0
Sales
Company Z
Sales
and
costs
Sales
revenue
Break-even
point
Total costs
Variable
costs
Fixed costs
0
Sales

CHAPTER 20

BUDGETARY CONTROL

20.1 GANBY'S GARAGES LTD

Vic Ganby had built up a thriving business. He had left the army in 1980 and used all of his capital to buy a small garage. He began by doing all the work himself - serving petrol, repairing and maintaining cars, and the paperwork. He built up a reputation for excellent service and quality workmanship. His business expanded rapidly. He extended the workshop and bought the building next door, turning it into a showroom for new car sales. He then bought two other garages in the area and a hire car business. His company now employed over 200 people and Vic appeared to be doing very well.

But Vic was a worried man. As he confessed to his friend Tom Robertson, 'I don't feel in charge any more. I don't know everyone in my business. I get complaints about poor work and bad service. I know nothing about the hire car business and I think one of my garage managers is fiddling the books. How can I control my business?'

Activity

What is Vic's main problem? Jot down some ideas.

His main difficulty is the *size* of his business. This makes it necessary for him to change the way in which he manages it. The small business can be run on an informal basis as the owner/manager will know everyone, will be aware of everything that is going on and will make all the decisions. But when a business grows, work and responsibility has to be given to other people, which makes it impossible for control to continue to be exercised informally. Vic may have problems, but think of a very large firm. For example GEC has 50,000 employees in Britain. How can companies of that size be controlled by their managers?

In this chapter we shall look at one of the ways in which this is done through a financial system known as *budgetary control*. We shall see how the system operates, some of the advantages to be gained from it, and discuss some of the pitfalls to be avoided. Whilst these ideas are very important in business, they can also be useful in helping you to organise your personal finances.

20.2 HOW DOES THE BUDGETARY CONTROL SYSTEM WORK?

It is based on the control loop idea. The principles of this are outlined in Figure 20.1, and it consists of the following stages:

1 *Preparation of plans*. Control cannot be exercised unless there are expectations against which actual results can be measured. For example, a production inspector at Clark's Shoes must know what are acceptable standards for the quality of a pair of shoes. He can then assess production against these expectations and decide whether each pair of shoes is acceptable. In the same way, expectations must be developed for a whole business. This process may start by setting targets, e.g. 'We want a return on capital employed of 25%' and then converting those into detailed plans or budgets. We shall look at this process in more detail later.
2 *Comparison with actual results*. In order to be effective information must be given to a manager as soon as possible after the event. So, to help control the activities of a business, regular figures are produced for managers, such as daily production statistics and weekly sales figures. For budgeting purposes, the financial year is usually split into *control periods*, usually a calendar month or a four-week period. The budgets are prepared for each control period and the actual results obtained as soon as possible after the period has finished. With modern computer systems this information can be produced very quickly indeed, which significantly improves the ability of managers to react to events and control their businesses.
3 *Analysis of variances*. This stage consists of investigating the reasons for differences between the planned and actual results. This is the most important stage in the process as it is where control can be made effective. A variance might be unfavourable because of inefficiencies within the business – this is highlighted by the system and it is up to the manager to do something about it. Alternatively, a variance may be caused by circumstances outside the control of the business, in which case the plans of the business may need to be altered. For example, a wage increase may be negotiated which is above the increase expected when the budgets were prepared.

This then is the principle of the control loop on which the budgetary control system is based. The idea is basic to a whole range of systems. For

Fig. 20.1 The control loop

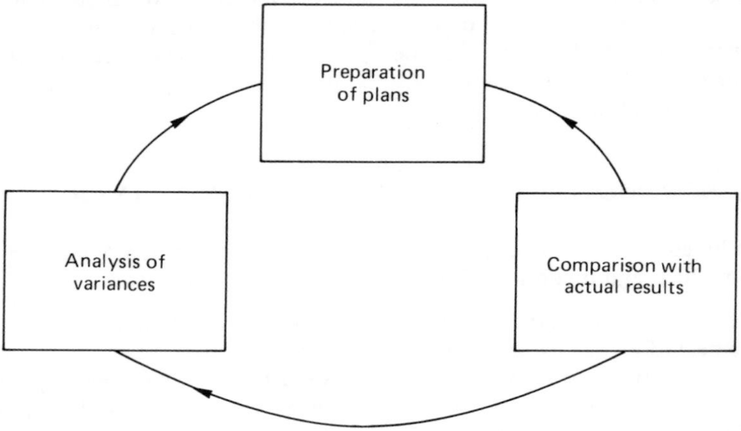

example, a ship will have a destination to go to and a route to follow - its plans; its progress will be measured by a range of navigational aids - the results; if the ship goes off its route the aids will inform the capital and enable him to take the necessary corrective action or change the route or destination if necessary - the analysis of variances.

20.3 **HOW ARE PLANS PREPARED?**

Activity

Let's think about this in relation to your personal finances. If you were asked to prepare a budget for your personal income and expenditure for the next year, how would you set about doing it? Jot down a few notes describing the steps you would take.

The steps you might take could be as follows:

- Summarise your income and expenditure for the previous year.
- Adjust those figures for various reasons:
  - definite events, e.g. increment on salary, a baby expected in the next few months.
  - likely events, e.g. increases in gas and electricity bills because of inflation.
  - desired events, e.g. you want to buy a new car in one month's time and have a holiday in the Canary Islands.
- Review the budget according to your criteria - does it look reasonable? Will the bank manager give you the overdraft? Does it give you the savings you want?

- Revise the budget as necessary until you are satisfied with the end results.

This is the sort of commonsense approach that might be taken and it is very similar to the way in which a business might tackle the preparation of budgets. This process is shown in Figure 20.2.

Fig. 20.2 The preparation of budgets

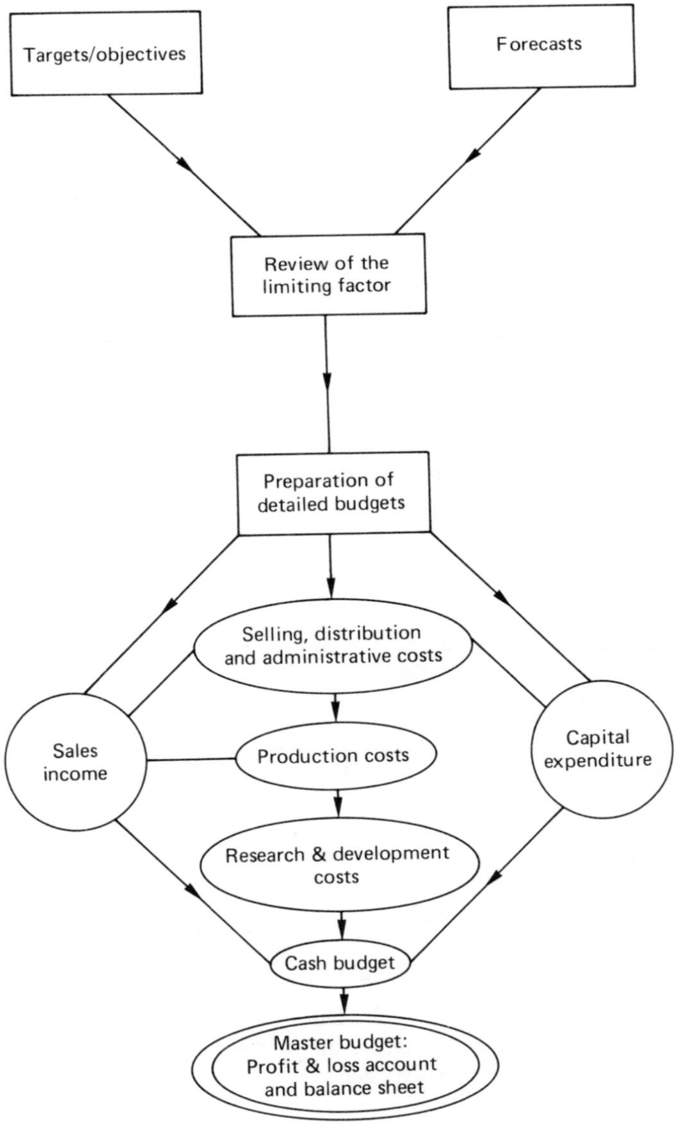

20.3.1 **Targets/objectives**

These will form the criteria by which the final budget will be measured. It is up to the board of directors to decide the main objectives that the budget must meet. Examples of targets and objectives could be:

- past performances – 'this company has had a return on capital employed of over 20% in the past five years, it must be over 25% in the next five years.'
- return to shareholders – 'the dividend must increase from5p per share to 7p per share next year and must be covered at least twice by profits.'
- market share – 'this must be improved by 2%.'
- benefits to employees – 'we want to give our employees a pay increase of 2% above the rate of inflation.'
- benefits to customers – 'we want to hold our prices steady for at least six months and launch ten new product lines in our stores.'

20.3.2 **Forecasts**

A forecast is an attempt to estimate the events which are likely to occur in the future. At this stage the emphasis will be on producing forecast trading and profit and loss accounts at various levels of sales to see what the results are. The more promising of these forecasts will then be followed through to cash flow and balance sheet forecasts to complete the picture.

The major problem for most businesses is forecasting sales as there are so many factors which can influence the level of sales which a business will obtain.

To illustrate this try the following:

Activity

Think about the sales of a brewing company. Make a list of some of the factors which can affect its sales.

A whole range of matters could be noted:

- level of competition and share of market
- effect of national economic conditions on people's spending
- distribution of sales outlets and local economic effects on spending, e.g. closure of large factories and a high level of unemployment in a particular area
- the weather
- production capacity or problems
- increases in duty by the Chancellor of the Exchequer
- advertising and promotion spending.

How then are sales forecasts made? Different businesses will use different techniques depending on the nature of their work. It is often a good idea to analyse sales into categories such as:

1 Regular business - the normal demand of regular customers.
2 Non-regular business - demand from new and one-off customers.
3 Unstable business -- unexpected demand for which allowance should be made.

The types of forecasting methods used in practice include such techniques as:

- market research, especially useful for new products
- statistical analysis of past sales leading to projected sales figures
- sales force method - asking individual salesmen to forecast their sales, totalling the results and adjusting them where necessary for factors known only to senior management, e.g. planned advertising.

If you wish to study this area in more detail, you should refer to the books in the Macmillan Master Series *Marketing* and *Statistics*.

20.3.5 **Review of the limiting factor**

Forecasts at various levels of sales will be made and then reviewed:

1 To see if they are practical, e.g. has the firm the capacity to produce sufficient goods to meet the sales forecasts?
2 To see if they achieve the firm's objectives.

Forecasts will only be unsuitable because something called the *limiting factor* has taken effect. This can be defined as something which limits the size of a business and restricts its growth. Examples might be the lack of orders because of competition or the lack of finance to increase production capacity. To develop this try the following:

Activity

What might cause (1) materials, (2) labour or (3) plant to act as a limiting factor on a business? Note down reasons for each one.

Each could reduce the ability of a firm to produce. Possible causes might include:

(1) Materials - lack of availability, poor quality, transport problems.
(2) Labour -shortage of people with the necessary skills, overtime bans.
(3) Plant - lack of investment, lack of flexibility in the plant purchased.

As can be seen from these examples the limiting factor will only affect a business if nothing is done to change it. For example, more spending on advertising might increase orders; production capacity can be increased by investing in the necessary resources. So at this stage decisions must be made on any spending required to ease the limiting factor.

20.4 **PREPARATION OF DETAILED BUDGETS**

A *budget* can be defined as a programme of action which management sets out to achieve in order to meet a given objective. It often represents a forecast after it has been adjusted for spending on the limiting factor. Allowance will also have been made for any other policies and plans which senior management want to implement. As can be seen in Figure 20.2, budgets will be prepared for each of the main account headings, leading to the cash budget and the master budget. These budgets are often broken down in various ways, for example:

- *by control period* - the annual budget will be split between the firm's control periods, giving weekly, monthly or quarterly budgets.
- *by responsibility* - the total budget will be broken up into smaller and smaller parts as each person in the hierarch is given responsibility for his section of the budget. This process is illustrated in Figure 20.3 in relation to the sales budget.

Fig. 20.3 Breakdown of sales budget by responsibility

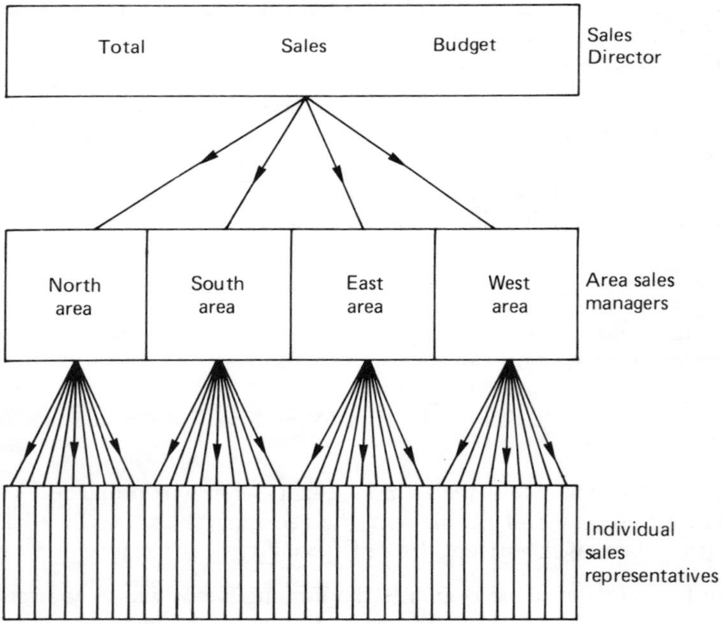

20.5 **WHAT DO BUDGETS LOOK LIKE?**

In general terms the budgets will look like a detailed set of accounts but with target rather than actual figures. They may also contain non-financial measures such as labour hours and units produced. Budgets vary greatly from one organisation to another so rather than attempt to reproduce a set of budgets here I would like to concentrate on one very important budget – the *cash budget*.

An illustration of a cash budget for three months is given in Figure 20.4.

The cash budget will be prepared from information contained in other budgets of income and expenditure which is then adjusted to a cash flow basis. The important points to remember when preparing cash budgets are:

1 Sales on credit cannot be treated as cash received until payments are made by debtors – assumptions about debtor collection periods must therefore be made.
2 Similar principles apply for payments to trade and expense creditors.
3 Depreciation must not be shown as a cash payment, although it will be included in the expense budgets. Any purchase of fixed assets must be included in full when the payment is made.

Fig. 20.4 Example of a simple cash budget

		January	*February*	*March*
Receipts:				
from cash sales		50,000	35,000	45,000
from debtors		120,000	105,000	100,000
	(A)	£170,000	£140,000	£145,000
Payments:				
creditors for materials		46,000	42,000	40,000
wages		55,000	55,000	55,000
variable overheads		12,000	11,000	10,000
fixed overheads		36,000	36,000	38,000
machinery		—	22,000	—
	(B)	£149,000	£166,000	£143,000
Net cash flow	(A)–(B)	21,000	(26,000)	2,000
Opening balance		2,000	23,000	(3,000)
Closing balance		£23,000	£ (3,000)	£ (1,000)

Note: Amounts in brackets indicate a net outflow of cash or a bank overdraft.

The cash budget is a very important document as it gives a warning of possible cash shortages. This enables overdraft or loan facilities to be negotiated in advance with the bank manager. It also indicates to potential lenders that a business is well managed because cash planning is taken seriously – a factor which may make them more willing to lend! So, for example, the cash budget in Figure 20.4 would show a bank manager that his business wishes to purchase machinery at a time when its cash income, probably because of seasonal factors, is in decline. Consequently, it needs a small overdraft for a short period until sales improve. On the face of it, this is a reasonable request.

To practise the preparation of cash budget, try this exercise:

Exercise 20.1

Alf Bradford is a sole trader who runs a hardware business. On 1 January he expects to have about £1,700 in the bank current account for the business. He gives you the following budget details:

1 Sales - payment to be received in the following month:

November	£14,200	March	£10,200
December	£16,400	April	£12,000
January	£13,000	May	£13,500
February	£8,400	June	£14,800

2 Wages, drawings and expenses - all paid in the same month:

January	£3,400	April	£3,400
February	£3,200	May	£3,600
March	£3,100	June	£3,800

3 Purchases - paid two months after purchase:

November	£4,200	March	£4,200
December	£4,000	April	£4,600
January	£3,600	May	£5,000
February	£3,800	June	£5,100

4 Alf expected to purchase a new van for the business in March, paying cash of £6,200, and machinery in April, paying cash of £24,000.

Prepare a cash budget for Alf's business for the six months, January to June.

20.6 WHAT ARE THE ADVANTAGES OF THE BUDGETARY CONTROL SYSTEM?

The main ones are likely to be:

Planning. Each year the senior management is forced to look ahead; this will help to anticipate possible problems. The performance of the business is also subjected to detailed review; weaknesses may be identified and plans developed to deal with them.

Co-ordination. All of the budgets must dovetail. Consequently, each function becomes aware of the requirements of others and the need to work together effectively. The analysis of variances will often highlight areas where co-ordination has broken down.

Financial responsibility. Each manager is likely to have a budget to work to and is responsible for managing it. This often makes non-financial employees more money conscious.

Control. It would help solve Vic Ganby's problems. Each of the individual budgets add up to the plan for the business as a whole and the variance analysis indicates when something is going wrong. The person responsible for the variance can then be made accountable.

20.7 **WHAT DISADVANTAGES ARE THERE?**

Inflexibility. There is the danger that if a budget is adhered to too rigidly, then stupid decisions can be made. There are many stories of salesmen not being allowed to go abroad to finalise a contract with a customer because the overseas expenses budget had been spent; as a result the firm has lost the contract.
Lack of commitment. This can occur if the people who have to implement the budgets are not given the opportunity to be involved in their preparation. If budgets are imposed from above there is not the same motivation to achieve them.
Excessive variances. These can occur when actual production and sales vary considerably from budget. There is the need then to introduce flexible budgeting - this recognises the difference between fixed and variable costs and allows budgets to be prepared for the actual level of activity achieved.

These problems can occur if budgeting system is not operated with common sense. However, as we have seen, there is much to be gained by the larger business if it operates a budgetary control system.
Try the following:

Exercise 20.2

2.1 Explain how the idea of the control loop can be applied to the management of a football team.
2.2 Match these two lists of terms and definitions:

Terms	*Definitions*
A Forecast	1 a programme of action to achieve an objective
B Limiting factor	2 an attempt to estimate likely future events
C Budget	3 restricts the growth of a business

2.3 Outline the process by which budgets are prepared by completing the following diagram:

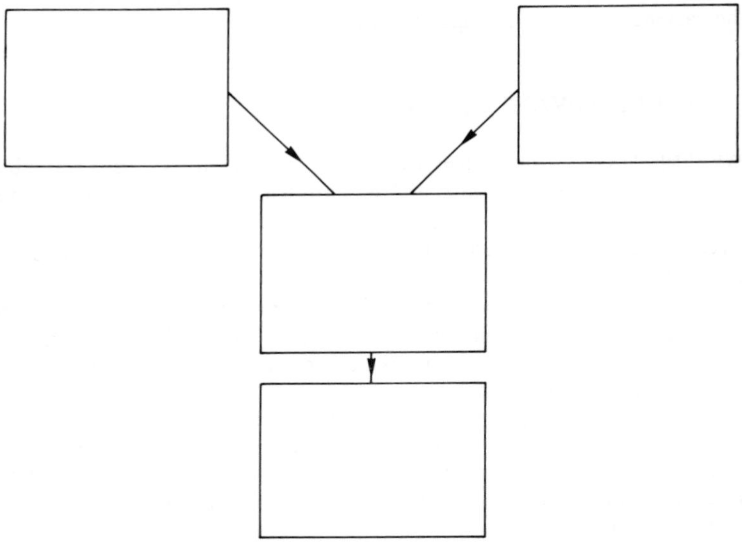

2.4 Tom Tweed wants to form his own company which will begin trading on 1 July. The figures he will be working to for the first three months are:

(a) The company, Tweeds Ltd, will issue 20,000 50p ordinary shares, payable in full on 1 July.
(b) One quarter's rent will be paid in advance on 1 July – £1,200.
(c) At first he will have to pay cash for stock. He anticipates purchases of: July £4,000; August £5,000; September £6,000.
(d) His sales during the three months are expected to be: July £6,000; August £7,500; September £9,000. Half the sales should be for cash and half on credit. The credit customers are expected to pay in the month following the sale.
(e) Wages and other expenses are expected to be £1,000 per month, paid during that month.
(f) Fixtures will be needed of £3,000, payable on 1 July.

Prepare the cash budget of Tweeds Ltd for the three months, July to September.

As with all accounting there is nothing better for improving your understanding than seeing the real thing.

Try the following:

Activity and discussion

The budgeting systems operated by different organisations vary enormously. See if you can get someone in your firm who is involved in the preparation and implementation of budgets to explain how it works. It would also help if you could see some examples of budget forms, i.e. budgets, actual results and variances. You will probably be surprised at the detail which is gone into but it does enable a manager to control his business!

ANSWERS

CHAPTER 1

Exercise 1.1

He acted as (a) when keeping a record of his earnings, etc. in his pocket book. Recording transactions is what book-keeping is all about.

He acted as (b) when proving to his parents on a sheet of paper that he could afford to run the bike. Reporting to interested parties is the function of a financial accountant.

He acted as (c) when using the information in his pocket book to decide things like when he could afford to have his mud-guard repaired. Using accounts as an aid to decision making is the work of a management accountant.

If you had any difficulty with this question, reread the definitions on page 3.

Exercise 1.2

His Inspector of Taxes, who will require evidence on which to base his assessment of how much tax he should pay. When people do not provide enough satisfactory evidence the inspector has power to estimate how much profits have been made and tax them accordingly. It is usual in such circumstances to make such an estimate err on the high side rather than the low. This usually brings characters like Ginger to their senses. Of course, Ginger does not have to employ an accountant to prepare a profit and loss account and balance sheet. He could do it himself. If he reads this book he might be able to do so.

Exercise 1.3

3.1 The missing words in order are: (a) book-keeping, books; (b) profit, loss, financial accounting; (c) management accounting; (d) accounting. If this caused any difficulty reread the definitions on pages 3 and 7.

3.2 Henry is a sole proprietor or sole trader because he alone owns the business.

3.3 The three examples that come most readily to my mind are:

(a) Money received and paid. Money is the lifeblood of all businesses and a close check must be kept on it.

(b) Amounts owing to suppliers. Credit is important to many businesses, none of which want to lose this facility. Care must be taken not to offend suppliers by being too slow in payment.

(c) Amounts due from customers. Many customers have to be asked more than once for the money they owe.

There are other examples on page 5 to which you can refer if necessary. A reason should occur to you for each one. Besides individual reasons you might also have given general ones. For example all such information is needed for an owner to know how successful he is. It will be needed to calculate profits and losses. Such information is also needed to satisfy the Inspector of Taxes. It is also useful in providing the material needed to aid decision making.

3.4 Your general knowledge together with what you have read in this chapter should have led you to say 'None'. If you have any doubts about this find out what each of them does and reconsider.

Exercise 1.4

(a) assets £15,000, (b) capital £14,000, (c) liabilities £25,000, (d) capital – £10,000.

Exercise 1.5

(a) These cars should be classified as fixed assets. They will last for a reasonable amount of time and, while they contribute to a firm's ability to make profits, it is not intended that profits should be made directly from any change in their value.

(b) These should be regarded as current assets. They are a means by which the garage is making a profit. Cars will be bought and sold and thus the value of this asset will often be changing. From the garage's point of view the cars will be part of their stock-in-trade, one of the things that they trade in.

Exercise 1.6

Balance sheet of Peter Bright as at 31 January 1990

	£	£		£	£
Assets			*Sources of finance*		
Fixed assets			*Capital*		42,530
Freehold property	40,000		*Long-term liabilities*		
Furniture and fittings	3,000		Mortgage	5,000	
			ABC Finance Ltd	3,000	
Delivery vehicle	2,000				8,000
		45,000			
Current assets			*Current liabilities*		
Stock	6,800		Trade creditors	2,350	
Trade debtors	1,900		Bank overdraft	1,000	
Cash	180				
		8,880			3,350
		53,880			53,880

Compare this balance sheet with yours. The following notes should help you if there are differences.

- The heading is important. It tells us that this is the position of Peter Bright at a certain date, 31 January 1990.
- If your calculation of the total assets differs from ours, one or more of the following is likely:

  (a) You have confused debts due to suppliers with debts due from customers. The latter is an advantage to the business in that payment can be expected. It is therefore an asset and is usually written as 'debtors' or 'trade debtors'. The former is a liability because the business owes its suppliers money and will soon have to pay them
  (b) You have included £1,000 as money in the bank. This is wrong because there is no money in the bank to be shown as an asset. In fact Peter Bright has overdrawn his current account by £1,000 and therefore owes this sum to the bank. It is a liability of the business.
  (c) You have made an error of addition.

- The assets are shown in order of permanence with fixed assets coming before current assets and cash (the only truly liquid asset) last of all.
- The mortgage and loan from ABC Finance Limited are not due for repayment in the current year and should be regarded as long-term.
- Trade creditors and bank overdraft are both current liabilities. The former is normally repayable within a month or so and the bank overdraft is repayable on demand if the bank manager so decides.
- Capital of the proprietor was the figure missing. It can be calculated by means of the book-keeping equation: total assets (£53,880) less total liabilities (£11,350) = capital (£42,530). However, you did not have to do a separate calculation to get this right. Provided all your other figures are correct, then £42,530 is the *only* figure which can be inserted to make the balance sheet balance. Remember the sources of finance must

equal the value of the assets. We call this the jigsaw method. Capital was the only piece missing and it had to be the right size to give the picture its completeness.

- The sources of finance are also shown in order of permanence with the most permanent finance (the proprietor's capital) coming first and the least permanent (the bank overdraft) last. While this is not essential for the accuracy of the balance sheet, it does fit in better with the assets side. It is considered to be good style. For this reason also it is worth making certain that the totals of the two sides of the balance sheet end up level with each other.

Exercise 1.7

2 Feb. Asset, bank + £500; liability, bank loan + £500.

Balance sheet of Tom Spear as at 2 Feb. 1986

	£		£
Bank	2,500	Capital	2,000
		Bank loan	500
	2,500		2,500

3 Feb. Asset, motor vehicle + £2,200; asset, bank – £1,600; liability ACE Motors + £600.

Balance sheet of Tom Spear as at 3 Feb. 1986

	£		£
Motor vehicles	2,200	Capital	2,000
Bank	900	Bank loan	500
		Creditor, ACE Motors	600
	3,100		3,100

4 Feb. Asset, bank – £50; asset, cash + £50.

Balance sheet of Tom Spear as at 4 Feb. 1986

	£		£
Motor vehicle	2,200	Capital	2,000
Bank	850	Bank loan	500
Cash	50	Creditor, ACE Motors	600
	3,100		3,100

5 Feb. Asset, stock + £200 (the term 'stock' is given to the asset which is bought and sold to make a profit); asset, bank – £200.

Balance sheet of Tom Spear as at 5 Feb. 1986

	£		£
Motor vehicle	2,200	Capital	2,000
Stock	200	Bank loan	500
Bank	650	Creditor, ACE Motors	600
Cash	50		
	3,100		3,100

6 Feb. Asset, stock – £80; asset, cash + £120; owner's capital + £40 (the latter is the profit which belongs to the owner).

Balance sheet of Tom Spear as at 6 Feb. 1986

	£		£
Motor vehicle	2,200	Capital	2,000
Stock	120	*add* Profit	40
Bank	650		
Cash	170		2,040
		Bank loan	500
		Creditor, ACE Motors	600
	3,140		3,140

Exercise 1.8

8.1 The missing words in order are: two, assets, sources, finance.
8.2 Assets = capital + liabilities.
8.3 Stock is reduced by £200 and cash is increased by £120 thus the total value of assets is reduced by £80. This £80 represents a loss which is borne by the owner of the business and is deducted from his capital. Thus the sources of finance are also reduced by £80.

If this caused difficulty, reread Bill's transaction of 6 July on page 15. He made a profit which was added to his capital. A loss, the opposite of profit, is shown by deducting it from the owner's capital.

8.4 Your balance sheet should have subtotals of £91,700 for fixed assets and £7,400 for current assets. The bank loan should be shown as a long-term liability and trade creditors as a current liability. In this chapter we have been more concerned with the changes taking place within a balance sheet than with its layout. However, the latter must not be forgotten. Return to the example on page 11 for help if necessary.

CHAPTER 2

Exercise 2.1

(a)

Delivery vehicles account		Cr	Dr	Cash account	
	3 May Cash	£4,000	3 May	Delivery vehicles	£4,000

The credit entry in delivery vehicles account shows the reduction in the value of an asset. The debit entry in cash account shows a corresponding increase in another asset.

(b)

Delivery vehicles account			Cr
	3 May	Parkhill Motors	£4,000

Dr	Parkhill Motors account		
3 May	Delivery vehicles	£4,000	

The credit entry in delivery vehicles account shows the reduction in the value of that asset. The debit entry in the account for Parkhill Motors shows another asset increasingly by the same amount. Note that selling on credit means the purchaser owes money to Tom. The purchaser is therefore a debtor to Tom. Debtors like Parkhill Motors are assets because it is expected that debtors will pay their debts.

(c)

Delivery vehicles account			Cr
	3 May	Parkhill Motors	£3,000
	3 May	Bank	£1,000

Dr	Parkhill Motors account		
3 May	Delivery vehicles	£3,000	

Dr		Bank account			Cr
3 May	Delivery vehicles	£1,000			

This time three accounts are affected. However, the total debit entries still equal the total credit entries. The credit entries in delivery vehicles account reduce the value of the asset by £4,000. The debit entry in the bank account shows an increase in this asset by £1,000. The debit entry in the account for Parkhill Motors shows that the remaining £3,000 is owed to Tom by that garage. This is also an asset to Tom.

Exercise 2.2

Dr		Premises account			Cr
1990		£	*1990*		£
1 July	Balance	84,000			

Furniture and fittings account

1 July	Balance	7,000	4 July	S. Moore	50
2 July	Bank	300	4 July	Cash	50
5 July	Bank loan	500			

Stock account

1 July	Balance	5,000	6 July	Cash	300
3 July	JLK	500			

Bank account

1 July	Balance	1,900	2 July	Furniture and fittings	300

Cash account

1 July	Balance	100			
4 July	Furniture and fittings	50			
6 July	Stock	300			
6 July	Owner's capital	100			

Dr Capital account Cr

		£			£
			1 July	Balance	82,000
			6 July	Cash	100

Bank loan account

			1 July	Balance	16,000
			5 July	Furniture and fittings	500

S. Moore account

4 July	Furniture and fittings	50			

JLK account

			3 July	Stock	500

Any difficulties you encountered probably occurred with the transactions of 4 July and 6 July.

On 4 July we have to show a reduction of £1 00 worth of furniture and fittings. As £50 is received in cash and £50 remains owing from Sally Moore there are two debit entries. The easiest way to show the reduction in furniture and fittings is to make two separate entries in this account as shown. Note that some owners may keep one single account for all their debtors, called sundry debtors' account, rather than a separate one for each as I have done here.

On 6 July cash had increased by £400, therefore the cash account has to be debited with this amount. However, we credit the stock account with only £300 since this is the actual worth of the stock sold. The remaining £100 is the profit on the deal and belongs to the owner. Therefore this is credited to his capital account. The simplest way of recording this transaction is by making two debits in the cash account – one for each of the separate credits.

Exercise 2.3

(a) Balance sheet; (b) ledger account; (c) debit balance; (d) debit . . . credit; (e) Double entry; (f) credit; (g) credit . . . debit.

Exercise 2.4

(a) Dr equipment, cr bank.
(b) Dr bank, cr motor vehicle.
(c) Dr stock, cr cash.
(d) Dr bank, cr cash.
(e) Dr cash, cr bank.
(f) Trade creditors, cr cash.
(g) Dr trade creditors, cr bank.
(h) Dr bank, cr cash.
(i) Dr cash, cr debtors.

Exercise 2.5

Premises a/c: Dr 1 May balance £33,000.
Equipment a/c: Dr 1 May balance £15,000; 2 May cash £500; Cr 4 May cash £2,000.
Debtors a/c: Dr 1 May balance £5,500.
Stock a/c: Dr 1 May balance £17,000; 3 May AJK £950; Cr 7 May cash £300.
Bank a/c: Dr 5 May £500 cash; Cr 6 May creditors £300; 2 May Cr equipment £1,500; 6 May creditors £300.
Creditors a/c: Dr 6 May bank £300; Cr 1 May balance £6,750.
Capital a/c: Cr 1 May balance £65,000; 7 May cash £200.
AJK a/c: Cr 3 May stock £950.
Cash a/c: Dr 1 May balance £1,250; 4 May equipment £2,000; 7 May £300 stock and £200 capital; Cr 2 May equipment £500; 5 May bank £500.

CHAPTER 3

Exercise 3.1

1 (a) Debit, (b) credit, (c) credit, (d) debit.
2 (a) Returns outward, (b) returns inward.

Exercise 3.2

(a) *Powa Electrics books*

Dr — Jim Hogg — Cr

		£			£
1 March	Balance	160	3 March	Sales returns	40
2 March	Sales	170			

Sales

			2 March	Jim Hogg	170

Sales returns

3 March	Jim Hogg	40			

(b) *Jim Hogg's books*

Powa Electrics

Dr					Cr
		£			£
3 March	Purchases Returns	40	1 March	Balance	160
			2 March	Purchases	170

Purchases

2 March	Powa	170			

Purchases returns

			3 March	Powa	40

Exercise 3.3

Transaction	*Dr*	*Cr*
(a)	Wages	Cash
(b)	Insurance	Bank
(c)	Bank	Insurance

Parts (a) and (b) should not have caused you any trouble. Both involve a credit entry to show a reduction in an asset account when payment is made and a debit in the expense account. Part (c) is less usual. Here the expense of insurance previously recorded by a debit in the insurance account must be reduced by the amount of the rebate. A credit entry is used to show this in the same way as a credit entry would be used to show the reduction of an asset. The corresponding debit entry will be made in the bank account because a cheque has been received and this will increase that asset.

Exercise 3.4

(a) Bank, (b) debtor, (c) cash, (d) debtor, (e) machinery.

Exercise 3.5

(a) Dr rates, cr bank.
(b) Dr purchases, cr Asta Suppliers.
(c) Dr office furniture or similar, cr cash.
(d) Dr bank, cr commission rec.

(e) Dr Asta Suppliers, cr discount rec.
(f) Dr commission received, cr bank.

Exercise 3.6

Bank a/c

		£			£
1 April	Balance	1,560	2 April	Rates	250
4 April	Rent received	60	3 April	Wages	620
7 April	Insurance	12	5 April	Insurance	120
			6 April	Rent received	10
			8 April	Drawings	100

Corresponding debit entries in rates a/c, wages a/c, insurance a/c (120), rent received a/c (£10) and drawings a/c. Corresponding credit entries in rent received a/c (£60) and insurance a/c (£12).

Exercise 3.7

(a) *Food Supplies ledger*

Jim Turner a/c

		£			£
1 June	Balance	250	6 June	Returns in	75
3 June	Sales	458	9 June	Bank	240
			9 June	Disct allowed	10

(b) *Jim Turner's ledger*

Food Supplies a/c

		£			£
6 June	Returns out	75	1 June	Balance	250
9 June	Bank	240	3 June	Purchases	458
9 June	Disct received	10			

Exercise 3.8

(a) *Zoe Clough's ledger*

Peter Blake a/c

		£			£
5 April	Bank	441	1 April	Balance	450
5 April	Discount recd.	9	3 April	Purchases	356
6 April	Returns out	20			

(b) *Peter Blake's ledger*

Zoe Clough a/c

		£			£
1 April	Balance	450	5 April		441
3 April	Sales	356	5 April	Discount allowed	9
			6 April	Returns in	20

Exercise 3.9

Balance sheet of Helen Berry as at 1 March 1989

	£	£		£
Fixed assets			*Owner's capital*	19,000
Premises	15,000			
Furniture and fittings	3,000			
		18,000		
Current assets			*Current liabilities*	
Bank	3,000		Busifinance Ltd	2,000
		21,000		21,000

Dr — Premises — Cr

1989		£	1989		£
1 March	Balance	15,000			

Furniture and fittings

1 March	Balance	3,000			

Bank

1 March	Balance	3,000	7 March	Northern Foods	980
5 March	Cash	80	9 March	Insurance	25

Capital

			1 March	Balance	19,000

Busifinance

			1 March	Balance	2,000

Purchases

2 March	Northern Foods	1,000			
2 March	AKJ	500			

Northern Foods

7 March	Bank	980	2 March	Purchases	1,000
7 March	Disct recd	20			

Dr		AKJ			Cr
		£			£
6 March	Purchases returns	100	2 March	Purchases	500

Sales

			3 March	Cash	50
			4 March	Cash	100
			8 March	N. Timms	100

Cash

3 March	Sales	50	5 March	Bank	80
4 March	Sales	100			
10 March	Rent received	20			

Purchases returns

			6 March	AKJ	100

Discount received

			7 March	Northern Foods	20

N. Timms

8 March	Sales	100			

Insurance

9 March	Bank	25			

Rent received

			10 March	Cash	20

CHAPTER 4

Exercise 4.1

Balance sheet of Mike Bishop as at 1 May 1989

	£	£		£
Fixed assets			*Sources of finance*	
Equipment and machinery		12,000	Owner's capital	17,200
Current assets			*Current liabilities*	
Stock	8,000		Petrofinance Ltd	4,000
Bank	1,000			
Cash	200			
		9,200		
		21,200		21,000

Dr — Equipment and machinery — Cr

		£			£
1989					
1 May	Balance	12,000			

Dr — Stock — Cr

		£			£
1 May	Balance	8,000			

Bank

1 May	Balance	1,000	5 May	Rent	160
4 May	Cash	1,500	7 May	PB Ltd	1,164
			7 May	Balance c/d	1,176
		2,500			2,500
8 May	Balance b/d	1,176			

Cash

1 May	Balance	200	4 May	Bank	1,500
2 May	Sales	600	7 May	Balance c/d	1,790
3 May	Sales	550			
4 May	Sales	720			
5 May	Sales	680			
6 May	Sales	540			
		3,290			3,290
8 May	Balance b/d	1,790			

Capital

			1982		
			1 May	Balance	17,200

Petrofinance Ltd

			1 May	Balance	4,000

Sales

7 May	Balance c/d	3,090	2 May	Cash	600
			3 May	Cash	550
			4 May	Cash	720
			5 May	Cash	680
			6 May	Cash	540
		3,090			3,090
			8 May	Balance b/d	3,090

Purchases

Dr					Cr
3 May	PB Ltd	1,200	7 May	Balance c/d	1,400
6 May	Greasoils	200			
		1,400			1,400
8 May	Balance b/d	1,400			

PB Ltd

7 May	Bank	1,164	3 May	Purchases	1,200
7 May	Discount recd	36			

Rent

5 May	Bank	160			

Greasoils Ltd

			6 May	Purchases	200

Discount received

			7 May	PB Ltd	36

Trial balance of Mike Bishop as at 7 May 1989

	Dr balances	*Cr balances*
	£	£
Equipment and machinery	12,000	
Stock	8,000	
Bank	1,176	
Cash	1,790	
Capital		17,200
Petrofinance Ltd		4,000
Sales		3,090
Purchases	1,400	
Rent	160	
Greasoils		200
Discount recd		36
	24,526	24,526

We have balanced only those accounts which contain more than one entry. In the others the sole entry stands out clearly and this is the balance of that account.

Exercise 4.2

Suspense account

Dr		£	Cr		£
30 June	Difference in books	50	12 July	K. Bryant	50

K. Bryant

12 July	Suspense account	50			

(a) The balance is the difference between the two sides of an account. The debit balance of 1 May indicates that B. John is a debtor to Edwards for £150.
(b) On 8 May, John settled the amount owing from last month. He paid £140 by cheque and was allowed £10 discount for prompt payment. The bank account will be found on page 6 of the ledger and the account for discount allowed on page 12.

Exercise 4.3

B. John 39

Dr			£				Cr £
1989				*1989*			
1 May	Balance b/d		150	8 May	Bank	6	140
17 May	Sales	21	250	8 May	Discount allowed	12	10
27 May	Sales	21	130	31 May	Balance c/d		380
			530				530
1 June	Balance b/d		380				

Exercise 4.4

A trial balance is a list of all the balances in the ledger accounts at a particular time. It is used to check on the accuracy of the entries. If correct, the total value of the debit balances should equal the total value of credit balances.

Exercise 4.5

You should have noticed that the balances for debtors, creditors, wages, sales and purchases were placed in the wrong column of the trial balance. If you change them around, the totals will agree at £61,000.

Exercise 4.6

Errors of omission, errors of commission, errors of principle, compensating errors and original errors.

Exercise 4.7

Dr	M. J. K. Smith		Cr
	£		£
M. Smith	60		

M. Smith			
		M. J. K. Smith	60

The debit entry in M.J. K. Smith's account removes the mistake and the credit entry in M. Smith's account corrects it.

CHAPTER 5

Exercise 5.1

(a) Debtors' ledger, (b) general ledger, (c) cash book, (d) general ledger. This should not have caused you too much trouble. Remember that, if there is no division of the ledger for a particular sort of account, it remains in the general ledger. If EBA had kept a creditors' ledger, Lindsay's account would have been in it. As they didn't the account will appear with numerous different accounts, including the wages account, in the general ledger.

Exercise 5.2

(c), (e) and (f) are real accounts because they are assets. (b) and (g) are nominal accounts, wages being an expense and rent received an income. (a), (d) and (h) are personal accounts. You may have encountered two classification problems here. *First*, it could be argued that as a debtor is an asset the account for Robin Withe might be classified as real rather than personal. The personal aspect takes priority, however, in this case, as the division between personal and impersonal accounts comes before the further subdivision of impersonal accounts into real and nominal. This should be clear if you look again at the diagram on page 50.

Second, how should capital be classified? It is regarded as a special kind of personal account recording the relationship of the business with a person – the owner. The owner's capital can be regarded as the sum owing to him by the business.

Exercise 5.3

Cash book

		Cash	Bank				Cash	Bank
1 May Balances	b/d	200	1,000	4 May	Bank	c	1,500	
2 May Sales		600		5 May	Rent			160
3 May Sales		550		7 May	PB Ltd			1,164
4 May Sales		720		7 May	Balances	c/d	1,790	1,176
4 May Cash	c		1,500					
5 May Sales		680						
6 May Sales		540						
		3,290	2,500				3,290	2,500
8 May Balances	b/d	1,790	1,176					

Note the diagonal line on the credit side between the last entry and the totals. This is done by some book-keepers to prevent an entry being made in an account in the wrong place after it has been balanced.

Exercise 5.4

Dr	Discount allowed		GL 21 Cr
	£		
1–15 May Sundry debtors	23.99		

Note that the reference made beneath the total of the discount allowed in the cash book told you that the discount allowed account could be found on page 21 of the general ledger. The credit entries corresponding to this one debit will be in the accounts of the customers or debtors who have been allowed the discounts. Hence the description 'sundry debtors'.

Exercise 5.5

Spareparts p.l.c.

Dr					Cr
		£			£
31 May	Bank	69.84	25 May	Purchases	72.00
31 May	Discount received	2.16			

Purchases

25 May	Spareparts	72.00			

Cash book

		disc	cash	bank
	31 May Spareparts	2.16		69.84

Note that the purchase of the exhaust on 25 May is recorded net of trade discount. The £8, which is 10% of £80, is deducted before entries are made in the accounts. When payment is made on 31 May the cheque is made out for £72 *less* the cash discount of 3%. Thus the cheque paid is for £69.84. The 3% discount received of £2.16 is shown in the account for Spareparts plc and also in the memorandum column in the cash book. At some time the latter will be added and a total for discounts received entered in the discounts received account in the ledger.

Exercise 5.6 *see page 286*

Exercise 5.7

Discount allowed total £14.00; discount received total £30.00; cash balance £395.83 (dr); bank balance £365.63 (dr).

CHAPTER 6

Exercise 6.1

1 (a) Invoice and credit note. These are sent by the seller to the purchaser.
  (b) Duplicates of the invoice and credit note. These are retained by the seller for his records.
2 (a) Cheque and copy of receipt.
  (b) Cheque counterfoil and receipt.

Exercise 6.2

Returns outward book 6

1989	Supplier	Credit note	Folio	£ p
8 July	EQP Ltd	82/24	CL9	38.29
10 July	Electose	82/25	CL7	49.54
23 July	Plugplies	82/26	CL22	56.20
28 July	Jones	82/27	CL14	17.47
29 July	Wilsons	82/28	CL27	38.25
31 July	Transferred to returns outward a/c		GL17	199.75

GL 17 Returns outward account Cr

	31 July	Sundry creditors	ROB 6	199.75

Exercise 5.6

Dr Cash book Cr

Date	Details	Folio	Discount allowed	Cash	Bank	Date	Details	Folio	Discount received	Cash	Bank
1 April	Balances	b/d		67.23	191.20	3 April	Bank	c		100.00	
2 April	Sales			138.00		4 April	Bentley		3.00		120.00
3 April	Cash	c			100.00	5 April	Royce		6.00		94.00
6 April	Sales			97.24		8 April	Wages			120.80	
7 April	W. Barnes		9.00		169.50	9 April	T. Ford		4.00	98.00	
10 April	Bank	c		75.00		10 April	Cash	c			75.00
11 April	R. Hewitt		5.00	95.00		12 April	Car insurance				78.90
13 April	Sales			120.62		14 April	Balances	c/d		274.29	92.80
			14.00	593.09	460.70				13.00	593.09	460.70
15 April	Balances	b/d		274.29	92.80						

Exercise 6.3

Journal

			£ dr	£ cr
9 May	Southern Electrical Factors a/c	DL4	600	
	Office equipment a/c			600
	Sales of electronic typewriter serial no. 68/54321	GL6		

Exercise 6.4

(a) No – they are subsidiary or supplementary to it.
(b) Books of original entry.
(c) Posting to the ledger.
(d) Sales book, sales journal.
(e) Purchases returns day book, purchases returns journal, returns outward day book, returns outward book, returns outward journal.

Exercise 6.5

(a) Purchases journal;
(b) Returns outward journal;
(c) Sales journal;
(d) Returns inward journal;

Exercise 6.6

Sales journal total £921.29; Sales a/c cr £921.29; Baxter a/c dr £218.35; Carter a/c dr £134.43 etc.

Exercise 6.7

Returns inward journal total £262.25; Returns inward a/c £262.25; Gregg a/c cr £28.79; Hector a/c dr £79.78 etc.

Exercise 6.8

(a) Dr motor vehicles; cr Abbot Motors.
(b) Dr sales; cr trading a/c.
(c) Dr T. Hall £1,200; cr delivery vehicle £1,000; cr profit on sale of vehicle £200.
(d) Dr bad debts; cr sundry debtors.
(e) Dr R. Bly £390; dr loss on sale of equipment £60; cr equipment £450.

CHAPTER 7

Exercise 7.1

Bank reconciliation statement

	£	£
Amended bank balance as per cash book		134.06
add Cheques not presented:		
	45.25	
	56.30	
	19.67	121.22
		255.28
less Lodgement not entered by bank		120.00
Balance as per bank statement		135.28

Exercise 7.2

Dr — Sales ledger (E–H) control account — Cr

		£			£
1 April	Balances b/d	15,321	1–30 April	Cash	720
1–30 April	Sales	18,640	1–30 April	Bank	12,930
			1–30 April	Discounts allowed	380
			1–30 April	Returns inward	621
			1–30 April	Bad debts	206
			30 April	Balances c/d	19,104
		33,961			33,961
1 May	Balances b/d	19,104			

As the totals agree, no error is revealed.

Exercise 7.3

Dr — Sales ledger control account — Cr

		£			£
1 May	Balances b/d	24,860	1 May	Balances b/d	190
1–31 May	Sales	92,340	1–31 May	Bank	86,420
31 May	Balances c/d	240	1–31 May	Discounts allowed	1,730
			1–31 May	Returns inward	960
			31 May	Balances c/d	28,140
		117,440			117,440
1 June	Balances b/d	28,140	1 June	Balances b/d	240

Exercise 7.4

(a) The most common are: cheques not presented for payment, bank charges, standing orders, direct debits and cheques paid into the bank which have not yet been cleared. It is also possible that one party or both may have made a mistake.

(b) The three stages are:
  (i) Compare the cash book and bank statement and list the differences.
  (ii) Bring the cash book up to date by entering those differences which are in the statement but not yet in the cash book.
  (iii) Draft a reconciliation statement to explain the remaining differences.

(c) (i) Sales book, returns inward book, cash book, journal and the sales ledger itself.
  (ii) Purchases book, returns outward book, cash book and the purchases ledger itself.

Exercise 7.5

Bank reconciliation statement

	£	£
Amended bank balance as per cash book		95.87
add Cheques not presented:	15.21	
	14.28	
	7.30	
		36.79
		132.66
less Lodgement not entered by bank		20.00
Balance as per bank statement		112.66

Exercise 7.6

Totals equal – no error revealed.

Exercise 7.7

Dr total £80,035; cr total £82,035 – therefore error in books.

CHAPTER 8

Exercise 8.1

You should have ticked both the revenue and the profit columns for (b), (c), (e), (g) and (h). These are examples of revenue expenditure. They do not provide a fixed asset to last for a long period of time and therefore must be included in calculating the profits of the business each year. Item (h) should be carefully noted. Repairs are defined as expenditure which restores an asset to the value at which it stood immediately prior to its needing attention. When a fixed asset is in need of repair it is not considered necessary to show the reduction in its value in its account. Consequently it would be wrong to show its value increasing when the repair has been carried out. Therefore, as a repair does not increase the value of an asset, it should be regarded as revenue expenditure.

Items (a), (d) and (f) involve expenditure on fixed assets, which are expected to last longer than one year. They are not deducted from one year's income to measure profit therefore and only the capital column should have been ticked.

Exercise 8.2

- *The profit made by a business is the difference between the total income or revenue earned and the total expenses incurred during a particular period of time.*

Statements (c), (d) and (g) are true; (a) is false because, although revenue expenditure is included, capital expenditure is not; (b) is false because, while receipts of income are included, capital receipts are not; (e) is false because it is assumed that repairs merely restore an asset to its original value before it was damaged: there is thus no increase in the value of the asset; (f) is false because this is an example of a capital receipt.

Exercise 8.3

	£	£
Revenue receipts		
Sales revenue – meals and drinks		20,000
less *Revenue expenditure*		
Cost of meals and drinks sold	7,000	
Rent and rates	500	
Depreciation of fixed assets	500	
Insurance	200	
Waiters' wages	4,000	
Gas and electricity	800	13,000
Profit		7,000

The way in which you display the information does not matter for now. The important thing is that you obtained the correct answer and excluded from the calculation the information which was not relevant. Purchase of equipment is capital expenditure. Loan from the bank and additional finance invested by the owner are capital receipts. Drawings are regarded as a direct reduction of capital. Hence these items should not have entered into your calculation.

Exercise 8.4

Trading and profit and loss account of Judy Brooks for the six months ended 30 June 1990

	£	£	£
Sales			16,000
less *Cost of goods sold*			
Opening stock		400	
Purchases	4,000		
less Returns outward	200		
Net purchases		3,800	
		4,200	
less Closing stock		600	
			3,600
Gross profit c/d			12,400
less *Expenses*			
Waiters' wages	3,000		
Rent and rates	250		
Depreciation on fixed assets	250		
Insurance	100		
Gas and electricity	500		
			4,100
Net profit			8,300

The item that may have caused most problems is returns outward, which is otherwise known as purchases returns. These are goods which have been bought but which, for some reason, are then returned to the supplier. We dealt with the relevant ledger entries on page 28.

Clearly, any purchases to be included in the cost of goods sold figure must be available for sale. Those which are returned before being sold must therefore be deducted from the purchases figure to arrive at true or net purchases.

Exercise 8.5

Dr — Purchases account — Cr

1989		£	*1989*		£
31 Jan.	Bank	600	30 June	Transferred to trading a/c	4,000
28 Feb.	Bank	600			
31 Mar.	Bank	600			
30 Apr.	Bank	600			
31 May	Bank	600			
30 June	Creditors	1,000			
		4,000			4,000

Exercise 8.6

Balance sheet of Judy Brooks as at 31 May 1990

	£	£	£
Fixed assets			
Furniture and fittings		6,000	
Equipment		4,000	
China etc.		800	
			10,800
Current assets			
Stock	600		
Debtors	100		
Cash at bank	400		
		1,100	
Less current liabilities			
Trade creditors		300	
Net current assets			800
Total assets less current liabilities			11,600
Financed by:			
Owner's capital		3,300	
Add Net Profit		8,300	
			11,600

Exercise 8.7

Gross profit £24,680; net profit £22,355.

Exercise 8.8

(a) and (b) gross profit £24,512.
(c) Stock a/c

1 May	Balance b/d	4,870	31 Oct.	Transferred to trading a/c	4,870
31 Oct.	Trading a/c	6,870	31 Oct.	Balance c/d	6,870
1 Nov.	Balance b/d	6,870			

Exercise 8.9

Gross profit £51,915; net profit £28,381; Balance sheet totals £49,881 (note: depreciation has already been deducted from fixed assets).

Exercise 8.10

Net profit £26,074; balance sheet totals £70,074.

CHAPTER 9

Exercise 9.1

Rent account

Dr					Cr
1989		£	*1990*		£
1 July	Bank	200	30 June	Transferred to profit and loss account	800
3 Oct.	Bank	200	30 June	Balance prepaid c/d	200
1990					
1 June	Bank	200			
2 Apr.	Bank	200			
4 June	Bank	200			
		1,000			1,000
1 July	Balance prepaid b/d	200			

Profit and loss account of Harry Wilson for the year ended 30 June 1990

	£
Expenses	
Rent	800

Balance sheet of Harry Wilson as at 30 June 1990

	£
Current assets	
Prepaid rent	200

As you were told that the premium amounted to £200 per quarter, and there are four quarters in a year, it is clear that £800 must be the true expense of rent incurred in the year ending 30 June 1990. The additional £200 must therefore relate to the next financial year and be brought forward as a debit balance in the rent account. It thus represents an asset to Harry at the end of June 1990. In the first quarter of his next financial year he will enjoy the use of premises for which he has already paid.

Exercise 9.2

Rent account

Dr					Cr
1989/90		£	*1990*		£
	Bank	944	31 Oct.	Profit and loss a/c	876
			31 Oct.	Balance prepaid c/d	68
		944			944
1990					
1 Nov.	Balance prepaid b/d	68			

Profit and loss account, year ended 31 October 1990

	£
Expenses	
Rent	876

Balance sheet as at 31 October 1990

	£
Current assets	
Prepaid rent	68

Exercise 9.3

(b) Profit and loss a/c £600, current asset £150 rates prepaid.
(c) Prepaid at 31.12.1986 £140, current asset £140 insurance prepaid.
(d) Trial balance £4,960, current asset £640 salaries prepaid.
(e) Trial balance £1,900, prepaid at 31.12.1986 £300.
(f) Prepaid at 31.12.1986 £120, profit and loss a/c £370.

Exercise 9.4

Dr — Wages account — Cr

1989/90		£	*1990*		£
	Cash book	30,000	31 Mar.	Profit and loss a/c	30,350
31 Mar.	Balance accrued c/d	350			
		30,350			30,350
			1 April	Balance accrued b/d	350

Profit and loss account year ended 31 March 1990

	£
Expenses	
Wages	30,350

Balance sheet as at 31 March 1990

	£
Current liabilities	
Accrued wages	350

Exercise 9.5

(b) Profit and loss a/c £700, current liability £300 rates accrued.
(c) Accrued at 31.12. £70, current liability £70 insurance accrued.
(d) Trial balance £700, current liability £100 wages accrued.
(e) Trial balance £600, accrued at 31.12 £300.
(f) Accrued at 31.12 £90, profit and loss a/c £510.

Exercise 9.6

Profit and loss account year ended 30 June 1990

	£	£
Advertising received	250	
less Prepayment	20	230

Balance sheet as at 30 June 1990

	£
Current liabilities	
Advertising received in advance	20

Exercise 9.7

Profit and loss account, year ended 31 Oct. 1990

	£	£
Advertising received	160	
add Accrual	40	200

Balance sheet as at 31 Oct. 1986

	£
Current assets	
Advertising due	40

Exercise 9.8

Trading and profit and loss account of the White Hart Hotel for the year ended 31 October 1990

	£	£	£
Sales			84,000
less *Cost of sales*			
Opening stocks		2,250	
Purchases		37,500	
		39,750	
less Closing stocks		3,000	
			36,750
Gross profit			47,250
Discounts received			105
Rent received		1,800	
less Prepayment		200	
			1,600
			48,955

less *Expenses*			
Salaries and wages	16,500		
add Wages accrued	200		
		16,700	
Advertising and insurance	1,905		
less Insurance prepaid	30		
		1,875	
Interest on loan accrued		450	
Rates		1,350	
Discount allowed		300	
Heat and light		825	
Sundry expenses		675	
			22,175
Net profit			26,780

Balance sheet of the White Hart Hotel as at 31 October 1990

	£	£	£
Fixed assets			
Leasehold premises		97,500	
Furniture and equipment		22,500	
			120,000
Current assets			
Stock	3,000		
Debtors	900		
Prepaid insurance	30		
Bank	1,500		
Cash	150		
		5,580	
Less current liabilities			
Creditors	750		
Wages accrued	200		
Interest accrued	450		
Rent received in advance	200		
		1,600	
Net current assets			3,980
Total assets less current liabilities			123,980
Financed by:			
Long-term liabilities			
Loan			15,000
Owner's capital (1 Nov. 1989)		85,800	
Add Net profit		26,780	
		112,580	
Less Drawings		3,600	
			108,980
			123,980

CHAPTER 10

Exercise 10.1

(a) Expense (or cost or loss), (b) asset, (c) fair (or true) picture, (d) writing off. If you got them all right, either you have a very good memory or you took the advice above and reread the section in Chapter 3. If you didn't get them right, read that section now.

Exercise 10.2

Bad debts account

Dr					Cr
1989		£	*1989*		£
1 Jan.–31 Dec.	Sundry debtors	140	31 Dec.	Transferred to profit and loss account	140

Provision for bad debts account

1989		£	*1989*		£
31 Dec.	Balance c/d	125	31 Dec.	Profit and loss account	125
			1990		
			1 Jan.	Balance b/d	125

Profit and loss account of Simon Robinson, year ended 31 Dec. 1989

	£
Expenses	
Bad debts	140
Provision for bad debts	125

Balance sheet of Simon Robinson as at 31 December 1989

	£
Current assets	
Debtors	2,500
less Provision for bad debts	125
	2,375

Exercise 10.3

Provision for bad debts account

Cr					Dr
1990		£	*1990*		£
1 Jan.–31 Dec.	Bad debts	110	1 Jan.	Balance b/d	125
31 Dec.	Balance c/d	75	31 Dec.	Profit and loss a/c	60
		185			185
			1991		
			1 Jan.	Balance b/d	75

Profit and loss account of Robinson, year ended 31 December 1990

	£
Expenses	
Provision for bad debts	60

Balance sheet of Robinson at 31 December 1990

	£
Current assets	
Debtors	1,500
less Provision for bad debts	75
	1,425

If you succeeded with this exercise you deserve a pat on the back. Provision for bad debts is usually regarded as the most difficult adjustment at this level. I will therefore exaplain again the process by which the above answer was achieved.

At the beginning of 1990 the credit balance of £125 in the provision account represented 5% of the debtors figure as at 31 December 1989. During 1990 bad debts actually written off against this provision amounted to £110, thus £15 of the provision was unused. At the end of 1990 you were told that the debtors amounted to £1,500 and that the provision was to be maintained at 5%. Thus the provision balance needed is £75, i.e. $^{5}/_{100} \times$ £1,500. As there is still a £15 balance within the provisions account it requires only £60 from this year's profit to obtain the balance needed. Note that the balance sheet entry uses the two balances in the ledger accounts after the profit and loss account has been prepared, i.e. debtors' £1,500 and provision £75.

Exercise 10.4

Dr — Bad debts account — Cr

		£			£
1990			*1990*		
1 Jan.–31 Dec.	Sundry debtors	110	31 Dec.	Transferred to profit and loss account	110

Provision for bad debts account

		£			£
1990			*1990*		
31 Dec.	Profit and loss account	50	1 Jan.	Balance b/d	125
31 Dec.	Balance c/d	75			
		125			125
			1991		
			1 Jan.	Balance b/d	75

Profit and loss account of Robinson, year ended 31 December 1990

	£
Expenses	
Bad debts	110
less Provision for bad debts	(50)

Balance sheet of Robinson as at 31 December 1990

	£
Current assets	
Debtors	1,500
less Provision for bad debts	75
	1,425

The figure of £50 in the profit and loss account for the provision is placed in brackets to indicate that it is a deduction from the expenses. As you can see the two entries combined; i.e. the actual bad debts of £110 and the provision adjustment of minus £50 give the same final result as obtained by method 1 – a net £60 is being deducted from profits to cover bad debts. As an alternative to deducting the provision adjustment from expenses you could add the £50 back into the profits. In effect what has happened is that the amount of debtors is less than last year. To retain a 5% provision therefore needs *less* finance than we already have in the provision account. A debit entry in the provision account for £50 reduces the credit balance to the sum we require. Thus with this method you must be prepared to make adjustments on either side of the provision account as needed. A credit entry will increase the provision and a debit entry will reduce it.

Exercise 10.5

Method 1

Dr — Provision for bad debts account — Cr

1991		£	*1991*		£
1 Jan.–31 Dec.	Bad debts	130	1 Jan.	Balance b/d	75
31 Dec.	Balance c/d	80	8 June	Cash book	30
			31 Dec.	Profit and loss account	105
		210			210
			1992		
			1 Jan.	Balance b/d	80

Profit and loss account of Robinson, year ended 31 December 1991

	£
Expenses	
Provision for bad debts	105

Balance sheet of Robinson as at 31 Dec. 1991

	£
Current assets	
Debtors	1,600
less Provision for bad debts	80
	1,520

Method 2

Dr — Bad debts account — Cr

		£			£
1991			*1991*		
1 Jan.–31 Dec.	Sundry debtors	130	31 Dec.	Transferred to profit and loss account	130

Dr — Bad debts recovered account — Cr

		£			£
1991			*1991*		
31 Dec.	Transferred to profit and loss account	—	8 June	Cash book	30

Dr — Provision for bad debts account — Cr

		£			£
1991			*1991*		
31 Dec.	Balance c/d	80	1 Jan.	Balance b/d	75
			31 Dec.	Profit and loss account	5
		80			80
			1992		
			1 Jan.	Balance b/d	80

Profit and loss account of Robinson, year ended 31 Dec. 1991

	£
Expenses	
Bad debts	130
Bad debts recovered	(30)
Provision for bad debts	5

Balance sheet of Robinson as at 31 Dec. 1991

	£
Current assets	
Debtors	1,600
less Provision for bad debts	80
	1,520

As you can see the balance sheet entry is identical whichever method is used. The entries in the profit and loss account do differ in form but the effect is the same, i.e. a 'net' effect of reducing profits by £105 in 1991. You can decide for yourself which method you prefer. Personally, I prefer the logic and greater simplicity of method 1. In examinations, however, you may not be given a choice. The way the question is worded may indicate that you have to follow one particular method.

Exercise 10.6

Trading and profit and loss account of A. Wilson for the year ended 31 December 1989

	£	£
Sales		150,000
less Cost of goods sold		
Opening stocks	60,000	
add Purchases	80,000	
	140,000	
less Closing stocks	70,000	
		70,000
Gross profit		80,000
Discount received		1,000
		81,000
less Expenses		
Salaries and wages	45,000	
Provision for bad debts	1,200	
Heating and lighting	2,500	
Advertising and insurance	1,800	
Rates	1,000	
Discount allowed	2,000	
Sundry expenses	2,000	
		55,500
Net profit		25,500

Balance sheet of A. Wilson as at 31 December 1989

	£	£	£	£
Fixed assets				
Premises			120,000	
Fixtures and fittings			10,000	
Motor vehicles			30,000	
				160,000
Current assets				
Stock		70,000		
Debtors	14,000			
less Provision	700	13,300		
Bank		8,500		
Insurance prepaid		200		
			92,000	

Less current liabilities			
Creditors	40,000		
Electricity accrued	500		
		40,500	
Net current assets			51,500
Total assets less current liabilities			211,500
Financed by:			
Long-term liabilities			
Mortgage			100,000
Owner's capital (1 Jan)		86,000	
Add Net profit		25,500	
			111,500
			211,500

As the provision for bad debts is the only really new element in the above review, we will explain how the profit and loss account and balance sheet entries were derived. We have used the first method you were shown. The actual bad debts of £1,000 left the provision of £500 deficient by £500. As a provision of £700 is needed at the end of the year (5% of £14,000 – outstanding debtors), £1,200 must come from this year's profits – £500 to make up the deficiency and £700 to establish the new provision. The account will look like this:

Dr — Provision for bad debts account — Cr

		£			£
1989			*1989*		
31 Dec.	Sundry debtors	1,000	1 Jan.	Balance b/d	500
31 Dec.	Balance c/d	700	31 Dec.	Profit and loss account	1,200
		1,700			1,700
			1990		
			1 Jan.	Balance b/d	700

When you are asked to prepare final accounts from a trial balance with adjustments it is not essential to do the individual ledger accounts. You can obtain the correct answer arithmetically, e.g.

	£
Opening provision	500
less Bad debts	1,000
Provision remaining (or deficit)	(500)
Provision needed	700
Therefore required from profit	1,200

If you used the second method of dealing with bad debts you would have ended up with two entries in the profit and loss account:

- £1,000 actual bad debts;
- £200 provision adjustment (to raise £500 to £700).

The balance sheet entry would have been the same.

CHAPTER 11

Exercise 11.1

(a) $\frac{\text{£13,000 less £1,000}}{\text{8 years}} = \frac{\text{£12,000}}{8} = \text{£1,500 per annum.}$

(b) Cost less accumulated depreciation to date = current value of asset, i.e. £13,000 less £6,000 = £7,000. Four years' depreciation will have been written off this asset by the end of 1989. Thus at £1,500 per annum a total of £6,000 will have been written off, leaving the machinery valued at £7,000.

Exercise 11.2

	£	£	£
1986	1,300	1,300	11,700
1987	1,170	2,470	10,530
1988	1,053	3,523	9,477
1989	948	4,471	8,529
1990	853	5,324	7,676

Since depreciation is very much an estimate, there is no point in calculating it in pence. The nearest £1 will always suffice when using this method.

Exercise 11.3

Machinery account

Dr		£			Cr £
1988			*1988*		
1 Jan.	Balance b/d	10,530	31 Dec.	Depreciation	1,053
			31 Dec.	Balance c/d	9,477
		10,530			10,530
1989					
1 Jan.	Balance b/d	9,477			

Depreciation on machinery account

		£			£
1988			*1988*		
31 Dec.	Machinery	1,053	31 Dec.	Transferred to profit and loss account	1,053

Profit and loss account, year ended 31 December 1988

	£
Expenses	
Depn on machinery	1,053

Balance sheet as at 31 December 1988

	£	£
Fixed assets		
Machinery	10,530	
less Depn for year	1,053	
		9,477

Exercise 11.4

Machinery account

Dr		£			Cr £
1988			*1988*		
1 Jan.	Balance b/d	13,000	31 Dec.	Balance c/d	13,000
1989					
1 Jan.	Balance b/d	13,000			

Provision for depreciation on machinery account

		£			£
1988			*1988*		
31 Dec.	Balance c/d	3,523	1 Jan.	Balance b/d	2,470
			31 Dec.	Depreciation	1,053
		3,523			3,523
			1989		
			1 Jan.	Balance b/d	3,523

Depreciation on machinery account

		£			£
1988			*1988*		
31 Dec.	Provision for depn	1,053	31 Dec.	Transferred to profit and loss account	1,053

Profit and loss account, year ended 31 December 1988

	£
Expenses	
Depn on machinery	1,053

Balance sheet as at 31 December 1988

	£	£
Fixed assets		
Machinery at cost	13,000	
less Depreciation to date	3,523	
		9,477

Exercise 11.5

$$\frac{30}{100} \times \frac{£5{,}000}{1} \times \frac{3}{4} = £1{,}125.$$

30% of £5,000 would give the amount of depreciation to be written off in 1989 if the asset had been used for a full year. As it was used for only nine months in 1989 the proportionate amount of depreciation to be written off is

$^9/_{12}$ or $^3/_4$.

Exercise 11.6

Trading and profit and loss account of M. Trigg for the year ended 30 June 1990

	£	£
Sales		90,000
less Cost of sales		
Opening stock	8,000	
add Purchases	60,000	
	68,000	
less Closing stock	10,000	
		58,000
Gross profit		32,000
Expenses		
Wages	4,000	
Depn on fixed assets	4,000	
Provision for bad debts	51	
General expenses	5,800	
		13,851
Net profit		18,149

Balance sheet of M. Trigg as at 30 June 1990

	£	£	£	£
Fixed assets at cost			40,000	
Less Aggregate depreciation			8,000	
				32,000
Current assets				
Stock		10,000		
Debtors	1,420			
Less Provision	71			
		1,349		
Cash		200		
Prepaid rent		200		
			11,749	
Less current liabilities				
Creditors		500		
Bank overdraft		100		
			600	
Net current assets				11,149
Total assets less current liabilities				43,149
Financed by:				
Owner's capital			26,000	
Add Net profit			18,149	
			44,149	
Less Drawings			1,000	
				43,149

CHAPTER 12

Exercise 12.1

two, more, capital, equally.

Exercise 12.2

(b), (c), (f). (a) is a sole trader, (d) is an unincorporated association, (e) is a public limited company.

Exercise 12.3

3.1 A partnership is a business which has two or more owners who each provide capital for the business and are usually liable for the debts of the business.

3.2 Main benefits – new ideas and new skills to modernise the business and obtain a greater variety and number of customers. Problems – personality clashes, change too rapid for Harry.

3.3 Refer to section 12.4. It would be important in a business like this, which requires both technical knowledge of computers and the ability to market and administer the business, to clarify the management responsibilities of each partner.
3.4 (a) F, (b) T, (c) F.

Exercise 12.4

4.1 two capital, capital.
4.2 two current, drawings.
4.3 appropriation.

Exercise 12.5

5.1 Mary receives £3,600 and Liz £900. £4,500/5 = £900. Mary = £4 × £900. Liz = 1 × £900.
5.2 Mary receives £4,400 and Liz £3,300. £7,700/7 = £1,100. Mary = 4 × £1,100 and Liz 3 × £1,100.

Exercise 12.6

6.1 (a) ii, (b) iv, (c) i – you need to do an appropriation account first which should give you a profit of £9,000; Steve receives 2/3 of £9,000.

6.2 *Capital a/c – P. Thomas*

	1 Apr. Bank 6,000

Capital a/c – F. Lock

	1 Apr. Bank 5,000

Current a/c – P. Thomas

31 Mar.	Drawings	3,300	31 Mar.	Appropriation a/c:	
31 Mar.	Balance c/d	2,335		Interest on capital	420
				Share of profits	5,215
		£5,635			£5,635
			1 Apr.	Balance b/d	2,335

Current a/c – F. Lock

31 Mar.	Drawings	3,200	31 Mar.	Appropriation a/c:	
31 Mar.	Balance c/d	3,165		Salary	800
				Interest on capital	350
				Share of profits	5,215
		£6,365			£6,365
			1 Apr.	Balance b/d	3,165

Profit and loss appropriation account

Salary – F. Lock		800	Net profit b/d	12,000
Interest on capital:				
P. Thomas (7% × £6,000)	420			
F. Lock (7% × £5,000)	350	770		
Share of profits:				
P Thomas (½ of £10,430)	5,215			
F. Lock (½ of £10,430)	5,215	10,430		12,000
				£ —

Exercise 12.7

7.1 There would need to be four capital accounts and four current accounts. The capital account would contain the transaction recording the agreed fixed capital contribution of a partner. The current account records the earnings of each partner, whether they be from a salary, interest on capital or share of profits, and the drawings each partner has made. Separate capital and current accounts are kept to make it easy to identify the two main elements of the firm's capital structure.

7.2 *Capital a/c – Jane*

	1 Jan	Bank 3,000

Capital a/c – Jill

	1 Jan	Bank 2,000

Current a/c – Jane

31 Dec.	Drawings	1,400	31 Dec.	Appropriation a/c:	
				Interest	300
31 Dec.	Balance c/d	2,200		Salary	3,300
		£3,600			£3,600

Current a/c – Jill

31 Dec.	Drawings	1,100	31 Dec.	Appropriation a/c:	
				Interest	200
31 Dec.	Balance c/d	1,300		Salary	2,200
		£2,400			£2,400

Profit and loss appropriation account

Interest on capital:			Net profit	6,000
Jane (10% × £3,000)	300			
Jill (10% × £2,000)	200	500		
Share of profits:				
Jane ($^3/_5$ × £5,500)	3,300			
Jill ($^2/_5$ × £5,500)	2,200	5,500		6,000
				£ —

Balance sheet as at 31 December

Capital accounts		
Jane	3,000	
Jill	2,000	5,000
Current accounts		
Jane	2,200	
Jill	1,300	3,500
		8,500

Exercise 12.8

Trading, profit and loss and appropriation account for year ended 30 April

	£	£	£
Sales			112,000
Opening stock		7,100	
Purchases		71,200	
		78,300	
Less Closing stock		8,090	
Cost of gods sold			70,210
Gross profit			41,790
Expenses:			
Depreciation of fixtures		100	
Depreciation of van		1,100	
Salaries		17,050	
Rent, rates etc (*Note 1*)		6,780	
Advertising		1,020	
Motor expenses		2,200	
Telephone and postage (*Note 2*)		1,010	
General expenses		1,730	30,990
Net profit			10,800
Interest on capital:			
Bill (12% × 6,000)		720	
Ben (12% × 4,000)		480	
Salary – Ben		2,000	
Share of profits:			
Bill (3/4 × 7,600)	5,700		
Ben (1/4 × 7,600)	1,900	7,600	10,800
			–

Current a/c – Bill

			30 Apr.	Balance b/d	2,750
			30 Apr.	Interest on cap.	720
30 Apr.	Balance c/d	9,170	30 Apr.	Share of profits	5,700
		£9,170			£9,170

Current a/c – Ben

			30 Apr.	Balance b/d	1,340
30 Apr.	Balance c/d	5,720	30 Apr.	Interest on cap.	480
			30 Apr.	Salary	2,000
			30 Apr.	Share of profits	1,900
		£5,270			£5,270

Balance sheet as at 30 April

	£	£	£
Fixed assets:			
Fixtures at cost	1,000		
Less depreciation	300	700	
Delivery van at cost	4,400		
Less Depreciation	2,200	2,200	
	(*Note 4*)		2,900
Current assets:			
Stocks		8,090	
Prepayment		800	
Bank and cash		17,680	
		26,570	
Less Current liabilities:			
Creditors	3,510		
Accrued expenses (*Note 3*)	1,070	4,580	
Working capital			21,990
			24,890
Capital accounts:			
Bill		6,000	
Ben		4,000	10,000
Current accounts:			
Bill		9,170	
Ben		5,720	14,890
			24,890

Note 1 This is calculated as follows:

6,580 from the trial balance
+1,000 the amount owing for rent outstanding

7,580
– 800 the amount of rates paid in advance of the next period

£6,780

Note 2 This charge is calculated by adding the charges not yet paid to the trial balance figure.

Note 3 Remember to include accrued expenses and prepayments in the balance sheet.

Note 4 Again, remember from your previous studies that the balance sheet should show the current value of your assets. The depreciation figure must therefore, include:

the provision at the start of the year	200 and	1,100
plus the charge for the current year	100 and	1,100
Figures in the balance sheet	£300	£2,200

If you have made errors in the non-partnership parts of the exercise then refer to the earlier chapters to clarify your understanding of the relevant part.

If you have got the whole exercise right – well done partner!

Exercise 12.9

9.1 Capital account balances – Gatting £24,000, Gower £30,000, Gooch £12,000. Current account balances – Gatting £10,000, Gower £5,000, Gooch £1,000.

9.2 Capital accounts – balances as given. Current account balances – Davies £1,000 DR, Harris £500, Lord £11,500.

9.3 Gross profit £57,000; Net profit £23,000. Balance sheet – FAs £58,000; CAs £25,000; CLs £5,000. Capital account – as given; Current accounts – Nicholson £8,400, Marriott £9,600.

CHAPTER 13

Exercise 13.1

1 and (c); 2 and (a); 3 and (d); 4 and (b).

Exercise 13.2

2.1 False, 2.2 True, 2.3 False, 2.4 True.

Exercise 13.3

formed, Registrar, Certificate, Incorporation.

Exercise 13.4

True – items 1, 2 and 5; False – items 3 and 4.

Exercise 13.5

5.1 Companies Acts 1985 and 1989. 5.2 (c) and (d); (a) is a sole trader; (b) and (e) are private limited companies. 5.3 Memorandum, Articles. 5.4 Refer to sections 13.5 and 13.6.

Exercise 13.6

6.1 fixed, dividend, ordinary. 6.2 (a) (i) – 5,000 × £1 = £5,000 × 20% = £1,000; (b) (ii) – £1 × 20% = 20p.

Exercise 13.7

debenture, fixed, lenders, security.

Exercise 13.8

8.1 (a) P; (b) A and BS; (c) A and BS; (d) BS; (e) A and BS; (f) P. 8.2 (a) True; (b) False; (c) True; (b) and (c) deal with a common belief that reserves or retained profits are cash. The fact that a company has retained profits means that its total net assets have increased, i.e. the total business is worth more. This can happen even when cash decreases. So reserves represent increases in all of the assets of the business, not just cash.

Exercise 13.9

9.1 *Balance sheet as at 1 January*

	£	£
Fixed assets		100,000
Current assets	75,000	
Current liabilities	25,000	
Working capital		50,000
Net assets employed		150,000
Authorised share capital		
150,000 ordinary shares		150,000
50,000 6% preference shares		50,000
		200,000
Issued share capital:		
100,000 ordinary shares		100,000
50,000 6% preference shares		50,000
		150,000

9.2 *Profit and loss appropriation account for year ended 31 December*

	£	£
Net profit		50,000
Proposed dividends:		
Ordinary	10,000	
Preference	3,000	
		13,000
Profit and loss account carried forward		37,000

Balance sheet as at 31 December

	£	£	£
Fixed assets			150,000
Current assets		90,000	
Current liabilities	40,000		
Proposed dividends	13,000	53,000	
Working capital			37,000
Net assets employed			187,000
Authorised share capital:			
150,000 ordinary shares			150,000
50,000 6% preference shares			50,000
			200,000
Issued share capital:			
100,000 ordinary shares			100,000
50,000 6% preference shares			50,000
			150,000
Reserves:			
Profit and loss account			37,000
Net capital employed			187,000

9.3 *Profit and loss appropriation account for year ended 31 December*

	£	£	£
Net profit			80,000
Profit and loss account brought forward			36,000
			116,000
Transfer to General Reserve		15,000	
Proposed dividends:			
Ordinary	37,500		
Preference	3,600		
		41,100	56,100
Profit and loss account carried forward			59,900

Balance sheet as at 31 December

	£	£	£
Fixed assets			350,000
Current assets		126,000	
Current liabilities:			
Other	50,000		
Proposed dividends	41,100	91,100	
Working capital			34,900
Net assets employed			384,900
Authorised share capital:			
300,000 ordinary shares			300,000
100,000 6% preference shares			100,000
			400,000
Issued share capital:			
250,000 ordinary shares			250,000
60,000 6% preference shares			60,000
			310,000
Reserves:			
General reserve		15,000	
Profit and loss account		59,900	74,900
Net capital employed			384,900

9.4 *Trading, profit and loss and appropriation account for year ended 31 December*

	£	£
Sales		165,000
Opening stock	1,200	
Add purchases	91,000	
	92,200	
Less Closing stock	1,400	
Cost of goods sold		90,800
Gross profit		74,200
Rent receivable (450 + 150)		600
		74,800
General salaries (18,000 + 200)	18,200	
Rates and insurance (500 – 50)	450	
Motor expenses	1,000	
Directors' salaries	19,000	
General expenses	2,500	
Depreciation on motor vans	1,300	
Debenture interest (450 + 450)	900	
Bad debts	600	43,950

Net profit			30,850
Profit and loss account at 1 January			12,900
			43,750
Transfer to general reserve		5,000	
Proposed ordinary dividend		3,000	8,000
Profit and loss account at 31 December			35,750

Balance sheet as at 31 December

	£	£	£
Fixed assets:			
Freehold buildings			80,000
Motor vans at cost		5,200	
Less Depreciation		4,300	900
			80,900
Current assets:			
Stocks		1,400	
Debtors		8,900	
Income due – rent		150	
Prepayment – rates		50	
Bank and cash		5,400	
		15,900	
Current liabilities:			
Creditors	7,400		
Debenture interest due	450		
Salaries due	200		
Proposed dividends	3,000	11,050	
Working capital			4,850
Net assets employed			85,750
Authorised and issued share capital:			
30,000 ordinary shares			30,000
Reserves:			
General reserve		5,000	
Profit and loss account		35,750	40,750
Long-term liability:			
6% debentures			15,000
Net capital employed			85,750

9.5 *Trading, profit and loss and appropriation account for year ended 30 June*

	£	£
Sales		240,000
Opening stock	30,000	
Add Purchases	180,000	
	210,000	
Less Closing stock	32,000	
Cost of goods sold		178,000
Gross profit		62,000
Rent receivable (1,000 + 1,000)		2,000
		64,000
Salaries (24,000 + 1,000)	25,000	
Rates and insurance	2,000	
Motor expenses	3,000	
Directors' salaries	6,000	
General expenses	5,000	
Depreciation on motor vans	3,000	
Debenture interest (1,000 + 1,000)	2,000	
Bad debts	2,000	48,000
Net profit		16,000
Profit and loss account at 1 July		21,000
		37,000
Proposed ordinary dividend		5,000
Profit and loss account at 30 June		32,000

Balance sheet as at 30 June

	£	£	£
Fixed assets:			
Buildings			36,000
Motor vans at cost		12,000	
Less Depreciation		6,000	6,000
			42,000
Current assets:			
Stocks		32,000	
Debtors		18,000	
Income due – rent		1,000	
Bank and cash		30,000	
		81,000	

Current liabilities:			
Creditors	14,000		
Debenture interest due	1,000		
Salaries due	1,000		
Proposed dividends	5,000	21,000	
Working capital			60,000
Net assets employed			102,000
Share capital:			
Ordinary shares			50,000
Reserves:			
Profit and loss account			32,000
Long-term liability:			
6% debentures			20,000
Net capital employed			102,000

CHAPTER 14

Exercise 14.1

A manufacturing firm obtains raw materials and components and converts them into finished products ready for resale.

Exercise 14.2

2.1 Refer to the definitions given in the text. 2.2 Tomato grower – (a) Direct materials, (b) Factory overheads, (c) Direct labour Newspaper – (a) Direct labour, (b) Direct materials, (c) Direct expenses.

Exercise 14.3

3.1 This will depend on the firm but should include the element of conversion. 3.2 (a) and (iii); (b) and (i); (c) and (ii). 3.3 (i) M; (ii) P(F); (iii) P(S); (iv) M; (v) M; (vi) P(S); (vii) P(F); (viii) T; (ix) M; (x) M; (xi) P(A); (xii) P(F) or P(S).

Exercise 14.4

4.1 Opening stock of raw materials + purchases – closing stock. See previous example.

4.2 *Manufacturing and trading account for the year ended 30 June*

	£	£	£
Opening stock of raw materials		4,200	
Add Purchases of timber		82,000	
		86,200	
Less Closing stock of raw materials		6,200	
Direct materials (*Note 1*)		80,000	
Direct labour		38,300	
Direct expenses – royalties		1,000	
Prime cost		119,300	
Factory overheads:			
Power, light and heat	1,650		
Rates	3,000		
Depreciation of machinery	1,850		
Salaries	15,700	22,200	
Cost of production		141,500	
Add Opening stock of finished goods		13,200	
		154,700	
Less Closing stock of finished goods		15,700	
Cost of goods sold		139,000	
Add Warehouse expenses:			
Wages	4,700		
Power, light and heat	800		
Rates	1,500	7,000	
Cost of sales			146,000
Sales			200,000
Gross profit			54,000

4.3 1,000 – the total of the two closing stocks.

Exercise 14.5

5.1 *Manufacturing and trading account for the year ended 31 December*

	£	£	£
Opening stock of raw materials		6,000	
Add Purchases		35,000	
		41,000	
Less Closing stock of raw materials		5,000	
Direct materials		36,000	
Direct labour		55,000	
Prime cost		91,000	

Factory overheads:			
Fuel and power	6,000		
Rates and insurance	3,000		
Depreciation of plant and machinery	8,000		
Salaries	24,000	41,000	
Cost of production		132,000	
Add Opening stock of finished goods		4,000	
		136,000	
Less Closing stock of finished goods		8,000	
Cost of goods sold			128,000
Sales			200,000
Gross profit			72,000

5.2 *Manufacturing, trading, profit and loss and appreciation account for the year ended 30 September*

	£	£	£
Opening stock of raw materials		6,000	
Add Purchases of raw materials		43,000	
		49,000	
Less Closing stock of raw materials		9,000	
Direct materials		40,000	
Direct labour		65,000	
Prime cost		105,000	
Factory overheads:			
Rates and insurance	3,000		
Light and heat	6,000		
Factory power	5,000		
Factory expenses	18,000		
Depreciation on plant and machinery	7,000	39,000	
Cost of production		144,000	
Add Opening work-in-progress		4,000	
		148,000	
Less Closing work-in-progress		5,000	
Cost of production		143,000	
Add Opening stock of finished goods		8,000	
		151,000	
Less Closing stock of finished goods		10,000	
Cost of goods sold			141,000
Sales			190,000
Gross profit			49,000

Administration expenses:			
Office and administration expenses	9,000		
Rates and insurance	1,000		
Light and heat	2,000	12,000	
Selling and distribution expenses:			
Salaries and commissions	14,000		
Salespersons' expenses	4,000		
Advertising	3,000	21,000	33,000
Net profit			16,000

5.3 Bradley's Bats Ltd

Manufacturing, trading, profit and loss and appropriation account for the year ended 31 October

	£	£	£
Opening stock of raw materials		5,300	
Add Purchases of raw materials		89,160	
		94,460	
Less Closing stock of raw materials		6,250	
Direct materials		88,210	
Direct labour		52,180	
Prime cost		140,390	
Factory overheads:			
Rent	2,400		
Salaries	14,630		
Light, heat and power (4,250 + 750)	5,000		
General expenses	4,730		
Depreciation on plant and machinery	12,000	38,760	
Cost of production		179,150	
Add Opening work-in-progress		10,200	
		189,350	
Less Closing work-in-progress		11,150	
Cost of production		178,200	
Add Opening stock of finished goods		16,120	
Purchases of finished goods		3,240	
		197,560	
Less Closing stock of finished goods		17,380	
Cost of goods sold		180,180	
Add Warehouse expenses		5,970	
Cost of sales			186,150
Sales			245,010
Gross profit			58,860
Decrease in provision for bad debts			650
			59,510

Administration expenses:			
General expenses	9,840		
Depreciation of fixtures and equipment	1,500	11,340	
Selling and distribution expenses (14,620 + 300)		14,920	
Finance expenses:			
Bank interest (1,200 + 450)		1,650	27,910
Net profit			31,600
Profit and loss account balance at 1 November			61,200
			92,800
Proposed dividends:			
ordinary		6,000	
preference		1,200	7,200
Profit and loss account balance at 31 December			85,600

Balance sheet as at 31 October

	£	£	£
Fixed assets:			
Office premises			76,500
Plant and machinery at cost		80,000	
Less depreciation		57,000	23,000
Fixtures and equipment at cost		15,000	
Less depreciation		6,500	8,500
			108,000
Current assets:			
Closing stocks –			
raw materials		6,250	
work in progress		11,150	
finished goods		17,380	
		34,780	
Debtors	51,000		
Less provision	2,550	48,450	
		83,230	
Current liabilities:			
Creditors	16,450		
Accrued expenses	1,500		
Bank overdraft	20,480		
Proposed dividend	7,200	45,630	
Working capital			37,600
Net assets employed			145,600
Share capital:			
40,000 ordinary shares			40,000
20,000 6% preference shares			20,000
			60,000

Reserves:	
Profit and loss account	85,600
Net capital employed	145,600

Check your answer carefully. Particular points to note are the decrease in the bad debts provision (only £550 is required and the existing provision was £200) and the proposed dividends in the balance sheet.

CHAPTER 15

Exercise 15.1

1.1 (b) is correct. 1.2 allocated, incurred, apportioned.

Exercise 15.2

	Winter sports		*Main sports*		*Other sports*
Opening stock for each department was:	£2,000		£6,000		£1,000
Divide through by 1,000 to simplify and give the ratio:	2	:	6 (a total of 9 parts)	:	1
The insurance of stock cost is £900 which is split	($^2/_9$ × £900) = £200		($^6/_9$ × £900) = £600		($^1/_9$ × £900) = £100

Exercise 15.3

3.1 To analyse the total figures of the business between its departments so that the management of the business has useful information on the performance of each main section of the business.

3.2 An allocated cost is one which can be charged in full to one department, i.e. it is incurred only for the benefit of that department.

3.3 Departmental profit or contribution is the surplus which remains after taking the cost of goods sold by the department and the direct cost of running that department away from its sales income. It is the surplus made before the deduction of the other general costs of running the business

3.4 The most sensible matching here would be:
(a) (iv); (b) (iii); (c) (ii); (d) (i).
If you had problems with any of these questions then re-read the relevant section in the text.

3.5 *Departmental trading and profit and loss accounts for the six months ended 28 February*

		Bedroom	*Kitchen*	*Other*	*Total*
Sales	(A)	20,000	40,000	60,000	120,000
Opening stock		4,000	8,000	15,000	27,000
Add Purchases		13,000	25,000	34,000	72,000
		17,000	33,000	49,000	99,000
Less Closing stock		3,000	9,000	14,000	26,000
Cost of goods sol	(B)	14,000	24,000	35,000	73,000
Gross profit	(A–B)	6,000	16,000	25,000	47,000
Advertising		1,000	2,000	3,000	6,000
Rates and insurance		800	1,200	2,000	4,000
Salaries		5.000	10,000	10,000	25,000
Other expenses		1,500	3,000	4,500	9,000
		8,300	16,200	19,500	44,000
Net profit/(loss)		£(2,300)	£(200)	£5,500	£3,000

3.6 *Yeovale Hardware Company Ltd*

Departmental trading, profit and loss and appropriation account for the year ended 31 July

		Hardware	*Timber*	*Total*
Sales	(A)	400,000	180,000	580,000
Opening stock		40,000	10,000	50,000
Add Purchases		240,000	70,000	310,000
		280,000	80,000	360,000
Less Closing stock		45,000	20,000	65,000
Cost of goods sold	(B)	235,000	60,000	295,000
Gross profit	(A–B)	165,000	120,000	285,000
Less Departmental costs:				
Wages and salaries		40,000	18,000	58,000
Departmental profits		£125,000	£102,000	227,000

Administration expenses	30,000	
Selling and distribution expenses	40,000	
Premises expenses	20,000	
Depreciation of fixtures and equipment	6,000	96,000
Net profit		131,000
Add Profit and loss account balance at 1 August		140,000
		271,000
Less Proposed ordinary dividend		16,000
Profit and loss account at 31 July		£255,000

Balance sheet as at 31 July

	£	£	£
Fixed assets:			
Freehold property			220,000
Fixtures and equipment at cost		60,000	
Less depreciation		24,000	36,000
			256,000
Current assets:			
Stocks		65,000	
Debtors		60,000	
Bank		40,000	
		165,000	
Current liabilities:			
Creditors	70,000		
Proposed dividend	16,000	86,000	
Working capital			79,000
Net assets employed			335,000
Share capital:			
50p ordinary shares			80,000
Reserves:			
Profit and loss account			255,000
Net capital employed			335,000

CHAPTER 16

Exercise 16.1

Assets = liabilities + capital.

Exercise 16 2

2.1 Incomplete records is where transactions are not recorded using a double-entry system. 2.2 The main reason tends to be because little time need then be spent on book-keeping. Other reasons may be lack of knowledge or dislike of double-entry book-keeping. 2.3 Assets = liabilities + capital; or capital = assets – liabilities.

2.4 *Statement of affairs at 1 January*

	£	£
Fixed assets:		
Furniture and fittings		850
Current assets:		
Stock	810	
Debtors	350	
Bank and cash	175	
	1,335	
Current liabilities	340	
		995
		1,845
Capital		1,845

Statement of affairs at 31 December

	£	£
Fixed assets:		
Furniture and fittings		1,250
Current assets:		
Stock	1,020	
Debtors	460	
Bank and cash	300	
	1,780	
Current liabilities	420	
		1,360
		2,610
Capital		2,610

Difference is £610 – £845 =	765
Add Drawings	1,200
Net profit	1,965

Exercise 16.3

Your approach should be as follows:

Total paid to suppliers, say	5,000
Less Amounts paid in settling liabilities from the previous period, i.e. opening creditors, say	1,000
	4,000
Add Amounts owing for purchases made but not yet paid for, i.e. closing creditors, say	2,000
Purchases	£6,000

Exercise 16.4

4.1 (b) £22,000 – £1,000 + £1,500 = £22,500.
4.2 (d) £10,250 – £750 + £1,000 = £10,500.
4.3 (a) £1,360 – £40 + £60 = £1,380.

Exercise 16.5

5.1 (1) *Statement of affairs at 1 January*

	£	£	£
Assets: Equipment		12,000	
Bank		5,000	
		17,000	
Capital		17,000	

(2) Calculation of sales:

Receipts from debtors	29,000
Add Closing debtors	3,000
Sales	32,000

Calculation of purchases:

Payments to creditors	15,000
Add Closing creditors	4,000
Purchases	19,000

(3) Bank balance = 1,000

(4) *Trading and profit and loss account for year ended 31 December*

	£	£	£
Sales			32,000
Purchases		19,000	
Less Closing stock		2,000	
Cost of goods sold			17,000
Gross profit			15,000
Expenses:			
Sundry expenses		5,100	
Depreciation of equipment		1,500	6,600
Net profit			8,400

Balance sheet as at 31 December

	£	£	£
Fixed assets:			
Equipment			15,000
Less Depreciation			1,500
			13,500
Furniture			1,000
			14,500

Current assets:			
Stock		2,000	
Debtors		3,000	
Bank		1,000	
		6,000	
Current liabilities:			
Creditors	4,000		
Expenses owing	100	4,100	
			1,900
			16,400
Capital:			
Opening balance			17,000
Add Net profit			8,400
			25,400
Less Drawings			9,000
			16,400

5.2 *Statement of affairs at 1 January*

	£	£	£
Fixed assets:			
Equipment			5,100
Vehicle			3,500
			8,600
Current assets:			
Stock		4,000	
Debtors		1,000	
Cash		50	
		5,050	
Current liabilities:			
Creditors	1,500		
Bank overdraft	500	2,000	
			3,050
			11,650
Capital			11,650

Calculation of sales:	£	*Calculation of purchases:*	£
Receipts from debtors	21,100	Payments to creditors	9,000
Less Opening debtors	1,000	*Less* Opening creditors	1,500
	20,100		7,500
Add Closing debtors	2,000	*Add* Closing creditors	2,000
Sales	22,100	Purchases	9,500

Trading and profit and loss account for year ended 31 December

	£	£
Sales		22,100
Opening stock	4,000	
Add Purchases	9,500	
	13,500	
Less Closing stock	5,000	
Cost of goods sold		8,500
Gross profit		13,600
Expenses:		
Assistant's wages	3,000	
Light and heat (300 + 50)	350	
Vehicle running costs	2,200	
Depreciation of equipment (5,100 + 1,000 – 5,500)	600	
Depreciation of vehicle (3,500 – 2,500)	1,000	7,150
Net profit		6,450

Balance sheet as at 31 December

	£	£	£
Fixed assets:			
Equipment (net)			5,500
Vehicle (net)			2,500
			8,000
Current assets:			
Stock		5,000	
Debtors		2,000	
Bank		600	
Cash		50	
		7,650	
Current liabilities:			
Creditors	2,000		
Light and heat owing	50	2,050	
			5,600
			13,600
Capital:			
Opening balance			11,650
Add Net profit			6,450
			18,100
Less Drawings			4,500
			13,600

5.3 *Statement of affairs at 1 January*

	£	£
Fixed assets:		
Furniture and fittings		1,000
Current assets:		
Stock	910	
Debtors	390	
Bank	3,550	
	4,850	
Current liabilities:		
Creditors	140	
		4,710
		5,710
Capital		5,710

Calculation of sales:	£	*Calculation of purchases:*	£
Receipts from debtors	6,640	Payments to creditors	2,420
Less Opening debtors	390	*Less* Opening creditors	140
	6,250		2,280
Add Closing debtirs	650	*Add* Closing creditors	320
Sales	6,900	Purchases	2,600

Trading and profit and loss account for year ended 31 December

	£	£
Sales		6,900
Opening stock	910	
Add Purchases	2,600	
	3,510	
Less Closing stock	1,200	
Cost of goods sold		2,310
Gross profit		4,590
Expenses:		
Wages (1,020 + 40)	1,060	
Rent and rates (1,650 – 140)	1,510	
General expenses	680	
Depreciation of furniture and fittings	100	
Bad debts	20	3,370
Net profit		1,220

Balance sheet as at 31 December

	£	£	£
Fixed assets:			
Furniture and fittings at cost			1,000
Less Depreciation			100
			900
Current assets:			
Stock		1,200	
Debtors		630	
Prepayment		140	
Bank (*Note 1*)		2,920	
		4,890	
Current liabilities:			
Creditors	320		
Wages owing	40	360	
			4,530
			5,430
Capital:			
Opening balance			5,710
Add Net profit			1,220
			6,930
Less Drawings			1,500
			5,430

Note 1 The closing bank figure is calculated by taking the opening balance + total receipts – total payments, i.e. 3,550 + 6,640 = 10,190 – 7,270 = 2,920.

Exercise 16.6

The correct items would be 2, 4 and 6. Items 1 and 5 are limited companies and 3 is a partnership – these will have profit-making as one of their main aims.

Exercise 16.7

constitution, rules, committee, manage, accounts, annual general meeting.

Exercise 16.8

(a) and (iii); (b) and (i); (c) and (iv); (d) and (ii).

Exercise 16.9

3 – fifty members at £10 each.

Exercise 16.10

10.1 Two or more people who have joined together to pursue a matter of common interest with no profit-making motive.

10.2 The main reasons are to regulate the affairs of a club, lay down rules for behaviour, administration and accountability and to ensure that members' interests are protected.

10.3 *Bar trading account for year ended 31 December*

	£		£
Opening balance	1,500	Takings	15,000
Add Purchases			
(10,000 + 2,000 – 1,000)	11,000		
	12,500		
Less Closing stock	2,500		
Cost of goods sold	10,000		
Add Barman's wages	3,000		
Cost of sales			13,000
Profit on bar			£2,000

10.4 A current liability. If the club was wound up at the end of 1989 that money would have to be returned to the subscribers.

10.5 Rent, £90. Subscriptions income, £4,420. Rates, £2,000.

10.6 *Bar trading account for year ended 31 December*

	£	£
Bar takings		22,970
Opening stock	920	
Purchases (16,980 + 1,380 – 1,300)	17,060	
	17,980	
Less Closing stock	960	
Cost of goods sold	17,020	
Add Steward's wages	2,500	
Cost of sales		19,520
Profit on bar		3,450

Income and expenditure account for year ended 31 December

	£		£
General expenses	1,760	Profit on bar	3,450
Repairs to premises	1,400	Subscriptions (1980 + 20)	2,000
Depreciation of furniture	350	Profit on socials	260
Surplus for the year	2,200		
	5,710		5,710

Balance sheet as at 31 December

	£	£
Fixed assets:		
Buildings		15,000
Furniture (1,600 + 1,900 – 350)		3,150
		18,150
Current assets:		
Bar stocks	960	
Bank and cash	1,435	
	2,395	
Current liabilities:		
Creditors	1,380	
		1,015
Net assets employed		19,165
Accumulated fund:		
Opening balance		16,965
Add Surplus		2,200
		19,165

CHAPTER 17

Exercise 17.1

Tesco Stores. Its ROCE has been constantly above 20%, although reduced from year 1's high level. BP's results have been variable with outstanding results in years 3 and 4 but significantly lower returns in the other years. Scottish & Newcastle's results have been consistent but at a lower level than Tesco.

A relatively low ROCE will indicate that there are weaknesses in either the profitability or productivity of the business. These can be assessed by using further ratios.

Exercise 17.2

You should have ticked items (b), (c) and (e). The fact that fewer items were bought and sold during the year would not affect the profit made on each item sold.

Exercise 17.3

Items (a), (c) and (d) all represent improvements in productivity.

Exercise 17.4

Number 3. His primary concern would be with the existing level of borrowing by the company.

Exercise 17.5

5.1

	1988		1989	
Slater's Stores				
Overall performance				
1 ROCE	$\frac{80}{200} \times 100$	= 40%	$\frac{80}{300} \times 100$	= 26.7%
2 Return on owner's equity	$\frac{42}{120} \times 100$	= 35%	$\frac{23}{140} \times 100$	= 16.4%
Profitability				
3 (a) Gross profit margin	$\frac{180}{600} \times 100$	= 30%	$\frac{220}{800} \times 100$	= 27.5%
(b) Mark-up on cost	$\frac{180}{420} \times 100$	= 43%	$\frac{220}{580} \times 100$	= 38%
4 Net profit margin	$\frac{80}{600} \times 100$	= 13%	$\frac{80}{800} \times 100$	= 10%
Productivity				
5 Sales per employee	$\frac{600}{20}$	= £30,000	$\frac{800}{25}$	= £32,000
6 Asset turnover	$\frac{600}{200}$	= 3 times	$\frac{800}{300}$	= 2.7 times
7 Stock turnover	420/(50+60/2)	= 7.6 times	580/(60+80/2)	= 8.3 times
8 (a) Debtor turnover	$\frac{600}{2}$	= 300 times	$\frac{800}{4}$	= 200 times
(b) Debtor collection period	$\frac{2}{1.643}$	= 1 day	$\frac{4}{2.192}$	= 2 days
Liquidity				
9 Current ratio	100:40	= 2.5:1	120:70	= 1.7:1
10 Acid test ratio	40:40	= 1:1	40:70	= 0.6:1
Investment				
11 Dividend yield	$\frac{10}{100} \times 100$	= 10%	$\frac{15}{100} \times 100$	= 15%
Capital structure				
12 Gearing ratio	$\frac{80}{200} \times 100$	= 40%	$\frac{160}{300} \times 100$	= 53%
13 Interest cover	$\frac{80}{8}$	= 10 times	$\frac{80}{16}$	= 5 times

5.2 Here are the detailed points we would make:

Overall performance. This is good, although it has worsened in 1989. *Profitability*. This has declined significantly in 1989 both at gross and net profit level. Stock turnover has improved and sales have increased by $33^1/_3$% on 1988. It may therefore be that selling prices have been held down in order to increase the level of sales being made. It also is noticeable that running expenses have increased at a greater rate than the increase in sales.

Productivity. Sales per employee have increased but this must be related to the increase in the rate of inflation to see if more items were actually sold per employee in 1989. The overall asset turnover has declined slightly due, in part, to the very large increase in fixed assets. Given that this is a stores business, it must be assumed that more premises have been acquired - no other fixed assets could account for such an increase. There has been a tight control on current assets - stock and debtor turnover rates have improved. Debtors are not very significant in this type of business as most transactions are for cash.

Liquidity. This was sound in 1988 but is now stretched. The acid test ratio is rather low but given that most stocks in stores are able to be sold for at least their book value, the company is probably sound. However, care should now be taken over the control of cash.

Investment. The dividend yield is adequate, especially as only he and his wife are shareholders. It is wise to leave the money in the business at present because of its tight liquidity.

Capital structure. There has been a significant increase in borrowing, presumably to pay for the purchase of premises. Because the net profit has remained constant the interest cover has been cut in two.

Conclusion. The company appears to have expanded rapidly with the purchase of premises financed by borrowing. This has required more staff and increased costs. Whilst sales have increased, profit margins have been cut to help this. It is likely that 1989's results have not yet seen the benefits of this expansion. The overall return on capital is good but John Slater must beware of liquidity problems. Tight control over costs and cash will be needed.

Exercise 17.6

6.1 Briefly he would want to see if he would be likely to be paid. The main ratios would be those concerned with the liquidity of the business, i.e. current and acid test ratios.

6.2 Because the accounting figures themselves don't clearly measure performance or key relationships. Ratios enable the assessment of a company by comparing one key figure with another.

6.3

	1988	1989
Current ratio	2.2 : 1	5.2 : 1
Acid test ratio	1.2 : 1	3.6 : 1

The current ratio has certainly increased (as has the acid test ratio) but it cannot be said to have 'improved'. In 1988 it was very satisfactory, in 1989 it is excessively high. In particular, the debtors' figure has increased enormously and would indicate that the company's credit control system has broken down.

6.4 The main points noted should include the following:

- The ROCE has been exceptionally high until 1989 when problems beset the company.
- The gross profit margin is relatively high but has declined substantially in 1988 and 1989. This may reflect the increasing competition the company has experienced as it has expanded, i.e. it has had to keep down or reduce selling prices in order to increase sales.
- This competition is also reflected in the slight slow down in stock turnover.
- The net profit margin has been declining steadily and has experienced a dramatic fall in 1989.
- This type of business is likely to spend a lot on research and development. This and other high costs together with the reducing gross profit margin may have resulted in the net profit margin fall.
- The liquidity of the business has been very high but has fallen to 'tight' levels in 1989. The management would have to ensure that there is no further decline, otherwise the company may suffer problems.
- Overall, there has been a decline in profitability due to increasing competition and high costs in a period of recession.

CHAPTER 18

Exercise 18.1

1.1 £900. To find profit we take the cost of the items sold from the sales value. Accounting accepts that a profit has been obtained when a legal obligation is made, i.e. those to whom Tony has made the sales are legally obliged to pay for the items at the end of the credit period.

1.2 Still nothing. Whilst Tony has made a profit on these sales he has not actually received any money for them, so his bank balance has not improved.

Exercise 18.2

2.1 £300. The profit on the one sale made.

2.2 £1 100 overdrawn. He will have paid cash for his replacement stock but has still not received any money from the sales made.

Exercise 18.3

Sources are 2, 4 and 5. Applications are 1 and 3. If you had any difficulties here check the items against the lists above.

Exercise 18.4

Cash flow statement for year ended 31 December

Sources of cash		
Cash from trading		7,000
Issue of shares		20,000
Loan		20,000
		47,000
Applications of cash		
Purchase of fixed assets	15,000	
Increase in stock	10,000	
Increase in debtors	15,000	
Decrease in creditors	2,000	42,000
Increase in cash		£ 5,000

Exercise 18.5

5.1 *Yes.* Mike would be getting people outside the business to put more money into it.

5.2 *Yes.* This is one of the main ways in which businesses can quickly improve cash flow in the short term. The details of credit control are outside the scope of this book but the main aim would be to chase up outstanding debtors more quickly and reduce the amount of credit given to customers. This may involve the use of 'incentives' such as cash discounts for payment within the credit period or 'threats' such as the withdrawal of further credit facilities, charging interest on overdue amounts and even legal action.

5.3 *No.* Holding more stocks would definitely not improve cash flow! The management of a business must decide on the level of stocks it wishes to hold bearing in mind its financial position, demand for its products, the level of service it wishes to provide etc. For example, Westlands PLC, manufacturers of helicopters, decided to invest substantial sums of money into stocks of raw materials and components in order to improve its competitiveness over delivery dates and its ability to support the sales of helicopters with adequate spares. This obviously was a use of cash which they were prepared to meet. But for firms with cash flow problems th usual approach is to reduce stock levels until their finances improve. To do this they will often analyse their stocks and try to eliminate slow-moving or obsolete items, reduce the average quantities held of all items, particularly expensive items etc.

5.4 *No.* The creditors have got the cash, it is not in the company's bank account! When a company is in trouble it will normally try to delay paying its suppliers. Whilst this is necessary then, it should not be made normal business practice as it is very easy to be put on blacklists which can make it difficult to obtain credit facilities in the future.

5.5 *Yes*, probably. Clearly if there is more cash coming in from each sale then the cash flow of the business should improve. However, it may be found that the increase in prices results in fewer items being sold which could then produce a worsening cash flow.

5.6 *Yes.* Less money would be spent.

5.7 *Yes*. By selling the factory the company would receive a large lump sum. It will then have to pay out smaller regular sums in rent on the lease.

As you can see from this list there are lots of ways in which cash flow can be improved. It is up to the management of a business to decide what are the most appropriate methods for the particular circumstances of that business.

Exercise 18.6

6.1 The reason is that in accounting a profit is accepted as being made when a legally binding contract has been made, i.e. where a sale on credit has taken place. However, the cash from the sale may not actually be received until weeks or months later.

6.2 Refer to Figure 18.1. Hopefully you were able to produce something similar.

6.3 *Cash flow statement for year ended 31 March*

Sources of cash		
Cash from trading		10,000
Issue of shares		20,000
Increase in creditors		9,000
		39,000
Applications of cash		
Purchase of fixed assets	18,000	
Increase in stock	12,000	
Increase in debtors	8,000	
Repayment of debentures	9,000	47,000
Decrease incash		£8,000

This agrees with the movement in the bank balance from £6,000 positive to £2,000 overdrawn.

The statement highlights the fact that whilst the company has paid for its new fixed assets through the issue of shares, it has not been able to cover the increases in stock and debtors from trading sources.

6.4 Clearly Tom needs to reduce his stocks without seriously affecting the reputation of his business. Examples of the action he might take could be to reduce the quantities he buys of each item of stock, to stop buying items which are not selling to arrange a sale at reduced prices of slow-moving lines and so get a quick inflow of cash etc.

CHAPTER 19

Exercise 19.1

Direct materials are those materials *used or contained* in the *finished* product.

Direct labour costs are the wages paid to those who actually *make or produce* the finished product.

Direct expenses are those incurred *specifically* for a particular unit of product.
Factory overheads are all those costs incurred in the *production* function of the business but are not directly traceable to a particular finished product.

If you had trouble with these definitions refer to Chapter 14 on manufacturing accounts.

Exercise 19.2

A and 3, B and 1, C and 2.

Exercise 19.3

3.1 A and 4, B and 3, C and 2, D and 1, E and 5.

3.2 Because you would be looking into the future you would have to use estimates as follows:

Direct material	– drawings and specifications priced by suppliers' quotations.
Direct labour	– estimates of production time at expected wage rates.
Direct expenses	– consider possible costs to be incurred.
Production overheads	– estimates of overheads to be incurred and of time to be worked would have to be carried out so that pre-determined overhead rates could be calculated and used.
Other overheads	– as for production.

3.3 Your completed worksheet should look like this:

Production overhead	£	Basis of apportionment	Machine shop	Assembly shop	Paint shop	Maint. dept.
Canteen expenses	2,400	No. of employees	800	1,000	400	200
Maint. wages	1,510	Actual	—	—	—	1,510
Rent	2,500	Area	1,000	750	500	250
Depreciation	1,200	Value of plant	400	600	100	100
Power	5,200	Horse-power	2,000	2,400	400	400
	£12,810		4,200	4,750	1,400	2,460
Apportionment of maintenance to production depts (equally)			820	820	820	(2,460)
			£5,020	£5,570	£2,220	£ NIL

3.4 Machine shop = £5,020/3, 100 = £1.62p per labour hour
Assembly = £5,570/3, 900 = £1.43p per labour hour
Paint shop = £2,220/1, 500 = £1.48p per labour hour

3.5 Job No. 86201 – *Cost statement*

Direct materials		22.67
Direct labour:		
Machine shop	12.00	
Assembly shop	7.50	
Paint shop	10.50	30.00
Prime cost		52.67
Production overheads:		
Machine shop (3 × £1.62)	4.86	
Assembly shop (2 × £1.43)	2.86	
Paint shop (3 × £1.48	4.44	12.16
Production cost		64.83
Other overheads		8.00
Total cost		72.83
Selling price		90.00
Profit		£17.17

Exercise 19.4

Examples would be: *Fixed* – insurance, car tax
Variable – petrol, oil
Semi-variable – repairs and maintenance.

Exercise 19.5

5.1 The variable cost is 50p per unit (£2,000 ÷ 4,000 units).
5.2 The total fixed cost is £1,000 (£5,000 – £4,000 (8,000 × 50p)).

Exercise 19.6

This is the extra cost per unit that the company would incur to make one workbench.

Exercise 19.7

7.1 (a) represents variable, (b) semi-variable and (c) fixed.
7.2 (a) How much will one unit cost to produce and sell?

Direct material	3.00
Direct labour	2.00
Production overheads (variable)	1.00
(40,000 × $^1/_4$ = £10,000 ÷ 10,000 units)	
Distribution cost	0.50
Marginal cost	£6.50

Each unit therefore gives a contribution of £8.50 – £6.50 = £2. The total contribution from the order would be 2,000 units times £2 = £4,000. The company should therefore accept the order.
(b) At present the company is making a profit of £20,000:

Sales income 10,000 × £12 =	120,000
Total costs	100,000
Profit	£20,000

The new order would increase this profit to £24,000. All of the fixed costs of the business are covered by its normal production. As a result the £4,000 is all profit to the business.

Exercise 19.8

40,000 units $\frac{(80,000)}{£2}$

Exercise 19.9 By calculation: Break-even point = $\frac{£14,000}{£6}$ = 2,333 units

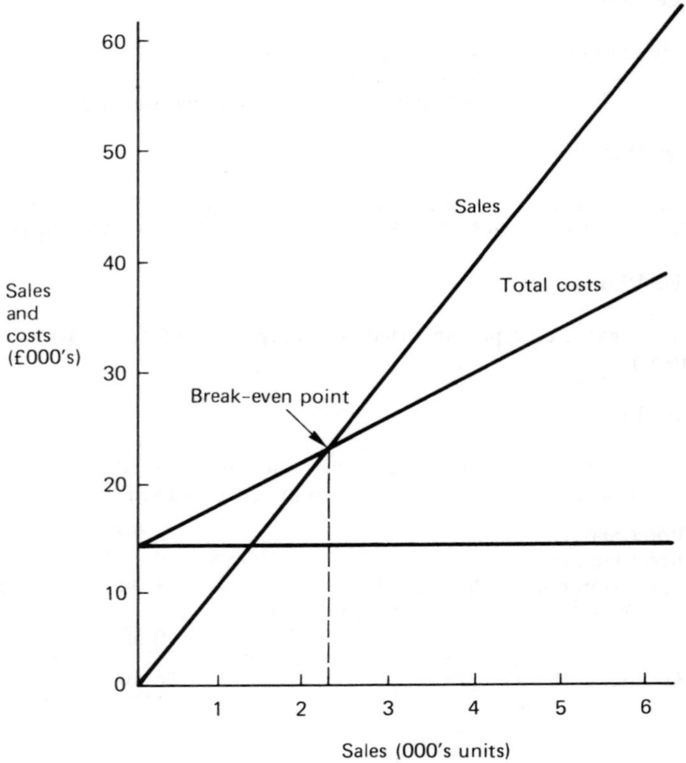

9.2 (a) The differences between these two companies lie in their cost structure and their break-even points. Company A has a low level of fixed costs, therefore its break-even point is easily met. Its variable costs are fairly high so that it has to sell a large volume of units to generate a good profit. Company Z is a much riskier business. It has a high level of fixed costs and therefore needs to work at a fairly high level of capacity to ensure that the company breaks even. Its variable costs are low however, which means that it generates a high profit very quickly.

(b) Company A might be typical of businesses in the retail trade, e.g. supermarkets, discount warehouses etc. Company Z might be typical of a chemical company or cosmetics manufacturer.

CHAPTER 20

Exercise 20.1

	Jan.	*Feb.*	*Mar.*	*Apr.*	*May*	*June*
Receipts from sales	£16,400	£13,000	£8,400	£10,200	£12,000	£13,500
Payment:						
wages etc	3,400	3,200	3,100	3,400	3,600	3,800
creditors						
for purchases	4,200	4,000	3,600	3,800	4,200	4,600
van and machinery	—	—	6,200	24,000	—	—
	£7,600	£7,200	£12,900	£31,200	£7,800	£8,400
Net cash flow	8,800	5,800	(4,500)	(21,000)	4,200	5,100
Opening balance	1,700	10,500	16,300	11,800	(9,200)	5,000
Closing balance	£10,500	£16,300	£11,800	£ (9,200)	£ (5,000)	£100

Exercise 20.2

2.1 Preparation of plans would be the acquisition of players, selection of teams, the development of tactics and style of play and finally the setting of targets, e.g. league position. Actual results would obviously be the performances of the team, individual players and particular tactics etc. Analysis of variances would be comparing performances with plans and deciding to change the team, change the formation used etc.

2 2 A and 2; B and 3; C and 1. Refer to the previous sections if you had problems.

2.3 Refer to Figure 20.2.

2.4 *Tweeds Ltd cash budget*

	July	*August*	*September*
Receipts:			
Sales – for cash	3,000	3,750	4,500
– on credit	—	3,000	3,750
Share capital	10,000	—	—
	£13,000	£6,750	£8,250
Payments:			
Purchases	4,000	5,000	6,000
Rent	1,200	—	—
Wages and other expenses	1,000	1,000	1,000
Fixtures	3,000	—	—
	£9,200	£6,000	£7,000
Net cash flow	3,800	750	1,250
Opening balance	—	3,800	4,550
Closing balance	£3,800	£4,550	£5,800

APPENDIX
GCSE QUESTIONS

1 Below are the ledger accounts as they appear in the books of R. Eastern, Butchers.

John Evans a/c

1986					
1 April	Balance b/d	£ 600	12 April	Cheque	£ 580
10 April	Goods	600	12 April	Discount	20
			16 April	Returns	10
			30 April	Balance c/d	690
		1,200			1,200
1 May	Balance b/d	690			

Welsh Meat Suppliers PLC a/c

18 April	Cheque	£ 600	1 April	Balance b/d	£ 650
18 April	Discount	50	20 April	Goods	400
30 April	Balance c/d	400			
		1,050			1,050
			1 May	Balance b/d	400

Vehicles and equipment a/c

1 April	Balance b/d	£10,000	10 April	Bank	£2,000
28 April	Meat trade Supply Association	5,000	30 April	Balance c/d	13,000
		15,000			15,000
1 May	Balance b/d	13,000			

You are required to take each ledger account in turn and briefly explain the meaning of each entry (taken in date order). Answer in the manner set out below:

John Evans a/c

1 April	John Evans owes R. Eastern	£600.
10 April	etc.	

(WJEC, specimen paper)

2 (a) The following accounts appeared in the books of Yvette Hague. Explain the transactions which gave rise to the entries.
Not more than a single sentence is necessary to explain each entry.

(i) A. Sowter a/c

16 Jan	Purchases returns	5	1 Jan	Balance b/d	65
			14 Jan	Purchases	90
28 Jan	Bank	65			

(ii) Purchases a/c

31 March	Sundries	724	30 March	Drawings	44

(iii) Drawings a/c

28 Feb	Bank	96			
30 March	Purchases	44			

(b) (i) Calculate the balance of Sowter's a/c and state what it means.
(ii) Assume that the Purchases and Drawings a/cs are closed on 31 March. State precisely the entry which will be made in each case.

(MEG, specimen paper)

3 The following *list* of balances was extracted from the books of Ian Brown on 31 March 1986.

	£
Premises	36,230
Stock, 1 April 1985	5,500
Drawings	2,224
Provision for doubtful debts	100
Returns outwards	350
Carriage outwards	85
Purchases	62,000
Sales	72,350
Sundry creditors	3,834
Bank	1,930
Discount received	25
Insurance	940

Sundry debtors	3,250
Rent and rates	2,500
Salaries and wages	7,000
Mortgage on premises	15,000
CAPITAL	?

Prepare a Trial Balance for Ian Brown.

(MEG, specimen paper)

4 (a) As the clerk in charge of petty cash you are required to enter the following transactions into a petty cash book, which should have *four* analysis columns headed as follows:

(i) Canteen
(ii) Travelling
(iii) Postage
(iv) Cleaning

The petty cash book is to be kept on the imprest system, the acount spent to be reimbursed at the end of each week. The open-cash float is £45.

1986			£ p
1 April	Voucher no. 123	Postage stamps	4 30
1 April	Voucher no. 124	Milk	52
2 April	Voucher no. 125	Bus fare	3 00
2 April	Voucher no. 126	Window cleaner	1 10
2 April	Voucher no. 127	Tea	60
3 April	Voucher no. 128	Registered letter	2 12
3 April	Voucher no. 129	Sugar	4 19
3 April	Voucher no. 130	Train ticket	2 40
4 April	Voucher no. 131	Broom	80
4 April	Voucher no. 132	Bus fare	2 14
4 April	Voucher no. 133	Polish	3 82
5 April	Voucher no. 134	Coffee	5 00
5 April	Voucher no. 135	Postage stamps	4 84
5 April	Voucher no. 136	Car expenses	

(b) If the balance in the petty cash book at 5 April failed to agree with the money in the cash box, what steps would you take to find the error(s)?

(WJEC, specimen paper)

5 (a) Why do businesses keep a cash book *and* a petty cash book?
(b) Explain clearly the meaning of the imprest system of petty cash.
(c) Record the following transactions in the cash book and petty cash book of A. Milne. The petty cash book should have three analysis columns: Postages; Stationery; Office Expenses.
On 1 January 1986 A. Milne's books showed the following balances.

	£
Cash	69.70
Bank overdraft	201.10
Petty cash (imprest)	50.00

1 Jan	Bought stamps: 20 at 17p each and 50 at 13p each.
	Sent cheque to G. Hammond £41 in full settlement of a debt of £42.80.
	Paid wages in cash £68.70. Cash sales £110.40.
2	Paid for shop cleaning £5.60.
	Bought goods and paid by cheque £21.20.
3	Postage on parcels £4.40.
4	Bought stationery for office £5.30.
	Received chque from W. May £96.
6	Paid rent by cheque £28.40. Cash sales banked £90.65.
7	Paid for milk £2.36. Bought envelopes £1.20.
8	The cheque received from W. May on 4 January was returned by the bank dishonoured.
	Paid all cash into bank except £30.00.
	The petty cashier was reimbursed in cash to restore imprest.

(d) Balance the cash book and petty cash book.

(NEA, specimen paper)

6 Your firm trades in office machinery and on 1 March 1981 its financial position was as follows:

	£		£
Freehold land and buildings	25,000	Cash at bank	2,000
Fixtures and fittings	6,000	Trade debtors	250
Stock on hand	15,000	Trade creditors	200

(a) Enter the above in the journal showing the capital at that date.

(b) Enter the following transactions for the month of March in the appropriate day books.

1 Mar	Sold 4 typewriters to Office Services, list price £80 each, allowing them 10% trade discount.
4	Bought 6 calculators from Webb & Co. at £12 each net.
12	Sold duplicating machine to J. Hoy for £350.
16	Sold 4 calculators to E. Mark, list price £20 each, allowing them 10% trade discount.
17	Office Services returned one damaged typewriter.
20	Bought 6 typewriters from Ace Co., list price £40 each. Allowed 15% trade discount.
25	Sold 2 duplicating machines to Mills & Co., list price £350, allowing them 10% trade discount.

N.B. Entries in the ledger accounts are not required.

(LEAG specimen paper)

7 (a) On 31 March 1985 Dermod Ruddock's debtors totalled £3,250. It was decided to write off the balance of A. Kitchen, £130, included in that total.

It was decided also to create a provision for doubtful debts equal to 2½% of the remaining debtors.

Show how these matters would be dealt with in Dermod Ruddock's Journal (narratives need not be given).

(b) During the next financial year, a payment of £50 was received on 30 September from the accountants of A. Kitchen following the latter's bankruptcy.
The following decisions were also made on 31 March 1986:

A to write off debtors' balances totalling £182
B to adjust the provision for doubtful debts to £90

Show how these matters would be recorded in the following accounts in Dermod Ruddock's books:

(i) A. Clixby's account.
(ii) Bad debts account.
(iii) Provision for bad debts account.
(iv) Profit and loss account for the year ended 31 March 1986.

(MEG, specimen paper)

8 (a) What is the purpose of a trial balance?
(b) Name and give examples of *four* types of errors which may be in a trial balance even though the totals are equal.
(c) The following trial balance was extracted from the books of Jane Smith on 31 March 1986.

	Dr	Cr
	£	£
Premises	50,000	
Motor vans	7,400	
Sundry debtors	1,680	
Sundry creditors		2,385
Purchases	160,260	
Sales		200,490
Wages	12,000	
Drawings	1,600	
Capital		30,000
	£232,940	£232,875

As the trial balance totals did not agree, the difference was posted to a suspense account. The following errors were discovered.

1 The purchase of a motor van had been entered in the motor van account as £3,860 instead of £3,680.
2 The total of the purchases book £32,543 had been posted to the purchases account as £32,453.
3 The proprietress had withdrawn £140 for private use during March which had been debited to the wages account.
4 A cash discount of £25 allowed by Diane Jones, a creditor, had not been entered in Diane Jones's account.

You are required to take the above information into account and show:

(i) journal entries to correct the errors;
(ii) the suspense account written up and balanced;
(iii) the corrected trial balance.

(NEA, specimen paper)

9 The following balance sheet was drawn up in draft form for Ken Boyce by his accountant.

Balance sheet as at 31 March 1988

	£		£	£
Capital	32,900	*Fixed assets*		
add Net profit	9,200	Shop fittings		12,400
	42,100	*Current assets*		
less Drawings	9,000	Stock	16,280	
		Debtors	10,500	
	33,100	Bank	1,220	
Current liabilities				28,000
Creditors	7,300			
	£40,400			£40,400

Soon after the preparation of the draft balance sheet, the following errors were discovered.

1. An invoice for a new display unit costing £2,200 had been posted in error to the purchases account.
2. A cheque for £60 received from David Brown had been posted in error to the account of Brian Brown.
3. Ken Boyce took goods from stock to the value of £400 for his own private use but no entries had been made in the books.
4. Bank service charges amounted to £80, but the accountant was not aware of this when he drew up the draft balance sheet.
5. A cheque received from A. Luxton for £240 in settlement of his account has been returned by the bank marked 'refer to drawer'.

You are required to:

(a) Prepare the journal entries required to correct these five errors.
(b) Draw up a statement to show the amended profit.

(WJEC, 1988)

10 A sole trader, L. Bright, receives a statement of his current account at his bank and finds that the figure for the balance does not equal that in the cash bank.

Bank statement balance £7,000
Cash book balance £2,800

It appears that several matters mentioned in the cash book have not been taken into account by the bank:

(i) cheques for £1,000, £500 and £2,000 have been issued and not cleared;
(ii) a direct debit entry in the cash book for £50 and a standing order for £75 have not yet appeared in the bank statement.

Certain entries in the bank statement do not appear in the cash book:

(i) the bank has entered charges for £25;

(ii) a payment by a debtor for £500 appears in the bank statement and not in cash book;
(iii) a dividend paid on shares for £100 has been sent direct to the bank and is in the statement.

(a) What is a bank statement?
(b) In what ways are standing orders and direct debits similar and in what ways are they dissimilar?
(c) Why do cash books and their related bank statements differ in content?
(d) Why are bank reconciliation statements prepared?
(e) Prepare a bank reconciliation statement to reconcile the cash book and the bank statement.

(NISEC, specimen paper)

11 (a) Prepare Clive Allen's 3-column Cash Book from the following information.

1986			£
1 April	Balance:	Cash	30.00; and
		Bank	10.00
13	Cash sales paid into bank, £600.00		
19	Received cheque from D. Smithies for £98.00 in settlement of his balance outstanding of £100.00		
20	Paid wages in cash, £10.00		
21	Paid insurance premiums by cheque, £31.00		
29	Cash sales, £350.00		
29	Paid G. Gutteridge by cheque the balance due to him, £120.00 less 2½% cash discount		
30	Received cheque from A. Blyth for £147.00 in settlement of his debt of £150.00		
30	Deposited all cash except £25.00 in the bank, together with Blyth's cheque.		

(b) Clive received the following bank statement on 3 May 1986:

Bank statement

Date	Particulars	Payments	Receipts	Balance
1 April	Balance			10.00
3	Sundry credits		600.00	610.00
19	Sundry credits		98.00	708.00
24	107651	31.00		677.00
30	D. D. Newton B.C.	60.00		617.00
30	Charges	17.00		600.00
1 May	Sundry credits		492.00	1,092.00

(i) Bring Clive's cash book up to date.
(ii) Prepare a statement reconciling the revised cash book balance with the balance on the bank statement.

(MEG, specimen paper)

12 (a) Briefly explain the difference between a bank statement and a bank reconciliation statement.

(b) *Cash Book* (Bank columns only)

1 Jan	Balance	600	18 Jan	D. Anderson	145
13 Jan	T. Francis	224	28 Jan	R. Patrick	72
31 Jan	L. Bond	186	30 Jan	B. Thompson	109

Bank Statement

		Debit	Credit	Balance
1 Jan	Balance			635
3 Jan	H. Turner	35		600
13 Jan	T. Francis		224	824
23 Jan	D. Anderson	145		679
31 Jan	Standing Order	30		649

Using the information given above:
(i) prepare a corrected cash book;
(ii) draw up a bank reconciliation statement.

(NEA, specimen paper)

13 The cashier of your firm has been absent owing to illness and no entries have been made in the cash book for the period 24–30 November. The cash book has three columns, for discounts, cash and bank.

On 23 November the balances on the cash book were: cash in hand £86 and cash at bank £420. There were no cash discount items in the cash book at that date. The following additional information is available:

24 November	Paid cash for stationery £8 and stamps £11.
25 November	Sent S. Davis a cheque for £280 and took £20 cash discount.
26 November	Received and paid into bank a cheque from T. Griffiths £432 accepted in full settlement of his debt of £470.
28 November	Banked a cheque from K. Stephens £506 on account.
29 November	Cashed a cheque £42 for office use.
30 November	Cash sales for the period 24–30 November, £544, paid direct to bank.

At the start of business on 1 December, there was £59 in the firm's cash box.

Required
(a) Preparation of the cash book for the period 24–30 November, bringing down the balances to December.
(b) An explanation of why you may be dissatisfied with the correctness of the cash balance.
(c) An explanation of where discount allowed and discount received will be posted from the cash book and how each of them will affect the net profit calculation.

On 3 December the bank supplies you with a statement, from which you extract the following items relating to the period 24–30 November but omitted from the bank columns in your cash book.
Cheque received from K. Stephens has been dishonoured by his bank;
Your bank has made a charge of £4 for its services;

Credit transfers by customers, totalling £480, have been paid direct to your bank.

Required

(d) A statement showing the calculation of the actual bank balance at 30 November.

(SEG, specimen paper)

14 Wendy peart has started business in the hotel and catering industry. She has acquired suitable premises and in addition to residential accommodation offers food and drink facilities to non-residents.

The following items are purchased by Wendy during her first month's trading.

Indicate, by placing a tick in the columns provided, whether in your opinion the items acquired are capital or revenue expenditure.

Item	*Capital*	*Revenue*
Hotel and outbuildings		
Furniture and fittings		
Television sets (hired from Telelone Ltd)		
Refrigeration equipment		
Food and drink		
Advertising		
Salaries of staff		
Motor car for manager		

(WJEC, 1988)

15 In which of the final accounts would the following ledger account balances appear? Tick the appropriate box.

Ledger Account	*Trading Account*	*Profit and Loss Account*	*Balance Sheet*
Bank overdraft			
Purchases			
Sales returns			
Rent received			
Carriage outwards			
Drawings			
Bad debts			
Capital			
Creditors			
Carriage inwards			

(WJEC, 1988)

16 Certain mistakes have been made in drawing up the trading and profit and loss account and the balance sheet of J. Tomlison, a sole trader.

Trading profit and loss account of J. Tomlison for the year ended 31 December 1985

	£		£
Purchases	10,200	Sales	11,860
Sales returns	70	Discounts received	100
General expenses	500	Closing stock	2,970
Opening stock	3,160		
Profit (net)	1,000		
	14,930		14,930

Balance sheet of J. Tomlison as at 31 December 1985

	£	£		£
Capital at 1.1.85	3,300		Trade debtors	1,840
Add long-term loan	1,200			
		4,500	Trade creditors	2,465
Drawings		300	Bank overdraft	415
Fixtures and fittings		610	Motor vehicles	2,660
Stock 31.12.85		2,970	Net profit	1,000
		8,380		8,380

Your are required to:

(a) Draw up the trading and profit and loss account in correct form clearly showing, within the trading and profit and loss account:

(i) the cost of goods sold;
(ii) the net sales;
(iii) the gross profit;
(iv) the net profit.

(b) Draw up the balance sheet in correct form clearly showing, within the balance sheet:

(i) the total of the capital account on 31 December 1985;
(ii) the total of the current liabilities;
(iii) the total of the fixed assets;
(iv) the total of the current assets.

(WJEC, specimen paper)

17 The following trial balance was extracted from the books of J. Robinson, a retailer on 31 May 1986.

Trial balance as at 31 May 1986

	Dr £	Cr £
Fixtures and fittings	5,000	
Motor van	2,000	
Stock (1/6/85)	6,520	
Debtors	1,140	
Cash in hand	80	
Cash at bank	2,040	
Creditors		3,050
Capital		14,000
Purchases	26,320	
Sales		44,400
Motor running expenses	510	
Wages and salaries	3,100	
Light, heat and power	850	
Rent and rates	4,200	
Advertising	940	
Drawings	9,000	
Rent received		860
Sundry expenses	610	
	62,310	62,310

You are required to prepare Robinson's trading and profit and loss account for the financial year ended 31 May 1986 together with a balance sheet at that date, taking into account the following adjustments:

(i) The closing stock was valued at £7,450.
(ii) There was an unpaid electricity account amounting to £120.
(iii) There was a prepayment on the rates to the value of £90.

(iv) Allow for depreciation on the motor van at the rate of 20% per annum.

(WJEC, specimen paper)

18 Yorkie, a haulage contractor, started business on 1 January 1986 and on that date purchased a motor lorry by cheque for £10,000. He decided to close his books each year at 31 December and to depreciate lorries at the rate of 10% per year on cost using the straight line method.

On 1 July 1987 he purchased on credit from Wolverton Motors another lorry for £12,000.

(a) Prepare the motor lorries account and the provision for depreciation on motor lorries account for the two years ended 31 December 1987.
(b) Prepare a balance sheet extract showing the entries for motor lorries at 31 December 1987.

(LEAG, 1988)

19 The following trial balance was extracted from the books of Jane Morgan, a boutique owner, at the end of her financial year, 31 May 1988.

Trial balance as at 31 May 1988

	Dr	Cr
	£	£
Capital		12,000
Sales		42,000
Purchases	21,500	
Fixtures and fittings (at cost)	18,000	
Opening stock	5,200	
Carriage inwards	120	
Returns inwards	230	
Trade debtors	5,390	
Trade creditors		1,780
Cash in hand	95	
Bank overdraft		4,240
Provision for depreciation (fixtures)		7,200
Drawings	7,000	
Wages	3,650	
Rent, rates and insurance	4,900	
Advertising	600	
Discount received		205
Interest paid	740	
	£67,425	£67,425

In preparing the year-end accounts, the following should be accounted for:

1. The stock at the end of the year was valued at £5,600.
2. Fixtures and fittings should be depreciated by 20% p.a. on cost.
3. Insurance paid in advance £60.

4. Interest due but not paid on the overdraft has been estimated at £120.

You are required to:
(a) Prepare Jane's trading account for the year ended 31 May 1988.
(b) Prepare Jane's profit and loss account for the year ended 31 May 1988.
(c) Draft Jane's balance sheet as at 31 May 1988.

(WJEC, 1988)

20 (a) The following balance remained in the books of Hill and Dale *after* the preparation of their profit and loss account for the year ended 31 March 1988.

Trial balance as at 31 March 1988

	Dr £	Cr £
Net profit		18,000
Capital accounts:		
Hill		30,000
Dale		20,000
Current accounts:		
Hill (as at 1.4.87)		102
Dale (as at 1.4.87)		118
Drawings accounts:		
Hill	10,000	
Dale	5,000	
Premises	32,000	
Fixtures	9,000	
Stock	4,425	
Debtors	7,687	
Cash at bank	2,242	
Creditors		2,134
	£70,354	£70,354

The partners have agreed the following profit-sharing arrangements:

1. Interest is to be allowed on capital at 10% per annum.
2. The following partnership salaries are to be appropriated:
   Hill £4,000; Dale £1,500.
3. Remaining profits to be distributed in the ratio of partners' capital.

Your are required to:
(i) Prepare the partnership appropriation account.
(ii) Complete the partners' current accounts.

(b) Give the title and brief details of any Act affecting the running of a partnership.

(WJEC, June 1988)

21 Henshaw and Harrison are in partnership as retailers. The trial balance below has been completed after preparation of the trading account.

Trial balance of Henshaw and Harrison as at 31 March 1988

	Debit £	Credit £
Premises	75,000	
Fittings at cost	3,500	
Motor vans at cost	2,000	
Capital 1 April 1987 Henshaw		40,000
Harrison		45,000
Current accounts 1 April 1987 Henshaw		1,320
Harrison	200	
Gross profit		25,672
Stock	2,275	
Creditors		4,200
Debtors	5,160	
Rates	1,320	
Lighting and heating	1,200	
General expenses	345	
Cash discount	290	
Cash at bank	3,360	
Cash in hand	942	
Drawings Henshaw	11,200	
Harrison	10,400	
Provision for depreciation on motor vans		1,000
	117,192	117,192

The following additional information is available at 31 March 1988

1 Rates prepaid £110.
2 Light and heat owing £95.
3 Vans are to be depreciated by 20% and fittings by 10% per annum on cost.
4 A provision for bad debts of 5% on debtors is to be created.
5 Partners share profits and losses equally.
6 Interest on capital is to be allowed at 9% per annum.

(a) For the year ended 31 March 1988 prepare Henshaw and Harrison's
 (i) profit and loss account, including appropriation section
 (ii) current accounts.

(b) Prepare Henshaw and Harrison's balance sheet as at 31 March 1988 distinguishing between fixed and current assets and current liabilities. The current account (balance only) of each partner should be included in the balance sheet.

(LEAG, May 1988)

22 Fox and Langton have been trading in partnership for a number of years. Their profit-sharing agreement is as follows:

(i) Fox is to receive a salary of £4,000 per annum;
(ii) remaining profits or losses are to be shared in the ratio, Fox : Langton, 2:3.

(a) On 31 December 1987, the end of the firm's financial year, the following balances were extracted from the books after preparation of the trading account.

	£
Capital accounts:	
Fox	22,000
Langton	28,000
Current accounts, 1 January 1987:	
Fox (debit balance)	1,260
Langton (credit balance)	380
Salaries	18,360
Gross profit	55,150
Discounts received	184
Drawings:	
Fox	10,220
Langton	11,920
Administration expenses	3,662
Fixed assets:	
at cost	76,000
provision for depreciation, 1 January 1987	28,000
Rent and rates	1,380
Advertising	958

(b) The following additional information is available.

(i) No entry has been made in the accounts for advertising charges £158 which had been paid by Langton from his private funds.

(ii) Salaries £124 are owing at 31 December 1987.

(iii) On 6 April 1987 a payment was made for rates, £672, for the year ending 31 March 1988.

(iv) It is the firm's policy to depreciate fixed assets by 15% per annum using the reducing balance method.

Required

1 An explanation of the purpose of partners' current accounts.

2 For the firm of Fox and Langton

(i) a profit and loss and appropriation account for the year ended 31 December 1987;

(ii) an extract from the balance sheet as at 31 December 1987 showing in detail the partners' capital and current accounts.

(c) The partners are not totally satisfied with their profit-sharing agreement and feel that some additional clauses could marginally alter the way profits are distributed to produce a fairer result.

Required

3 Advice for the partners on *two* additional clauses (other than partnership salaries and profit-sharing ratio) which could be included in their partnership agreement. Explain the purpose of each of the clauses chosen and state the double entry which will be required if they are adopted.

(SEG, June 1988)

23 Galloway Ltd has an authorised capital of 250,000 ordinary shares of £1 each.

(a) At the end of its financial year, 30 April 1988, the following balances remained in the Company's books after preparation of trading and profit and loss accounts.

	£
Motor vehicles:	
at cost	38,400
provision for depreciation	16,300
Net profit for year	36,600
Freehold premises at cost	190,000
Stock in trade	32,124
Share capital: 200,000 ordinary shares of £1 each, fully paid	200,000
Insurance prepaid	280
Profit and loss account balance brought forward	3,950
Wages and salaries due	774
General reserve	24,000
Trade creditors	3,847
Trade debtors	4,782
8% Debentures	15,000
Rent receivable outstanding	175
Bank overdraft	1,830
Furniture and equipment:	
at cost	44,000
provision for depreciation	7,460

The directors have proposed
(i) the transfer of £5,000 to the general reserve
(ii) a final dividend on the ordinary shares of 12.5%.

(b) Galloway Ltd's directors are making an assessment of the company's performance for the year. They are concerned by a decline in both profitability and liquidity despite an increase in turnover.

Required

1 *Three* significant differences between ordinary shares and debentures.

2 For Galloway Ltd:
  (i) a profit and loss appropriation account for the year ended 30 April 1988
  (ii) a balance sheet as at 30 April 1988 in a form which shows clearly:
  total shareholders' funds
  working capital.

3 Concerning the company's performance:
  (i) Name *one* ratio which could be used to assess profitability.
  (ii) State *two* possible reasons why the profitability ratio may have declined despite increased turnover.
  (iii) Name *one* ratio, other than working capital ratio, which could be used to assess liquidity.

(iv) Give *four* suggestions as to how working capital could be increased during the year ahead.

(SEG, June 1988)

24 The following information relates to the manufacturing business of James & Margaret Gunning:

	£
Stocks at 1 January 1987:	
Raw materials	11,060
Work-in-progress	6,210
Indirect wages	8,340
Lighting, heating and power	3,500
Factory rent and rates	2,900
General factory expenses	2,550
Manufacturing wages	25,640
Factory insurance	1,875
Carriage inwards	700
Purchases of raw materials	40,610
Plant and machinery at cost	55,000
Stocks at 31 December 1987:	
Raw materials	4,010
Work-in-progress	3,800

Notes:

(a) The plant and machinery is to be depreciated at 10% on cost.

(b) Lighting, heating and power to be apportioned between factory and office in the ratio 3:2.

(c) Factory rates paid in advance £300.

(d) Factory insurance premium for the last quarter of the year is due.

(i) Prepare a manufacturing account which shows clearly:
   (a) Cost of raw materials used
   (b) Prime cost
   (c) Factory cost of finished goods produced.

(ii) If 50,000 units were produced during the year what was the manufacturing cost per unit?

(iii) What is meant by:
   (a) Direct costs;
   (b) Indirect costs;
   (c) Work-in-progress?

(NISEC, May 1988)

25 Sarah Douglas has recently started a small bakery business. She makes high quality loaves and bread rolls which she supplies to local retail bakers, hotels and restaurants.

(a) The following information is available about the business for its first month of operation, March 1988.

   (i) The business uses rented accommodation for production purposes at an annual charge of £1200; rates per annum are £840. Sarah purchased equipment at a cost of £13,840; she estimates that the equipment will have a four-year lifespan and have a scrap value of £400.

(ii) During the first month of operation, basic materials (flour, yeast, etc) costing £1,350 were received from suppliers; of these all but £130 were used in production.
(iii) Sarah employs a part-time assistant who carries out much of the routine work involved in preparing and baking the bread. The assistant's wages for March 1988 totalled £450.
(iv) A local firm has been used for collecting basic materials from suppliers and delivering orders to customers; their charge for March 1988 was £440. Sarah estimates that one-quarter of this figure represents the cost of collecting material from suppliers.
(v) Electricity consumed during March 1988 cost £120.
(vi) In March 1988 all production was sold; selling price was established by adding 25% to the cost of production.

Required
1 For Sarah Douglas's business:

(i) a detailed manufacturing account for the month ended 31 March 1988 which shows the prime cost and total cost of production;
(ii) a trading account for the month ended 31 March 1988.

(b) Sarah Douglas believes she can increase sales in the months ahead if she can become more competitive. She would like advice on the implications of steady growth on the pricing on her products.

Required
2 Advice for Sarah Douglas by giving:

(i) The meaning of the terms fixed cost and variable cost. (Illustrate your answer with *two* examples of fixed costs and *two* examples of variable costs selected from the information above.)
(ii) An explanation of the importance of the distinction between fixed and variable costs when choosing prices as production grows.

(SEG, June 1988)

26 Kingston's is a manufacturer of a children's toy called 'Playtime'.
(a) The following details relate to the business's financial year ended 30 September 1988.

	£
(i) Raw materials per unit	2.60
Direct labour per unit	3.20
(ii) Other costs paid during the year	
	£
Factory power	5,800
Factory indirect labour	14,300
Factory insurance	3,390
Rates	8,560

(iii) Factory insurance, £180, was prepaid at 30 September 1988.

(iv) Seven-eighths of the amount paid for rates should be allocated to the factory.

(v) Machinery which cost £44,800 is used in the production process; depreciation should be provided at 12.5% per annum on cost.

(vi) Total production for the year under review was 28,000 units.

Required

1 Kington's manufacturing account for the year ended 30 September 1988 in a form which shows clearly:
prime cost
total cost of production.

2 A calculation of the cost of producing one unit during the year ended 30 September 1988.

3 An explanation of how you would treat a closing stock of work-in-progress in the final accounts and balance sheet of a manufacturer.

(b) Compared to the previous year, sales of 'Playtime' have increased by 25% and profits have increased by 30%. Market research has, however, predicted a sharp decrease in sales for the year ending 30 September 1989.

Required

4 An explanation of why the increase in Kington's profits for the year ended 30 September 1988 have been proportionately greater than the increase in production.

5 Your view as to the likely effect on profits of the sharp decrease in Kington's sales predicted for the year ending 30 September 1989. (Give reasons to support your answer.)

(SEG, November 1988)

27 Karnail Singh is in business as a wholesaler. Although he has not kept a full set of accounting records, the following details are available.

	1 April 1987	*31 March 1988*
	£	£
Premises	10,000	10,000
Fixtures	2,000	2,200
Stock	4,500	5,500
Trade debtors	700	900
Bank	650 (Dr)	?
Trade creditors	1,350	1,650
Expense creditors	200	300
Capital	16,300	

The summary of his bank account is as follows.

Receipts	£
Cheques from debtors	10,300
Payments	
Cheques to suppliers	9,200
Expenses	500
Drawings	1,600
Fixtures	400

You are required to prepare the following:
(a) the bank account, so as to calculate the bank balance at 31 March 1988;
(b) the accounts or statements showing the calculations of
   (i) credit sales;
   (ii) credit purchases;
   (iii) expenses;
(c) the trading and profit and loss accounts for the year ending 31 March 1988;
(d) the balance sheet as at 31 March 1988.

Stationery to be used is as follows:
(a) ledger or three-column paper;
(b) ledger or three-column paper or lined answer sheet;
(c) and (d) journal paper.

(NEA, June 1988)

28 Pauline Fox is an electrician operating from rented premises. Her financial year ends on 31 March. She does not keep full accounting records but a summary of her bank account for the year ended 31 March 1988 is as follows.

	£		£
Balance at 1/4/87	2,187	Payments to suppliers	15,715
Receipts from customers	26,546	Drawings	6,200
		Rent	2,300
		Rates	550
		Insurance	231
		Motor vehicle repairs and expenses	873
		New equipment	2,225
		Balance at 31/3/88	639
	28,733		28,733

Fox provides the following additional information

	As at 31 March 1987	*As at 31 March 1988*
	£	£
Stocks of materials	2,873	3,528
Insurance paid in advance	124	140
Motor expenses owing	247	334
Trade creditors	2,516	3,318
Amounts due from customers	3,729	3,974
Motor vehicle (at cost less depreciation)	4,200	–
Equipment (at cost less depreciation)	5,475	–
Capital account (Cr. balance)	15,825	–

You find that all the receipts from customers during the year had been banked except for £2,294 which Fox used to buy materials and £1,800 taken for her personal use. Depreciation is to be written off equipment at 10% per annum and off the motor vehicle at 20% per annum, calculated on the book values at 31 March plus additions during the year.

Questions

(a) Making the necessary adjustments, prepare Fox's
 (i) Trading and profit and loss account for the year ended 31 March 1988.
 (ii) Balance sheet as at 31 March 1988, distinguishing between fixed and current assets.

(b) (i) Calculate Fox's working capital at 31 March 1988.
 (ii) Using *two* appropriate ratios, measure the liquidity of the business.

(MEG, June 1988)

29 The assets and liabilities of the Cricketers Club at 31 March 1987 were:

premises £300,000; equipment £1,560; cash £892; bar stocks £641; subscriptions in advance £45; creditors for bar supplies £225.

(a) Prepare an opening statement of affairs at 1 April 1987 listing assets and liabilities, and calculating the accumulated fund as the balancing item.

Receipts and payments during the year ended 31 March 1988 were:

Receipts subscriptions £1,812; bar sales £5,500.
Payments rates £1,500;creditors for bar supplies £3,220; equipment £940; insurance £94; general expenses £39.

(b) Prepare the club's receipts and payments account for the year ended 31 March 1988.
At the end of March 1988, the following further information was available.
1 20% depreciation is to be applied to all equipment.
2 Creditors for bar supplies £800.
3 Insurance prepaid £24.
4 Bar stocks £906.
5 Rates owing £150.
6 Subscriptions in arrears £22.

(c) Prepare an account showing the club's profit and loss on the bar for the year ended 31 March 1988.

(d) Prepare the club's income and expenditure account for the year ended 31 March 1988, including details of the items relating to the bar.

(e) Prepare the Cricketers Club balance sheet as at 31 March 1988, distinguishing between fixed and current assets and current liabilities.

(LEAG, May 1988)

30 The financial position of the Llanfair Sports Club on 31 March 1987 was as follows:

	£
Club house	11,000
Equipment	2,820
Subscriptions unpaid	60
Cash at bank	820

The club had only one liability at that date, an amount due to Super-games Limited for £610.

A summary of the club's receipts and payments for the year to 31 March 1988 is given below:

Receipts	£	*Payments*	£
Balance	820	Super-games Limited	610
Subscriptions:		Rent for playing field	880
Year ended 31.3.87	60	New equipment	880
Year ended 31.3.88	3,760	Light and heat	530
Year ended 31.3.89	50	Casual wages	1,800
Receipts from:		Insurance	206
Dances	1,020	Expenses of:	
Tournaments	1,420	Dances	740
		Tournaments	1,360
		Balance	124
	£7,130		£7,130

In preparing the accounts the following matters should be taken into account:

1. Equipment should be depreciated at the rate of 10% per annum.
2. Insurance was paid in advance to the value of £16.
3. Subscriptions unpaid at 31 March 1988 amounted to £70.
4. The playing field is leased from the local authority at a monthly rental of £80.

You are required to:

(a) Prepare an income and expenditure account, for the year ended 31 March 1988.

(b) Calculate the accumulated fund as at 31 March 1988.

(WJEC, June 1988)

31 In the summer of 1987 the head teacher of Calloden School gave permission to the sixth form to establish a social club.

(a) The following information is available for the club's first year of operation, 1 September 1987 to 31 August 1988.

(i) On 1 September 1987 the club was made a gift of £500 cash from school funds. (The gift should be treated as a capital receipt.)

(ii) The membership subscription was set at £3 per member per annum. However, it was decided to offer a special £4 membership to any first-year sixth-former who joined the club for two years. The number of students who joined was:

Second-year sixth-formers one-year membership	72
First-year sixth-formers	
one-year membership	66
two-year membership	35

All subscriptions were paid by members on joining the club.

(iii) A room has been set aside for use by the club and for which a token rent of £96 per annum is charged. The rent is payable in three equal instalments. By August 1988 all but the third instalment had been paid. The club paid £230 for redecoration of the clubroom and £440 for new furniture and fittings. It was agreed that the redecoration should be regarded as a revenue expense and that the furniture should be depreciated by 15% on cost.

(iv) The members run a coffee and snack bar. The following details are available:

	£
Payment for equipment	420
Cash takings received	2,768
Payments to suppliers	1,325
Wages paid to part-time assistant	740

On 31 August 1988 there was a stock of unused supplies valued at £150 and an invoice for £245 from one of the suppliers had not been paid. It was decided that the equipment should be depreciated by 10% on cost.

(v) During the year a number of discos were held which raised £1,260; the costs which have all been settled amounted to £730. Half of the profit made on the discos was donated to charity.

(vi) Other expenses paid during the year were:

	£
Cleaning	250
Secretarial and administration charges	54

(vii) At 31 August 1988 the club's balance of cash at bank was £564.

Required

For the Calloden School Social Club:

1 an account to show the profit or loss made by the coffee and snack bar for the year ended 31 August 1988;

2 an income and expenditure account for the year ended 31 August 1988;

3 a balance sheet as at 31 August 1988.

(b) The club committee have plans to expand facilities during the next few years and will need to increase income. However, they have ruled out running additional discos or other social activities because of the time required in their organisation.

Required

4 Advice for the committee on *five* ways in which the club could increase its income over the next few years which will not involve running additional social activities.

(SEG, November 1988)

32 The summarised trading and profit and loss accounts for both John and David, together with their balance sheets as at their year-end 30 April 1988, are shown below.

Trading and profit and loss accounts

	John	*David*		*John*	*David*
	£	£		£	£
Opening stock	4,000	14,000	Sales	64,000	76,000
Purchases	32,000	38,000			
	36,000	52,000			
Final stock	5,000	16,000			
Cost of goods sold	31,000	36,000			
Gross profit	33,000	40,000			
	£64,000	£76,000		£64,000	£76,000
Expenses	21,400	28,800	Gross profit b/d	33,000	40,000
Net profit	11,600	11,200			
	£33,000	£40,000		£33,000	£40,000

Balance sheets

	John	*David*		*John*	*David*
	£	£		£	£
Capital:			Fixed assets	41,000	38,000
including net profit	48,000	55,000	Stock	5,000	16,000
			Debtors	1,500	6,200
			Bank	4,100	2,200
Current liabilities:					
Creditors	3,600	7,400			
	£51,600	£62,400		£51,600	£62,400

John and David are rivals in similar businesses. David feels that the above accounts show that he is the better businessman.

You are required to:

(a) Calculate the four ratios given below, correct to *one* place of decimals, for both John and David.

(b) Comment on the accuracy of David's boast.

Ratios

1. Gross profit as % of sales.
2. Net profit as % of sales.
3. Current ratio.
4. Return on capital employed.

(WJEC, June 1988)

33 Boundary Products Limited is a specialist sports equipment wholesaling company. The information set out in the table below relates to its trading activities for the last three years.

Years ended 31 December

	1985	*1986*	*1987*
Sales	250,000		
Opening stock			
Purchases		208,000	
Closing stock	12,000		
Gross profit		70,000	
Fixed expenses	17,500		
Variable expenses			
Net profit			33,000

You are given the following additional information relating to each year's operations.

1985: (1) The gross profit was 20% of sales;
(2) All purchases were of items costing £5 each and 39,600 were bought;
(3) Variable expenses were 25% of gross profit.

1986: (1) The ratio of gross profit to sales increased by 5% compared with 1985;
(2) The ratio of variable expenses to gross profit was 30%;
(3) Net profit was 11% of sales;
(4) Purchase prices were unchanged from 1985.

1987: (1) Sales increased by 10% compared with 1986;
(2) The ratio of gross profit to sales was the same as in 1986;
(3) The cost of purchases increased by 20% per item. There were 1,500 items in stock at the year end, all valued at the new price;
(4) Fixed expenses were £2,000 more than in the previous year.

Questions

(a) Copy out the table and use the information provided to calculate the figures required. Use your calculations to complete the table.

(b) (i) What is meant by a firm's 'rate of stockturn' (or stock turnover ratio)? What is its significance?
(ii) Calculate the rate of stockturn for Boundary Products Ltd, for the years 1985, 1986 and 1987.

(MEG, June 1988)

34 On 31 May 1988 Fiona Maxwell presents you with copies of balance sheets of two engineering firms. She says that she is thinking of expanding her light engineering business by taking over one of these firms and she asks you for advice. The balance sheets are shown below.

Metal Products Ltd balance sheet as at 30 September 1987

	£
Premises, at cost	15,000
Machinery, at cost	5,000
Stock at cost (market value £3,000)	2,000
Debtors	1,800
Bank balance	200
	24,000
Share capital: authorised and issued	19,360
Undistributed profits	2,640
Creditors	2,000
	24,000

Forge Engineering Ltd balance sheet as at 30 June 1987

	£	£
Premises, at cost		35,000
Machinery, at cost, less depreciation		15,000
Stock at cost (market value £12,000)		20,000
Debtors	9,000	
Less provision for doubtful debts	1,000	8,000
		78,000
Share capital: authorised and issued		63,800
Undistributed profits		4,200
Creditors		8,000
Bank overdraft		2,000
		78,000

Using a lined answer sheet, prepare a report which should include the following points.

(a) A criticism of the information shown in the balance sheets.
(b) An explanation of additional accounting information which is required.
(c) Any calculations which you think would be useful.
(d) A recommendation as to whether either firm should be taken over, giving your reasons.

(NEA, June 1988)

35 The trading and profit and loss accounts of two separate businesses, of similar size and engaged in the same trade are given below.

Trading and Profit and Loss Accounts for year ended 31 December 1987

	Smith Ltd	Jones Ltd		Smith Ltd	Jones Ltd
	£	£		£	£
Opening stock	4,000	4,500	Sales	54,000	40,250
Purchases	?	?	*Less* Returns	600	250
	?	?			
Less Closing Stock	?	4,000			
Cost of goods sold	?	?			
Gross profit	?	?			
	?	?		?	?
Total expenses	?	?	Gross profit	?	?
Net profit	8,000	2,000			

Additional information:

	Smith Ltd	*Jones Ltd*
Capital employed	£20,000	£20,000
Rate of turnover of stock	12	not given
Gross profit margin on net sales	$33^1/_3$%	20%

(a) Prepare the above trading and profit and loss accounts, including all the missing figures denoted by question marks.

(b) Calculate for each business

(i) net profit expressed as a percentage of net sales;
(ii) total expenses expressed as a percentage of net sales;
(iii) return on capital employed.

(c) Using the information available give two reasons why you feel one of the businesses produced a better performance than the other, during the period concerned.

(d) The comparison made above is between one business and another business. State *two* other means of comparison frequently used to evaluate the performance of a business.

(e) (i) Using examples, explain what is meant by the term *liquidity*.
(ii) How would you measure a firm's liquidity?

(LEAG, May 1988)

36 Study the following break-even chart and answer the questions which follow.

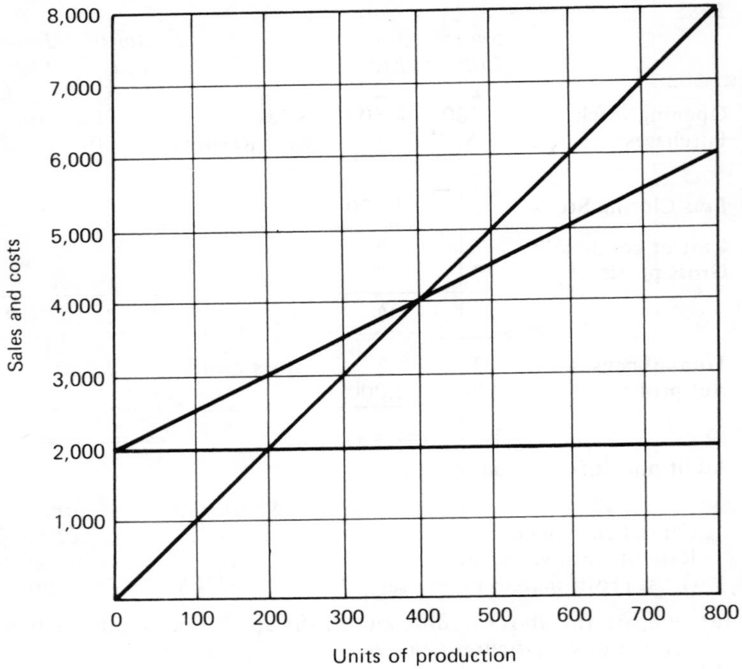

(a) Label the following on the break-even chart:
  (i) Sales revenue line.
  (ii) Total costs line.
  (iii) Fixed costs line.
  (iv) Area of loss.
  (v) Area of profit.

(b) Indicate the break-even point on the chart.

(c) How many units of production are required to break-even?

(d) What is the value of sales at break-even point?

(e) What is the margin of safety in units of production?

(f) If fixed costs were to increase by £1,000 what would be the sales value of the new break-even point?

(g) Why does a business prepare a break-even chart?

(NISEC, May 1988)

37 Claire Jones starts a trading business on 1 November 1987 by introducing £10,000 into the business bank account. The following are her plans for the first six months:

(a) Purchases are expected to be:

Nov	*Dec*	*Jan*	*Feb*	*March*	*April*
£2,150	£1,700	£1,800	£1,700	£1,800	£1,700

She plans to pay suppliers 2 months after the month of purchase.

(b) Sales (all on credit) are expected to be:

Nov	*Dec*	*Jan*	*Feb*	*March*	*April*
£1,000	£1,250	£1,250	£2,500	£3,000	£2,500

Debtors are expected to pay one month after invoice date.

(c) Rent of premises will be £250 per month, payable on 1st day of each month.

(d) She plans to purchase a delivery van in January at a cost of £3,900, to be paid for in equal instalments: January, February, March.

(e) Trading and general expenses are payable as they arise and are expected to be £450 per month on average.

(f) Drawings are expected to be £400 per month.

(i) Explain why Claire should prepare a cash budget.

(ii) Write up the firm's cash budget for the six-month period ending 30 April 1988.

(iii) Claire anticipates being offered an 'agency' which would involve initial costs of £1,500 in April. Do you consider it feasible? Explain your decision.

(NISEC, May 1988)

INDEX